New Casebooks

SHELLEY: *Frankenstein* Edited by Fred Botting
STOKER: *Dracula* Edited by Glennis Byron
WOOLF: *Mrs Dalloway* and *To the Lighthouse* Edited by Su Reid

DRAMA

BECKETT: *Waiting for Godot* and *Endgame* Edited by Steven Connor
APHRA BEHN Edited by Janet Todd
MARLOWE Edited by Avraham Oz
REVENGE TRAGEDY Edited by Stevie Simkin
SHAKESPEARE: *Antony and Cleopatra* Edited by John Drakakis
SHAKESPEARE: *Hamlet* Edited by Martin Coyle
SHAKESPEARE: *Julius Caesar* Edited by Richard Wilson
SHAKESPEARE: *King Lear* Edited by Kiernan Ryan
SHAKESPEARE: *Macbeth* Edited by Alan Sinfield
SHAKESPEARE: *The Merchant of Venice* Edited by Martin Coyle
SHAKESPEARE: *A Midsummer Night's Dream* Edited by Richard Dutton
SHAKESPEARE: *Much Ado About Nothing* and *The Taming of the Shrew* Edited by Marion Wynne-Davies
SHAKESPEARE: *Romeo and Juliet* Edited by R. S. White
SHAKESPEARE: *The Tempest* Edited by R. S. White
SHAKESPEARE: *Twelfth Night* Edited by R. S. White
SHAKESPEARE ON FILM Edited by Robert Shaughnessy
SHAKESPEARE IN PERFORMANCE Edited by Robert Shaughnessy
SHAKESPEARE'S HISTORY PLAYS Edited by Graham Holderness
SHAKESPEARE'S ROMANCES Edited by Alison Thorne
SHAKESPEARE'S TRAGEDIES Edited by Susan Zimmerman
JOHN WEBSTER: *The Duchess of Malfi* Edited by Dympna Callaghan

GENERAL THEMES

FEMINIST THEATRE AND THEORY Edited by Helene Keyssar
POSTCOLONIAL LITERATURES Edited by Michael Parker and Roger Starkey

New Casebooks Series
Series Standing Order
ISBN 0–333–71702–3 hardcover
ISBN 0–333–69345–0 paperback
(*outside North America only*)

You can receive future titles in this series as they are published by placing a standing order. Please contact your bookseller or, in case of difficulty, write to us at the address below with your name and address, the title of the series and the ISBN quoted above.

Customer Services Department, Macmillan Distribution Ltd,
Houndmills, Basingstoke, Hampshire RG21 6XS, England

New Casebooks

MARLOWE

EDITED BY AVRAHAM OZ

First published 2003 by
PALGRAVE MACMILLAN
Houndmills, Basingstoke, Hampshire RG21 6XS and
175 Fifth Avenue, New York, N. Y. 10010
Companies and representatives throughout the world

PALGRAVE MACMILLAN is the global academic imprint of the Palgrave
Macmillan division of St. Martin's Press, LLC and of Palgrave Macmillan Ltd.
Macmillan® is a registered trademark in the United States, United Kingdom
and other countries. Palgrave is a registered trademark in the European
Union and other countries.

ISBN 0–333–62498–X hardback
ISBN 0–333–62499–8 paperback

This book is printed on paper suitable for recycling and made from fully
managed and sustained forest sources.

A catalogue record for this book is available from the British Library.

Library of Congress Cataloging-in-Publication Data

Marlowe/ edited by Avraham Oz.
    p. cm. — (New casebooks)
  Includes bibliographical references (p.)and index.
  ISBN 0–333–62498–X (cloth)
    1. Marlowe, Christopher, 1564–1593—Criticism and interpretation.
I. Oz, Avraham. II. New casebooks (Palgrave Macmillan (Firm))

PR2673.M36 2003
822'.3–dc21
                                                                2003053279

10   9   8   7   6   5   4   3   2   1
12   11 10 09 08 07 06 05 04 03

Printed in China

To TAL
As ever

Contents

Acknowledgements

The space is too short to include the full amount of the editor's gratitude. The late Eric Pendry was perhaps the first to introduce me to the intriguing world of Marlowe, working on his edition of Marlowe while directing my dissertation on Shakespeare. Martin Coyle has demonstrated formidable patience and astute guidance. Anna Sandeman and her Palgrave Macmillan crew were helpful in completing this volume, a project assisted by a special grant from the University of Haifa and the devoted efforts of my research assistant, Jennie Tabak. As always, Tal, my wife and friend, provided the support and comfort needed to work and create. This project, as many others, is dedicated to her.

The editor and publishers wish to thank the following for permission to use copyright material:

Emily C. Bartels, for material from *Spectacles of Strangeness: Imperialism, Alienation, and Marlowe* by Emily C. Bartels (1993), pp. 4–26, by permission of the University of Pennsylvania Press; Catherine Belsey, for material from *The Subject of Tragedy: Identity and Difference in Renaissance Drama* by Catherine Belsey, Methuen (1985), pp. 55–75, by permission of Taylor and Francis Books Ltd; Dympna Callaghan, for 'The Terms of Gender: "Gay" and "Feminist" Edward II' in *Feminist Readings of Early Modern Culture: Emerging Subjects*, ed. Valerie Traub, M. Lindsay Kaplan, and Dympna Callaghan (1996), pp. 281–97, by permission of Cambridge University Press; Thomas Cartelli, for '*Queer Edward II*: Postmodern Sexualities and the Early Modern Subject' in *Marlowe, History, and Sexuality: New Critical Essays on Christopher Marlowe*, ed. P. Whitfield White (1998) pp. 213–21, by permission of AMS Press, Inc; Sara Munson Deats and Linda S. Starks, for '"So Neatly Plotted, and so Well Perform'd": Villian as Playright in Marlowe's Jew of Malta', *Theatre Journal*, 44 (1992), 375–89. Copyright © 1992 The Johns Hopkins University Press, by permission of The Johns Hopkins University Press; Jonathan Dollimore, for material from *Radical Tragedy: Religion, Ideology and Power in the Drama of Shakespeare and his Contemporaries* by Jonathan Dollimore, Harvester Wheatsheaf (1989), pp. 109–19, by permission of the author; Stephen Greenblatt, for material from *Renaissance Self-Fashioning: From More to Shakespeare* by Stephen Greenblatt (1980), pp. 291–307, by permission of The University of Chicago Press; Michael Hattaway, for 'Christopher Marlowe: Ideology and Subversion' in *Christopher Marlowe and English Renaissance Culture*, ed. Darryll Grantley and Peter Roberts, Scolar Press (1996), pp. 198–217, by permission of Ashgate Publishing Ltd; Avraham Oz, for material from *Strands Afar Remote: Israeli Perspectives on Shakespeare*, ed. Avraham Oz, University of Delaware Press (1998), pp.151–76, by permission of Associated University Presses; Alan Sinfield, for material from *Faultlines: Cultural Materialism and the Politics of Dissident Reading* by Alan Sinfield (1992), pp. 230–7. Copyright © 1992 The Regents of the University of California, by permission of Oxford University Press and University of California Press; David H. Thurn, for 'Economic and Ideological Exchange in Marlowe's *Jew of Malta*', *Theatre Journal*, 46 (1994), 157–70. Copyright © 1994 The Johns Hopkins University Press, by permission of The Johns Hopkins University Press.

Every effort has been made to trace the copyright holders but if any have been inadvertently overlooked the publishers will be pleased to make the necessary arrangement at the first opportunity.

General Editors' Preface

The purpose of this series of New Casebooks is to reveal some of the ways in which contemporary criticism has changed our understanding of commonly studied texts and writers and, indeed, of the nature of criticism itself. Central to the series is a concern with modern critical theory and its effect on current approaches to the study of literature. Each New Casebook editor has been asked to select a sequence of essays which will introduce the reader to the new critical approaches to the text or texts being discussed in the volume and also illuminate the rich interchange between critical theory and critical practice that characterises so much current writing about literature.

In this focus on modern critical thinking and practice New Casebooks aim not only to inform but also to stimulate, with volumes seeking to reflect both the controversy and the excitement of current criticism. Because much of this criticism is difficult and often employs an unfamiliar critical language, editors have been asked to give the reader as much help as they feel is appropriate, but without simplifying the essays or the issues they raise. Again, editors have been asked to supply a list of further reading which will enable readers to follow up issues raised by the essays in the volume.

The project of New Casebooks, then, is to bring together in an illuminating way those critics who best illustrate the ways in which contemporary criticism has established new methods of analysing texts and who have reinvigorated the important debate about how we 'read' literature. The hope is, of course, that New Casebooks will not only open up this debate to a wider audience, but will also encourage students to extend their own ideas, and think afresh about their responses to the texts they are studying.

John Peck and Martin Coyle
University of Wales, Cardiff

Introduction

AVRAHAM OZ

'To enter upon the Marlovian stage,' Emily Bartels writes at the outset of her fascinating account of strangeness in Marlowe, 'is to enter a landscape filled with strangers and strange lands.'[1] The alleged spy from Canterbury, the 'Muses' darling' for his verse, as his elder contemporary George Peele dubbed him just after his death,[2] has long aroused controversy among critics regarding both his character and his work. His brilliance as a writer, however, has never been doubted. Like many of his fellow dramatists in the second generation of Elizabethan dramatists, Marlowe was born to the ranks of the lower bourgeoisie, small tradesmen and craftsmen. His father, John Marlowe, originating from a little village near Faversham, in Kent, moved to Canterbury around 1556 and practised as a shoemaker. In 1561 he married Katherine from the Arthur family of Dover. Christopher, his second child and elder son, was educated first at small local schools, but in 1579, when he turned 14, he was admitted to King's School, one of the most privileged schools in Canterbury. In 1580 he received another scholarship, from the foundation of Matthew Parker, Archbishop of Canterbury, to Corpus Christi College, Cambridge, where he read the Bible, the Reformation theologians, philosophy and history, gained his BA degree in four years and his MA degree in 1587.

During these years and after, two major developments affected and shaped Marlowe's life and career: first, he disappeared from Cambridge for long periods to carry out some secret, rather mysterious missions for the Elizabethan government. Since those missions took him to Rheims, the stronghold of Catholicism (possibly to spy on the activities of English Catholics living in exile), it led the Cambridge University authorities to believe that he had been converted to the old religion (there are some who believe he had, in fact). This almost jeopardised the conferring of his MA degree, which was in danger of being denied both on that ground as well as on his long absences from his studies. Only the intervention of the Queen's Privy Council on his behalf saved his degree.

Second, Marlowe became a public figure in London, counted among the gentry, associating with such figures as Sir Philip Sidney and Sir Walter Ralegh (the founder of the colony of Virginia in the New World, and the rival of Essex for the Queen's favours) and mixing with playwrights such as Thomas Kyd, with whom he shared a room, Robert Greene and Thomas Nashe. In the same year that he took his MA degree (1587), his *Tragedy of Tamburlaine, Part One* was probably performed on the London stage, which made him overnight a recognised and much appreciated playwright in the capital. This kind of social mobility, typical of Tudor England, seems to have influenced the conception of Tamburlaine, who rises from a simple shepherd to become an Emperor. Indeed, most of Marlowe's major characters constantly fashion themselves into a conspicuous social stature, and yet this not simply by their own action: as Linda Gregerson notes, the Tudor subject 'was always a crux and an interpellation of power', always, that is, an embodiment and effect of the social and political forces operating in the culture.[3]

The forces affecting Marlowe's major characters and which propel them into the regions of desire, empire and mystery, seem open-ended and of eternal magnitude. So, too, with Marlowe's own career which closed on Wednesday evening, 30 May 1593, the day of his death in an affray in a Deptford tavern, Eleanor Bull's house, at the hand of one Ingram Frizer. At the age of 29, Christopher Marlowe was a more accomplished and successful playwright than his close contemporary, William Shakespeare. While the latter, but two months his junior, could brag at that moment of one historical tetralogy, three or four early comedies, and a flawed if promising tragedy, Marlowe's accumulated achievement clearly overshadowed the early Shakespearean crop. His death, however, was not an event significant enough in the life of the Elizabethan monarchy to arouse public interest.

And yet the end of Marlowe's life was not unprepared for, by the public scandals in which he was involved. Marlowe was proclaimed a notorious troublemaker on several occasions. In 1589 he was sent to Newgate Prison, charged with the murder of one William Bradley, but he was acquitted a fortnight later. But his quick temper was yet to commit him to more trouble. In 1592 an injunction was brought against him for a street fight, in which another man was killed. While he was attending one of his secret missions, this time in the Netherlands, Marlowe was deported back on the charge of counterfeiting gold coins. Thomas Kyd, who was arrested for keeping heretic papers, claimed they belonged to his former room-mate, which caused Marlowe to be summoned before Queen Elizabeth's Privy Council, by whom he was 'commanded to give his daily attendance on their lordships, until he shall be licensed to the contrary'.

What makes Marlowe so important, though, is not his life, however fascinating its details, but his work. Contrary to the impression created by the fact of a mere handful of friends who attended his burial at the church of St Nicholas in Deptford on 1 June, in an unmarked grave, Marlowe was a popular playwright both in the positive and the condescending senses of the term. His plays filled the 'Theatre' and the 'Rose' theatres, offering their audiences the most palatable dishes of the popular stage, with strong sensations and spectacular scenes, blood and violence (even though we are often warned not to equate our modern shock at, say Tamburlaine's actions, with that of its original audience),[4] all-devouring desire and assertions of their most cherished communal creeds. A pioneer in the formative years of early modern English drama, Marlowe was at once a daring dramatist and great poet. 'Marlowe, like Spenser', wrote Leigh Hunt in 1844, 'is to be looked upon as a poet who had no native precursors ... He prepared the way for the versification, the dignity, and the pathos of his successors ... Marlowe and Spenser are the first of our poets who perceived the beauty of words ... as a habit of the poetic mood, and as receiving and reflecting beauty through the feeling of the ideas.'[5] Some of those ideas as well as Marlowe's politics and dramatic skill are the subject of this New Casebook.

Significantly, the earlier Casebook on Marlowe in the Macmillan series, edited by Professor John Russell Brown, had, as its last piece, Stephen Greenblatt's now classic chapter on Marlowe in his seminal work *Renaissance Self-Fashioning*. Greenblatt's following article, on *The Jew of Malta*, capitalism and antisemitism, published ten years later and already a classic study in itself, is a major pivot of the present collection, which marks a flourishing period for Marlowe scholarship and criticism. Within the narrow scope of this collection I have included articles (alas, not as many as I would have liked to) representing various approaches typical of the period it attempts to include, and have also sought to cover the three major tragedies – *Dr Faustus, The Jew of Malta* and *Edward II* – as well as the *Tamburlaine* plays within the range of this collection, in the light of the growing interest in them in recent years, both on stage and in the classroom. Unfortunately, I have not been able to include any essays about the intriguing tragedy *Dido, Queen of Carthage*, which tells of the love affair between the Classical North African Queen and the Trojan Aeneas, who turns his back and leaves her; nor have I been able to include essays on the fragmentary *The Massacre at Paris* (a dramatic account of the 1572 Massacre of French Hugenots by Catholics on St Bartholomew's Day), the poems, of which the most famous is *Hero and Leander* (left unfinished at his death, and later completed by George Chapman), or the translations of Lucan's *Pharsalia* and Ovid's *Elegies*. These nevertheless provide an essential background for the tragedies and for the modern criticism that seeks to read the plays in their cultural, historical and textual context.

The opening essay of the volume takes a general overview of Marlowe's work. Emily Bartels' introduction to her seminal work on Marlowe insists on the strange and estranging spectacles informing his dramatic work. His preoccupation with the 'other', she argues, coming as and when it does, is no accident, for Marlowe's representations respond to an increasingly dominant cultural obsession with foreign worlds and peoples, emerging with England's nascent imperialism. Michael Hattaway's article (essay 2) discusses Marlowe as a political writer, demonstrating how his dramatic work displays within the playhouse what had been carefully kept off-stage elsewhere, 'in that theatre of power that we know as the Elizabethan court, where elaborate rituals were deployed in order to imply that far more than might was needed to create right'. Like Bartels, Hattaway is interested in the overall picture of the Marlovian stage and its subversive art. My own essay which follows (3), is, by contrast, the one article in this collection devoted to Marlowe's early masterpiece, the two parts of *Tamburlaine the Great*, a text whose prestige in recent decades both on stage and in

critical acclaim drew it rapidly into the inner boundaries of canon-
ical drama. The article attempts to relate the *Tamburlaine* plays to
Marlowe's strategy of mimicry, where faces and maps, prophetically construed, reflect an early modern sense of nationhood and
desire for Empire within the mirror of barbarism inherent in their
newly accommodated civility.

Essays 4, 5 and 6 are devoted to *The Jew of Malta*. The first is
the above mentioned article by Stephen Greenblatt, which reads
Marlowe's play in the light of Marx's 'On the Jewish Question'.
Marx is compared to Barabas' hypothetical son, who, as a reaction
to his father's deeds, publishes an antisemitic pamphlet suggesting
that the greed and self-interest inherent in Judaism is nothing but
the 'practical essence of Christianity, the thing itself stripped of its
spiritual mystifications'. The fact that both works use the figure of
the perfidious Jew, Greenblatt suggests, provides a powerful interpretive link between Renaissance and modern thought. Coming
from a different angle, Sara Munson Deats and Lisa S. Starks read
The Jew of Malta play against the controversy over the theatre at
the time, showing that Marlowe shared with Shakespeare and
Jonson a deep ambivalence toward his own medium, self-reflexively
probing, censuring, and celebrating his dramatic art – an ambivalence toward his art and his profession which is most vividly embodied in the character of Barabas, the surrogate playwright and
villain. David Thurn (essay 6) approaches the play from the perspective of the 'economical model' rather than the 'containment'
one, arguing that, not being limited to the notion of a single mode
of power conceived as an instrumental, totalising exercise of political or juridical authority, the economic model can better accommodate exchanges among relatively autonomous areas within the
social structure. An exchange theory, Thurn maintains, can support
a more historically precise account of the circulation of force and
value within a culture whose practices cannot always be described
in the rather grand terms of power, subversion, and containment,
or subsumed under the rubric of a monolithic sovereign authority.

Doctor Faustus is the subject of the following group of articles.
Jonathan Dollimore (essay 7) marks the tension in the play
between the moral and theological imperatives of a severe
Christian orthodoxy and an affirmation of Faustus as 'the epitome
of Renaissance aspiration'. *Dr Faustus* is best understood not as
an affirmation of Divine Law, nor conversely of Renaissance Man,
but an exploration of subversion through transgression. Catherine

Belsey (essay 8), exploring the orthodoxies of liberal Humanism, places *Doctor Faustus* in the context of her discussion of knowledge in the transition from medieval conceptions of the term into the Renaissance. She demonstrates the presence of allegorical voices within the soliloquy in which Faustus talks himself out of repentance and in his final soliloquy. She also describes the assumptions about syllogism as a means of knowledge, underlying Faustus's rejection of divinity. Alan Sinfield's project (essay 9) offers to show that the play, though amenable to a determined orthodox Calvinist reading, still might do more to promote anxiety about such doctrine than to reinforce it. *Faustus* is in his view entirely ambiguous – altogether open to the more usual, modern, free-will reading. The theological implications of *Faustus* are radically and provocatively indeterminate.

The last two essays are on *Edward II*. Dympna Callaghan (essay 10) juxtaposes the treatment of Edward II's story by Marlowe to that of Elizabeth Cary, in order to differentiate queer and feminist readings of that narrative. Indeed, Marlowe and Cary can only anachronistically be described as 'gay' and 'feminist' – feminist and queer cultural representations and identities, she suggests, do not have early modern equivalents. However, Callaghan continues, 'one can lay claim to these terms in order to ascertain those continuities that do exist within the sexualised terms of gender'. Thomas Cartelli (essay 11) studies the affinities of Derek Jarman's film *Edward II* (1991), after Marlowe's play, with contemporary queer theory. Jarman makes a series of political interventions that do, Cartelli maintains, improve on Marlowe by substituting a clearly positioned emphasis on gay victimisation and empowerment in place of Marlowe's generally unpositioned fascination with power and the powerful.

Together, this group of articles represents a good deal of the various perspectives on Marlowe through which his work was received and read within the last two decades of the twentieth century, an age in which both critical theory and new evaluations of early modern Britain from feminist, new historical, postcolonial and cultural materialist concerns have enriched our reception of his major dramatic work. That reception may have been drastically altered by the events of 11 September 2001, and their aftermath, in which Tamburlaine's Western successors reversed the course of his imperial hybris which reminded one once more that both evil and grandeur are never abstract, but always rely on the vast resources of human imagination; a reminder that Marlowe's world of violence and death, racial hatred and terrifying power, is very much the world we still live in, a world both strange yet familiar in its images.

Notes

1. Emily C. Bartels, *Spectacles of Strangeness: Imperialism, Alienation and Marlowe* (Philadelphia, 1993), p. 3 (see essay 1).

2. George Peele, 'Marlowe, the Muses' darling', from 'The Honour of the Garter', in *The Works of George Peele*, ed. A. H. Bullen (London, 1888), vol. II, 319–20.

3. Linda Gregerson, *The Reformation of the Subject: Spenser, Milton, and the English Protestant Epic* (Cambridge, 1995), p. 82.

4. See, for example, Stevie Simkin, *Marlowe: The Plays* (Basingstoke, 2000), p. 80.

5. Millar Maclure (ed.), *Marlowe: The Critical Heritage 1588–1896* (London, Boston and Henley, 1979), p. 91.

1

Strange and Estranging Spectacles: Strategies of State and Stage

EMILY C. BARTELS

> But that was in another country.
>   (*The Jew of Malta*, IV.i.43)

Imperialism, stereotypes, and the state

To enter upon the Marlovian stage is to enter a landscape filled with strangers and strange lands. One after another of Christopher Marlowe's plays focuses on a character type alienated from or marginalised within English society, and several situate that figure within a foreign setting. Their central characters include a Scythian barbarian, a black magician, a Machiavellian Maltese Jew, a homosexual king, and an African queen: their landscapes range from Carthage, to Malta, Persia, Babylon, Egypt, and beyond. Even the European settings seem markedly unfamiliar: England becomes a locus of uncertain authority, ruled by a homosexual king (Edward II) and his favoured 'minions' and contested by haughty, overpowering, and questionably noble nobles; Paris, a site of riots, massacres, and murders, also ruled by a homosexual king (Henry III); and Germany, a place where felonious, and potentially damnable, conjurations are admired rather than abhorred, and where devils are likely to appear. The extravagant spectacles (which, on one occasion, allegedly scared spectators from the theatre), the 'great and thundering speech' (*Tamburlaine*, 1:I.iii) of Marlovian blank verse, as well perhaps as the vernacular itself, which Steven Mullaney has suggested as a 'strange tongue', contributed also to the alterity of these alien worlds and figures.[1]

This preoccupation with the 'other', coming as and when it does, is no accident. For Marlowe's representations respond to an increasingly dominant cultural obsession with foreign worlds and peoples, emerging with England's nascent imperialism. As society attempted to come to terms with competing cultures and to establish its place beside and above them, it produced a discourse of difference, a discourse that interrogated and enforced the crucial, self-affirming distinctions between self (Europe, England, 'representative man', the status quo) and other (foreign cultures, nonconformists, alternative values). Marlowe participates in this self-scrutiny by producing his own 'spectacle[s] of strangeness'.[2] What makes his plays so remarkable, so subversive, and indeed, so important is that they combat his society's attempts to prove the alien inexorably alien and expose cultural stereotypes and discriminations as constructs, strategically deployed to authorise the self over and at the expense of some other.

While the Spanish and Portuguese began to develop a substantial trade network in non-European countries during the early sixteenth century without England's competitive intervention, the economic depression of the 1550s helped catalyse Elizabethan interest in the new goods, new markets, new jobs, and eventually new homes that such expansionism promised.[3] Though England had no explicit imperialist agenda, the mid-sixteenth century witnessed relentless searches for north-east and north-west passages to the East as well as for *Terra Australis*, development of trade with Russia, India, the East and far East, and exploration and colonisation of the recently discovered 'New World'. Figures such as Sir Francis Drake and Sir Walter Ralegh held prominent positions not only on the seas but also in the court, urging the nation forward, or rather outward, to the resources beyond.

Emerging with this impetus was an intensified desire for knowledge of unknown or partially known domains, a desire answered and evidenced by the energetic contemporary production of cross-cultural descriptions. Joannes Boemus's *Omnium gentium mores*, for example, which describes the 'aunciente maners, customes, and lawes, of the peoples enhabiting the two partes of the earth, called Affricke and Asie', had circulated throughout Europe in several languages beginning in 1520 and continuing for almost a century after, and was translated into English in 1555 as *The Fardle of Facions*.[4] John Leo Africanus's 'famous worke', *The Geographical Historie of Africa*, which details the 'exceeding strange creatures' and 'notable things' (customs, races and religions, natural resources and material wealth, geographies and histories) of Egypt and Africa, had been similarly disseminated across Europe and was popularised in England and in English by John Pory's 1600 translation.[5] Travel literature also became eminently popular, particularly under the aegis of Richard Hakluyt, whose 'life, from 1552 to 1616, paralleled the rise of a larger England' and whose well-known collection of the 'principal navigations' undertaken from the 1540s onward and covering a vast array of places – from Russia, to Africa, America, and the Caribbean – vigorously promoted that rise.[6] In addition to these textual collections, displays of foreign artifacts, and sometimes even people (Indians, Moors, and Turks), became fashionable during the mid-sixteenth to mid-seventeenth centuries, as England began to gather the 'infinite riches' of the outside world into its own 'little room'.[7]

Yet as recent studies of colonialist discourse have suggested, the 'knowledge' that Europe produced about other worlds, during the early modern period as through the colonialist and even postcolonialist eras, was far from neutral. Instead it was vitally connected with Europe's self-image and self-authorisation especially, though not exclusively, as Europe began to move toward empire. Europe's growing expansionism at once required and threatened the crucial gap between self and other that could 'justify' the domination of other worlds. Encounters with other cultures, though recorded at times along with longstanding myths about cannibals, 'Anthropophagi, and men whose heads/[Do grow] beneath their shoulders' (*Othello*, I.iii.143–4) and with 'actual' scenes of marvels, unearthed foreign subjects with fairly normal appetites and anatomies, interested like their European 'guests' in self-protection and profit.[8] However the levels of difference and similarity were actually experienced (something which is finally impossible to recuperate), cross-cultural discourse insisted repeatedly on difference.[9]

So too on the home front, within Europe and England, where the division between self and other was also in danger of breaking down. In England's case (which is what I am most concerned with here), the pressure to define and display a superior nation produced within domestic texts, such as the chronicled histories, a similar institution of difference, fostering the illusion of a state fully able to separate the 'we' from the 'they', to effectively identify, contain, and control transgression.[10]

In his seminal study, *Orientalism*, Edward Said introduced important ways in which European colonialist discourse produces its object as 'other', creating through projection and negation an inferior and uncivilised 'theirs' ripe for the domination of a superior, civilised and civilising 'ours'.[11] For Said the other is not real but imaginary, mapped out more by ideology than by geography, though finally bounded as a real terrain by the imperialism promoted through that ideologic mapping.[12] Though eminently useful, Said's world picture is itself bounded by its own ideology, dividing its territory into West and East, self and other, and leaving out the complicating presence of the 'third world' of Africa (as Christopher Miller has pointed out) and of a fourth, the 'New World', neither of which can be accommodated within a self/other binarism.[13] Nor, as both Miller and Homi Bhabha have argued, does Said's model allow adequately for the ambivalences present in depictions not only of these other 'other' worlds, but also of the Orient itself.[14] For though imperialist discourse masquerades as being monologic, stable, and sure, it is marked by significant contradictions.

This is nowhere clearer than in the case of cultural and crosscultural stereotypes which were vital to early modern England's production of both self and other and to its early move towards empire. Behind each iteration of these constructs lies a will to knowledge and a will to power, a desire to bound off absolutely and so to exploit, dominate, or suppress an identifiable other. As Bhabha has argued, stereotypes produce a kind of 'radical realism' and assert, through an excess of signification, a degree of probability and predictability beyond 'what can be empirically proved or logically construed'.[15] The stereotype seems to fix the other, to consolidate all we know about that other and all we need to know. Yet while these constructs take and give shape under the pretence of precision, fixity, and singularity, they are as polymorphic as they are perverse and contribute to a discursive field that is abstract, unstable, and conflicted.

Consider, for example, early modern conceptions of the Jew, who was sometimes a devil, sometimes (merely) an anti-Christian infidel, sometimes a cunning villain, sometimes a child-murderer, sometimes a usurer, sometimes some of the above, and sometimes none. Though Shylock and his prototype, Barabas, love their ducats at least as much as they do their daughters, Shakespeare's Jew is a usurer while Marlowe's is not. And while Barabas is all too ready to murder his daughter, along with anyone else who gets in his way, Shylock attempts murder only by law, according to a legitimate (though outrageous) contract. The Turk, too, came in various shapes and sizes, appearing as anything from an empire-mongering barbarian to a diabolical villain. On Marlowe's stage alone, Turks range from Ithamore, the *Jew of Malta*'s base and scurrilous slave who has a 'more the merrier' attitude toward murder, especially of Christians; to the imperious Calymath (of the same play), who would rather dominate Malta's Christians than kill them; to *Tamburlaine*'s Bajazeth, who displays the villainous excesses of the one and the imperiousness of the other, and stands ever ready to 'glut [his] swords' (III.iii.164) and 'let thousands die' (III.iii.138) in the name of empire. To complicate the matter further, these stereotypes had to compete with more positive though less publicised images – of the Jew, for example, as a victim of the state, scapegoated in times of financial crisis, or of the Turk as a masterful leader, whose forces were significantly better organised and equipped than those of the English.[16]

While the stereotype is produced as if it were *the* definitive type, what is clear in representations of these and other others is that the difference they prescribe is as variable as it is familiar. For Bhabha these discrepancies expose a deep ambivalence embedded in colonialist discourse, predicted anxiously on desire as well as fear, defence as well as mastery. Along similar, though deconstructionist rather than psychoanalytic lines, Miller has argued that Europe's bifurcated vision of Africa expresses Europe's own conflicted attitude toward the other, the self, and the possibility of 'maintaining an identity in discourse'.[17]

These studies, in exposing the disturbances within colonialist representations, usefully complicate Europe's expression of itself and suppression of the other, pressing us beyond Said and the assumption that colonialist discourse is always hegemonically in charge of itself and taking account of psychological and linguistic uncertainties that insistently disrupt self/other binarisms and the stereotypes constructed around them. Yet while the discrepancies within circumscriptions of the other may in part evolve from these pressures, they also serve strategically to further the colonialist cause, to amplify the critical difference between 'them' and 'us'.

For in the first place, because each iteration of a type stands in conflict with a field of others, it produces a figure who is ultimately unknowable. The 'other' is pressed out of the grasp of knowledge precisely at the moment that he or (less often) she is given a fixed place within it. The problem is translated not as a gap in 'our' perspective or perception but as an incriminating gap in 'their' nature. While Shakespeare's Romans repeatedly typecast Cleopatra as a strumpet, Enobarbus offers a far more alluring vision of the erotic Egyptian queen floating upon the Nile on her barge. Yet though his depiction is rich with detail, Cleopatra gets lost amidst it, as an object beyond the forms of art and nature, creating an unfillable and unnatural 'gap in nature' (*Antony and Cleopatra* II.ii.218).[18] Throughout as here, the more the characters talk about her, setting one image against another, the less definable she becomes, dangerously evading the Romans'/'our' language and knowing, like the crocodile Antony describes that is 'shap'd ... like itself', 'is as broad as it hath breadth' and so on (II.vii.42–3). Though the play alerts us to the gaps within the discourse, it also contributes to them and puts Cleopatra beyond our grasp, a figure a little less than kin and more than kind, who is neither the strumpet Philo and Demetrius create nor the erotic goddess Enobarbus sees, but rather is as erratic as she is alluring.

Beyond unknowability, all that can be known for sure about the 'other' points to where the self/other binarism leads: to the idea of the other as abstractly but unquestionably negative. Though stereotypes enlist a specificity that seems to ring 'true', the inconsistencies between and within them leave us with only the broadest and most negative outline. In most cases, the only constant among the other's various guises is that he or she is in some way villainous or threatening at the least, whether because of greed, deception, excessive sexuality, murderous actions, or lack of faith (which means, in early modern discourse, Christian or Protestant faith). And it is that constant that prevails.

Indeed, it seems no coincidence that different alien types, such as the Moor and the Turk, the sodomite and the witch, are confused and conflated within early modern discourse, for their abstract negativity matters more than their specific dimensions. Othello, when calling up the ultimate image to condemn himself before his suicide, identifies himself not as a Moor but as a Turk, a 'malignant and a turban'd Turk' who 'beat a Venetian and traduc'd the state' (*Othello*, V.ii.353–4) and whom Othello allegedly killed. In evoking the image, the Moor partially redeems himself, reminding his audience that he has been a loyal defender of the Venetian state. At the same time, however, he underscores his otherness by 'turning Turk' (something he fears), aligning himself with a figure who has been Venice's quintessential other, as if all others are interchangeable and interchangeably malign.

It is impossible to know finally how consciously stereotypes were set in conflict and articulated through incriminating abstraction. Yet the fact that it was happening in domestic as well as cross-cultural discourse, to figures such as the magician and the sodomite who were more familiar and more available for inspection and circumspection, suggests that the insistent obfuscation of the 'other' was not just a product of distance. And while part of the confusion may have arisen from mixed feelings, it nonetheless supported the imperialist cause, exposing the possibility of 'maintaining an identity' – an alien identity – 'in discourse' through and not despite its indeterminacies. From a practical perspective alone, on the home front the vagueness about what constituted various transgressions not only did not impede prosecution; it also aided it. Because sodomy, for example, was cloaked in layers of abstractions and conflated with all sorts of other 'crimes', the charge became a useful way of indicating social and political dissidence whose troubling offences were less easy to criminalise. So, too, in the case of black magicians, who could be produced from radical intellectuals or religious dissenters on fairly specious grounds.

Critics have been hesitant to ascribe racism and homophobia to early modern culture, in large part because the idea of race and homosexuality seemed poorly formed at best.[19] Yet that poor formation enabled rather than hindered prejudicial ideologies. Racism, homophobia, xenophobia and the like, though they did not yet have a local habitation or name, had their beginnings here, within cross-cultural and domestic discourses whose uncertainties amplified difference, allowing the self to impose its terms of supremacy on the world, over the alien abroad and the alien at home.

Marlowe, stereotypes, and the stage

It is from and against this hegemonic circumscription of unstable but nonetheless inalienable 'alien' types that Christopher Marlowe writes. Before Marlowe brought his infamous array of aliens to centre stage, the English theatre was itself threatening to become a place where stereotypes were prominently fashioned and fixed.

Early drama (still being performed in Marlowe's day) had built itself on Biblical typology in which the abstract, figural significance of characters mattered more than their specific material embodiments. Even as its characters were humanised with various degrees of local and comic colour, that humanisation itself served to fashion a type rather than an individual. In the mystery plays, Noah, for example, was given a vociferously unbelieving wife, who became a prototype of the shrew, and though the rash, outrageous Herods of the cycles invoked Mohamed's name and power, in their anti-Christian lust for murder and revenge, they provided material for the stock type of the Jew.[20] To bring such types into the mystery plays was to make divine 'truths' familiar and accessible, but it was also to inscribe difference, to give the 'other' a place which seemed as real as it was stable.

So too in the case of the moral plays, which gained prominence in the decades before Marlowe and which capitalised on 'others' in order to enforce political 'truths'. In Thomas Preston's *Cambyses*, for example, the 'wicked' king of Persia exemplified the Oriental barbarian; as David Bevington has argued, his contemptible excesses served to caution magistrates against tyranny and to school subjects in absolute obedience to their leaders, who presumably could never be as severe.[21] Yet the message was not only that 'our' rulers should not and would not be so tyrannical, but that other/Eastern rulers, categorically, would.

It was not just for the purpose of morality but also for the purpose of profit that the alien found such an accommodating home in the theatre. Because of its licensed social and geographic marginality, the theatre was one of the few and most accessible arenas where a large portion of the populace could safely 'see' the wonders of the world.[22] And because what they were looking for were 'wonders', the more other the better. In bringing such figures as Cambyses, Muly Hamet, Tamburlaine, and Cleopatra to centre stage, dramatists, including Marlowe, capitalised on public interest.[23] In so doing, they re-enacted the imperialist appropriations happening around the world, turning difference into spectacle and spectacle into profit.

Marlowe himself was no stranger to spectacle, especially in *Doctor Faustus*, which performed conjurations that were otherwise outlawed and that were assigned 'real' effects and 'real' devils.[24] *Tamburlaine*, too, is centred on othering displays, not just of words but of excesses of wealth, bloodshed, torture, and death. Indeed, all of Marlowe's plays in some ways put strangeness audaciously before the spectators' eyes.

Yet while Marlowe himself exploited the cultural fascination produced and promoted along with imperialism, he did so in a way that challenged the idea of otherness and helped turn the theatre into a place where hegemonic constructs were more often questioned than confirmed, more often subverted than supported. It seems no coincidence that after Marlowe the stock type begins to lose its prominence on the Renaissance stage, except perhaps in the case of women, which is also excepted in Marlowe. After Barabas, the outrageous Herods of the mystery plays give way to Shylock who, in his controversial set piece (*The Merchant of Venice*, III.i.53–73) at the least, highlights the sameness of the Jew.[25] And though Shakespeare gives us Aaron, the diabolical Moor in *Titus Andronicus*, he later gives Othello, a figure caught between a discourse on sexuality and a discourse on race and unable to contain or be contained by either. It is only in Jonson that the stock type prominently reclaims centre stage, but then as an agent of satire and parody, whose self-conscious fictionality is clear.

Until recently, critics have read Marlowe's 'spectacles of strangeness' symbolically, as part of a 'sublime landscape of imaginative aspiration', as a sign of the seemingly infinite possibilities that the protagonists are compelled, insistently and excessively, to master.[26] Yet the plays speak more immediately to an important cultural phenomenon that touched Marlowe himself. As a spy, possibly an associate of the freethinking School of Night (if it existed), probably a homosexual, and certainly a playwright, Marlowe was alienated within his society and demonised by accusations that are by now a well-known part of the Marlowe myth.[27] His fellow dramatist Robert Greene attacked him for 'daring God out of heaven with the atheist *Tamburlan*', and when Thomas Kyd, Marlowe's one-time room-mate and colleague, was arrested for possessing heretical papers, he ascribed them to Marlowe, who was then summoned before the Privy Council. After his death, the defamation seemed only to escalate: Kyd accused him of harbouring 'monstrous opinions', and the informant Richard Baines, in a 'note' that was the most incriminating evidence against him, of blasphemy, sodomy, and so on.[28]

What is also an increasingly well-known part of the Marlowe story is that these allegations, in case after case, were self-serving and coercive, if not coerced. Kyd, for example, promoted his colleague's reputation of atheism to escape being indicted for such 'vile opinion[s]' himself and had much to gain, theatrically speaking, in seeing this rival playwright put away. And not only was Baines known as 'a troublesome, clamorous, and wilful vexer of divers her majesty's subjects', in the habit of 'bringing malicious suits "to put the said defendants to great costs, wrong, and travail" ', his note, as David Riggs has argued, may have been coerced by the Privy Council who needed a scapegoat for sedition.[29] For Christian moralists, Marlowe's death provided an excellent example of the wages of sin.

Jonathan Goldberg has suggested that in rebelling Marlowe came to fill the transgressive space that society had constructed for him.[30] What is most interesting about that space is that it, like that of stereotypes, was significantly open-ended, producing a rebel capable of a seemingly infinite array of subversive activities, social, sexual, political, and religious, and providing a living instance of the uses indeterminacy was being put to in the construction of the 'other'. The Baines note alone makes Marlowe guilty of being an atheist, a papist, a sodomite, an alchemist, and a tobacco addict. If Riggs is right, the Privy Council's real agenda was to blame someone for publicly (in the Dutch Church libel) threatening a massacre against resident foreigners. While the revolt, according to the libel, was to be carried out in *Tamburlaine* style, Marlowe's complicity with it was otherwise unsubstantiated.[31]

The Baines note, with its plethora of charges, provided the perfect remedy, building Marlowe into a figure of such proportions that his criminality, though in no way related to the alleged crime, could not be questioned. Gabriel Harvey, himself not inconsequentially a rival author, defamed Marlowe as a 'hawty man' who feared neither God nor the devil and admired only 'his wondrous selfe'; to amplify his otherwise specious attack on Marlowe's 'toade Conceit', Harvey blurs impiety, if not atheism, into it, conflating and inflating its impact.[32] For decades, critics attempting to locate the 'real' Marlowe, have piled charge on top of charge and have made him increasingly unknowable and increasingly other. They have, for example, aligned him with conspiratorial activities of various sorts, including those of the School of Night and of supporters of the Scottish James VI's claim to the English throne.[33] Such charges, put together, expand Marlowe's subversiveness into uncertain but limitless proportions.

It is impossible to know, of course, how cognisant Marlowe was of his own demonisation. That he may have cultivated his infamy is suggested by the 'facts' that he (allegedly) voiced 'monstrous opinions', kept himself in 'the sinister company of men involved in spying or double-dealing', and was entangled in at least four public instances of disorderly conduct, the last ending in his death.[34] His plays flagrantly make public spectacles of publicly unaccepted practices (atheism, conjuration, sodomy), successfully 'daring' viewers and critics to recognise the transgressive nature of his subjects.[35] Yet however much he participated in the construction of his otherness, his plays suggest a keen awareness of and resistance to his society's manipulations of difference. Whether or not the plays protest against Marlowe's own personal exploitation within an increasingly discriminatory social nexus, as they turn to other worlds they turn against imperialism and expose rather than fulfil the cultural stereotypes enabling and enabled by imperialist endeavours.

Stephen Greenblatt was the first to rehistoricise Marlowe, to set 'the acquisitive energies of English merchants, entrepreneurs, and adventurers' in the foreground of the plays and to link Marlowe's fascination with 'the idea of the stranger in a strange land' with European imperialism.[36] For Greenblatt, Marlovian heroes share and reflect those energies as they attempt to map the bounds of their own existences, 'to invent themselves' against a void of 'neutral and unresponsive' space, and, through 'a subversive identification with the alien', 'to give life a shape and a certainty that it would otherwise lack'.[37] As important and enabling, and as grounded in history, as this story of self-fashioning is, Greenblatt's argument moves away from the context of imperialism, suggesting that what the characters face and what the plays address is a sort of existential crisis, that we are all, in fact, homeless and alienated and must construct ourselves in order to exist.

While Marlowe's focus includes this identity crisis, it is directed more specifically toward an alienation being imposed from without rather than being experienced from within – an alienation keyed to the historical moment of England's emergent imperialism and given shape through cross-cultural and domestic stereotypes. What problematises identity under these circumstances is not just that self-defining boundaries dissolve, but that alienating boundaries persist and are reinforced as relentlessly and authoritatively as self-constituting acts. What finally is most subversive here is not the characters' or the playwright's identification with *the alien*, but the insistence that such an identity does not, of itself, exist.

The Marlovian world picture

Although Marlovian drama centres on a diverse array of landscapes and of heroes, with widely varying means and ends, it employs common patterns of representation that work to expose and resist the processes of discrimination. In play after play, Marlowe places the spectators in an uncomfortable position, intellectually and emotionally, and, by creating significant discrepancies between culturally inscribed meanings and the meanings applicable on the stage, demands that they suspend not only their disbelief but their expectations and biases. He familiarises unfamiliar worlds and defamiliarises familiar ones, situates his aliens within contexts in which their signal traits of difference are not different, and at once provokes and frustrates the spectators' attempts to distinguish the established 'ours' from the threatening 'theirs'. In addition, he evokes emotional responses that are 'strange' rather than 'automatic' by encouraging audience sympathy, if not admiration, for heroes and spectacles which are socially or politically incorrect.[38]

While these manipulations problematise the process of discrimination, the plays also thematise it. In each case, Marlowe's representations of the alien are about the representation of the alien, and the arbitrary, uncertain, and strategic ways in which difference is constructed, deconstructed, and even reconstructed by the 'other' as by those who share his or (in Dido's case) her stage in answer to their own self-empowering agendas. In producing a staged world where the meanings that give meaning to the extra-theatrical environment no longer apply and where discrimination itself is incriminated as a self-authorising ploy, Marlowe sets culturally inscribed terms of difference in crisis and insists that they be questioned if not rejected, reassessed if not reformed.[39]

The representation of place is particularly important to this process and functions ideologically to unsettle spectator expectations, not only through its foreignness, but also through its familiarity. Our understanding of how precisely settings were set up on the Elizabethan stage is thwarted by the sparsity of performance records and artifacts. Some critics, such as A. M. Nagler, have argued for a 'realistically' ornamental setting with painted, illusionistic backdrops; others, such as Alan Dessen, for the openness, flexibility, and neutrality of the staged space; and others, such as Michael Hattaway, for a middle ground of scenic illusion created metonymically by portable and non-portable properties.[40]

Yet regardless of how elaborately or sparsely, metonymically or illusionistically, specifically or neutrally settings were signified by scenery and props, the idea of place was largely symbolic.[41] To create a setting was to establish a nexus of non-spatial conditions and preconditions beyond those that could be actually accommodated on stage – to signal time and temporal shifts, historical contexts, general cultural or situational characteristics (a 'tavern world' metonymically represented by a tavern, perhaps also represented metonymically by a table and a mug), ideological divisions between peoples and worlds (Capulets versus Montagues, Rome versus Egypt), metaphysical or psychological situations (the alienation of Edward II in prison or of Lear on the heath).

For Marlowe, the choice of settings from Africa to the Mediterranean to the East turns our attention to the key sites of England's imperialist exploits and so to the issue of imperialism. On a more symbolic level, however, his representation of those settings breaks down the barriers of difference, showing that the worlds out there are not so different from Europe. Greenblatt has argued that in *Tamburlaine* 'all ... spaces seem curiously alike' and that on the Marlovian stage generally 'space is transformed into an abstraction' that signals its 'essential meaninglessness'; although characters attempt to impose shape and significance on it, this backdrop remains 'neutral and unresponsive', exposing the vacancy of self that they struggle to overcome.[42] Marlovian space is, in some ways, shapeless, but the lack of differentiation between its worlds functions on a less abstract level to suggest the meaninglessness not of space but of the bounds imposed upon it. The point is not that space is meaningless, but that the differences assigned to it are empty, overdetermined, or arbitrary, at best.

In the decades before Marlowe, the Elizabethan stage witnessed an outbreak of 'tyrant plays' such as *Damon and Pythias* and *Cambyses*, which, though they provide a 'mirror for magistrates' and their subjects, emphasise and exploit the foreignness of their settings.[43] Other worlds provided a place where tyranny, in particular, could be dramatised in all its excesses and the message of obedience pressed to an extreme.

What makes Marlowe's plays stand out within this context is that their foreign worlds are not only 'Englished'; they make a point of that Englishing. *Dido, Queen of Carthage*, for example, announces the resemblance between its African landscape and England: Iarbas, in a complaint to Jove, makes 'all the woods Eliza to resound' (IV.ii.10) – a phrase that Edmund Spenser will canonise as part of the English literary tradition – bringing out an embedded parallel between Carthage's queen (whose Phoenician name was 'Elissa') and England's. That he is an African king complaining to a pagan god and invoking a name that is otherwise suppressed emphasises the incongruity, as ours and theirs suggestively collide in a space that excludes neither.

Though exotic beings would be expected to appear more readily in Africa than in Europe or even the East, they do not, and the play makes a point of that fact. When Aeneas first steps foot on the Carthaginian shore, his immediate concern is 'whether men or beasts inhabit' here (I.i.177). When Venus greets him shortly after, dressed as a Tyrian huntress in 'bow and quiver' ready to 'overtake the tusked boar in chase', and looking for her 'sisters' 'clothed in spotted leopard's skin', she evokes the Amazons who figured as 'exotic curios' in descriptions of Africa (I.i.184–208).[44] The potential exoticism of the scene is undermined as quickly as it is suggested, however, by the fact that this is only a 'borrow'd shape' (I.i.192) transparent to the staged and unstaged audiences. Aeneas, who soon recognises her, avows that he 'neither saw not heard of any such' (I.i.187), and for the rest of the play neither do the spectators, who are thus alerted to its lack.

The ordinary texture of this and other of Marlowe's other worlds becomes particularly clear in contrast to that of the exotic landscapes within Spenser's *Faerie Queene*, the first three books of which emerged during Marlowe's lifetime.[45] Although part of that difference is necessarily dictated by the constraints of performance and fostered by the licence of allegory, the comparison nonetheless reminds us that the playwright's strange lands exclude the monsters and marvels, the giants and dragons and metamorphosed beings, available for the imaginative refashioning of the self.

Reciprocally, Marlowe's European worlds are notably defamiliarised. *Faustus*'s Germany contains not only devils but also dragons, included on the 1598 property list of the Admiral's men and possibly brought on stage (or suspended above it) to show Faustus 'whirling round' the universe in a 'chariot burning bright, / Drawn by the strength of yoked dragons' necks' (III Prologue II, 5–6).[46] The exceedingly rapid tempo of *The Massacre at Paris*, with one act of violence following immediately and surprisingly upon another, though perhaps an aberration of the text, creates a sort of Monty Python world picture. And, as I have suggested above, the presence of a homosexual king on the French throne, as on the English throne of *Edward II*, also distances these kingdoms from Elizabethan (though, of course, not Jacobean) England.

Critics have often distinguished *Edward II* (sometimes along with *The Massacre at Paris*, which is more often ignored) from Marlowe's other plays in part because of its English setting and the historical base, which also lends familiarity; in Edward II's England, characters and issues seem 'the most naturally human', or, what has been taken as the equivalent, the most 'Shakespearean'.[47] The 'other' worlds, in contrast, are viewed as decidedly other – as, for example, escapist terrains where spectators need not confront otherwise inescapable fears, issues, or selves, at least not at close range.[48] This division resurrects bounds that the plays themselves resist. Indeed the English king Edward has a prototype in Persia, in the figure of Mycetes, who, like Edward, loves his minions. What characterises Marlovian landscapes is not a one-dimensional cultivation of strangeness or familiarity but an insistent incorporation of the strange within the familiar – an incorporation that proves geographic bounds arbitrary measures of difference and insists that the spectators suspend categorical assumptions about what is ours and what, theirs.

'Which is the merchant here? And which the Jew?'

This suspension is demanded even more forcefully by the representation of character, for Marlowe evokes cultural stereotypes only to set them in contexts that defy the uniqueness of those types. Significantly, each of the plays initially situates its alien figure in a space of difference.

In *Tamburlaine*, *Doctor Faustus*, and *The Jew of Malta*, the heroes are introduced in all their otherness in the separate and potentially authoritative space of the prologue. Before we see Tamburlaine, we are warned that the 'Scythian' will 'threaten the world with high astounding terms, / And scourg[e] kingdoms with his conquering sword' (Prologue 4–6). When he appears, he exoticises himself, throwing off his shepherd's 'weeds' to uncover a 'cotte with coperlace' and 'breches of crymson velvet' beneath and announcing his intention to 'be a terror to the world' (I.ii.38,41).[49] The Jew of Malta is introduced by Machevill, who unabashedly offers a catalogue of his own subversive policies and blasphemous beliefs, and then surreptitiously begs the spectators not to 'entertain' Barabas 'the worse / Because he favours me' (Prologue 34–5). Though Machevill proves an unreliable narrator, his prologue nonetheless sets the Jew in space of otherness, and when Barabas is then discovered in a long nose and possibly a red wig and beard (which, after him, became the stock costume of the stage Jew), fondling his 'heaps of gold' (stage direction) and declaiming against Christians, that impression is more than reinforced. And while Gaveston gets no prologue, he, in effect, creates his own as he stands on the outskirts of court, anticipating the homoerotic pageants he will use to entertain his 'dearest friend', the king (*Edward II*, I.i.2).

Yet, while the plays consciously emphasise these characters' distinguishing types, they place them in contexts in which they are more like than unlike those who share their stage. The fact that *Edward II* offers two 'others' (Gaveston and Edward) is only the beginning. Everyone in Carthage seems to be a stranger in one sense or another – from Aeneas who explicitly defines himself as such, to Dido, an exile from Tyre, to Iarbas, the African king. Tamburlaine, the barbarian, is surrounded by barbarians whose desires to rule the universe seem no more moderate than his; and his episodic and incessant engagement in battles creates a sense that there will always be one more conqueror, like one more country, to conquer. Faustus is alone as he makes his choice to study magic, but he is soon joined and tutored by the infamous black magicians, Valdes and Cornelius, and parodied by the unlearned Robin, who uses one of his 'conjuring books' to produce 'a roaring piece of work' (II.ii.2, 11–12). And while Barabas may be the only prominent Jew in Malta, the island is peopled with Machiavels, Christians as well as Turks among them, whose desires for money and property are no less pronounced and whose strategies for procuring them, no less devious, than his.

On the Marlovian stage, where stereotypical traits of difference are marks of sameness, alien status cannot be categorically assigned. For, to borrow Christopher Miller's words, 'a state where everything is other is a state where the word "other" has lost its oppositional power and no longer means anything'.[50] The comic elements mixed into Marlowe's tragedies keep them from generating the same darkness that is found on the Jacobean stage, but the pervasive corruption that defines the societies in the plays of John Webster, Cyril Tourneur, John Ford and the like, and that destabilises the division between right and wrong has its antecedent in Marlowe.[51] Instead of showing us how the 'other' half lives, murders, and deceives, Marlowe and his Jacobean predecessors situate the other as the status quo and, without necessarily valorising or condemning subversive standards, make them the norm against which other values and behaviours must be measured.

While disallowing automatic discriminations thus, Marlowe's plays also set up oppositions that at once prompt the viewers to discriminate and prohibit them from doing so. Each play centres on a confrontation between the alien and some other(s) who are not alien-identified, setting up what seems a 'conflictual, hierarchically structured field' but, significantly, without privileging either term.[52] Marlowe refuses to fault Aeneas, as does Dido, for deserting her in her love, or Dido, as do the Trojans, for detaining Aeneas from his duty; to damn Faustus for transgression, as do the devils, or laud his conjurations, as do the heads of state; to deride Edward as weak or tyrannical, as do the nobles, or exonerate him, as does his son. The point is not merely that the plays are ambivalent toward their alien 'heroes' but that they make a point of that ambivalence and expose the indeterminacy, relativity, and subjectivity of judgments which do not.

Tamburlaine provides one of the clearest examples of this strategy, for as it shifts from country to country, conflict to conflict, barbarian to barbarian, it makes it clear that in the world of the empire, one ruler's establishment is another ruler's other. Part 1 introduces Persia as 'the establishment', with Mycetes on its throne and Tamburlaine, the 'incivil' (I.i.40) outsider, threatening its borders. Yet it is the king's brother, Cosroe, who first usurps the throne, and when Tamburlaine then conquers him, it is unclear which side we should support, the 'sturdy Scythian thief' (I.i.36) or the original traitor. Before we have time to decide, the focus shifts from Persia to the further reaches and rulers of the East, where it is as hard to choose sides as to map them. Though Tamburlaine defeats the imperialising Turkish emperor, Bajazeth, for example, he himself has his eye not only on Persia, Africa and endless other worlds, but also on 'all the ocean by the British shore' (III.iii.259), leaving us unsure whether to cheer or regret the victory.

So, too, in *The Jew of Malta*, whose shifting oppositions similarly problematise our allegiance to any one side. The Christian governor, Ferneze, first joins with the Turks, then turns against them; first disenfranchises the Jew, then joins with him, then deceives and destroys him. The Jew first embraces then betrays the Turks, and first betrays and then embraces the Christians, making it as difficult for us to see the sides as to choose between them. Though the oppositions are more stable in *Edward II*, the idea of right is not. The primacy of a legitimate but homosexual monarch is set in competition with that of an established but seditious baronage, and though, in the end, the power of the monarchy is restored, the issue of which faction was at fault for the intervening chaos is never resolved. Once again, as the scene moves from one side and one set of protests and allegations to the other, we are made aware that 'contraries' can both be true, even if both cannot be right.[53]

Marlowe complicates this situation further by encouraging transgression responses that implicate the audience as disturbingly complicitous, whether intentionally or not, in the 'unlawful things' enacted onstage, placing the spectators in a compromised position between cultural standards that condemn and responses that condone. The final chorus of *Faustus* cautions us not to practise but 'only to wonder at unlawful things' (Epilogue, 6) and suggests our voyeurism is innocuous if not innocent.[54] Like the German emperor who asks Faustus to conjure spirits, we, too, beg for a show to 'wonder at', the more spectacular (even, or especially, if illegal) the better.

Significantly, Marlowe's heroes dominate the staged stage, directing the action, producing the spectacles, claiming the spectacular speeches, and monopolising everyone's attention. And while their illicit activities 'should' invoke our disapproval, their control over the production makes our enjoyment dependent upon them and their exploits, however subversive, illegal, or ungodly.[55] We need Barabas to poison a convent full of nuns or to trick one friar into 'killing' the dead body of another for our amusement, even though it aligns us with the fiendish Ithamore, who also delights in (and worships his master's nose for) excessive villainies. And, though an indignity to the idea of monarchy, we need Tamburlaine to bridle captive kings for his chariot and our astonishment.

When these heroes die, we are encouraged to feel sympathy rather than triumph or relief. In representing Edward II's death, for example, Marlowe turns the king into victim by detailing the torture and torment orchestrated by his captors, culling details from an additional source, Stow's chronicles, in order to do so. We might respond to the deaths of Barabas and Tamburlaine with some relief, because, unlike Faustus and Edward who are progressively disempowered and who finally express regrets, Barabas and Tamburlaine continue almost mechanically to deceive and destroy until the last possible moment. The characters who survive, however, promise to give us more of the same treachery or terrorism, but without the same attracting theatricality. Though Ferneze may steal Barabas's final plot and trap him in the cauldron constructed for the Turks, he can never be as cunning, elusive, or intriguing as the Jew.

While our sympathies are drawn toward figures we should love to hate, they are also turned from those figures' victims, particularly in *The Jew of Malta* and *Faustus* where tragedy is heavily mixed with comedy. Barabas's most egregious crime is the poisoning of his daughter, Abigail, a crime that plays into the belief that Jews ritualistically murder[ed] children. Yet the fact that she is killed along with a convent full of nuns, and almost (if Ithamore had his way) a monastery full of monks, turns the tragedy into farce, our sympathy into laughter. The thinness of her characterisation, like that of the friars, Don Lodowick, and Don Mathias, and the cultivated scurrility of Pilia-Borza, Bellamira, and Ithamore, all murdered by the Jew, create a distance between their interests and ours, their victimisation and our sympathy. This same distance also emerges in *Faustus*, for the only victims of Faustus's magic (besides Faustus himself) are the comic figures such as the Pope and the horse-courser, who seem to get what they deserve. Marlowe's plays do foster an estrangement, not between their exotic worlds and England, but rather, and more subversively, between the viewers and their world, pressing them to question established categories of meaning, to suspend their biases, and to see the other as part of the self, the merchant as the Jew.

The subject of alienation

Marlowe's plays not only frustrate discrimination; they also thematise it. The Marlovian world picture is 'spectacular' in a literal sense: its spectacles provide a means not just of displaying strangeness, but of exhibiting the ways in which the 'strange' is displayed. Though Marlowe refuses to support prefabricated discriminations, the secondary characters do not, and it is amid their conflicting constructions of self and other that the primary characters must negotiate an identity. Our attention is turned, as Greenblatt has suggested, to their self-fashioning, but it is self-fashioning with a difference. Instead of acting against a 'neutral and unresponsive' void, each of Marlowe's heroes is surrounded by characters who are constructing themselves against him or her and whose representations the hero constructs himself or herself against.

The singular prominence that the central characters claim within these texts has prompted critics to give them comparable priority within interpretations, to focus on the outstanding aspects that set them apart from or within the staged environment: their hyperbolic language, ambitions, or histrionics, their obsessive desires to transgress or transcend, their repeated attempts to define themselves or a place for themselves in their own self-aggrandised, though ultimately self-abnegating, terms, and so on. While such readings do, to some extent, take into account the dramatic transactions between the primary and secondary characters, the dominance that they give, almost automatically, to the hero tends to reduce the importance of the surrounding society.

Yet it is not only the viewers and critics offstage but also the spectators onstage who are preoccupied with the hero, and it is their preoccupation, in addition to and in competition with his or her self-representation, that not only directs our gaze but emerges as the object of it. What emerges under the gaze is the fact that the sometimes aggrandising and sometimes demonising discriminations that these characters impose upon the alien are constructed in answer to their own agendas. When Tamburlaine is not exhibiting his 'working words' or 'sights of power', other characters are commenting on those exhibitions, valorising them (and him) if they want to join with him and demonising them (and him) if they want to defeat him. Barabas, too, is surrounded by discourses which attempt to define him as 'the Jew' and so to appropriate his money, his daughter, or his schemes. In *Faustus*, when morality figures are not appearing out of nowhere to label the 'good or bad' of Faustus's fortunes, rulers, devils, and scholars are. And even though sodomy was an unspeakable sin, Edward II's barons find a way to speak it, to defame the king and his 'minions', and so to justify civil war.

Ironically, what the texts (and the wide discrepancies between interpretations of them) make most clear about the heroes is that their underlying motives are ultimately unknowable, even as they articulate and act upon specific desires (Barabas for money, Faustus for magic, Edward II for 'minions', and so on) in ways that suggest a uniformity of mind or purpose. Although their professed preoccupations with a certain object initially define their actions, neither their words nor their deeds remain centred on that goal. Instead they 'swell beyond' it, as Michael Goldman has argued – not necessarily or exclusively toward 'the possibility of entire bliss' as he posits, but rather toward some more elusive end.[56] Barabas seems intent on gathering infinite riches into his little room; yet as he gains more wealth and power than the governor and directs his revenge against allies and enemies alike, he makes us unsure when (or whether) enough will be enough and what is 'enough' for him. Edward declares that he will 'either die, or live with Gaveston' (*Edward II*, I.i.138), but his quick embrace of the Younger Spenser, coming even before there could be any funeral baked meats for Gaveston, alters our impression of what Edward is and has been after. Tamburlaine is perhaps the most single-minded of the lot, but his thoughts, too, turn from conquering kingdoms to 'entertain[ing] divine Zenocrate' (*Tamburlaine*, 2:II.iv.17) to acting as the scourge of God or terror of the world.

In making his aliens so elusive, Marlowe runs the risk of reinforcing the unknowability that stereotypes themselves produce beneath the guise of absolute knowability. Yet Marlowe uses that unknown as a way of highlighting the instability of the 'knowledge' imposed upon it, exposing the discrepancies between and within the terms the secondary characters use to fix the hero's difference, to produce a self-affirming other. In setting the elusiveness of the aliens in conflict with those terms, Marlowe insists upon uncertainty where competing characters write certainty, gaps where they write knowledge.

It is within this context of conflicting discourses that Marlowe's aliens emerge, and from it that they must (and do) distinguish themselves, that they must, that is, create their own terms of difference and identity. In each case, they exploit the terms imposed upon them and use difference as a means to power. Though they, like Marlowe himself, are made to fill the space of subversion that their societies open for them, they also reconstruct that space and, by playing into and against expectations, turn those constructs against themselves. The crucial question to be asked of Marlowe's aliens is not whether they are 'good or bad', but how they and others fashion themselves as such, and to what ends.

Marlowe's plays do not attempt to recuperate the 'subaltern' voice; instead their focus is on the means of appropriation that silence and occlude that voice, creating in its stead an other who speaks of and for Europe.[57] In Marlowe both Europeans and non-Europeans figure as the subjects and objects of alienation. In taking on both, Marlovian drama reinforces what each play affirms individually: that what is out there and what is here are not so different after all, despite the plethora of contemporary representations invested in proving the contrary.

Alienated subjects

Before examining how Marlovian drama works to undermine cultural biases, however, it is necessary first to acknowledge that in some cases these strategies break down and encourage rather than refute such biases, however consciously or unconsciously. For indeed, while in the abstract and for the most part the plays unfix prescribed bounds of difference, in certain instances they do not. Though the problem may derive in part from hazards inherent in their methodologies, it also suggests that Marlowe, despite the radicality of his position, was nonetheless conditioned by his era and partially subject to the prejudicial tendencies he was otherwise subverting. These inconsistencies do not ultimately disrupt the subversive ideology of his plays, but they do show how powerful and coercive were the forces he was resisting and how necessary and remarkable that resistance was.

Methodologically, in producing strange spectacles to show how spectacles were produced to estrange, the plays run the risk of seeming to present the strange for strangeness's sake, despite their familiarisation strategies, and of distracting attention from their ideological purposes. Ithamore's outrageous representations of the Jew, for example, turn our attention from the fact that he manipulates stereotypes to the comic terms in which he does so, as he turns Barabas into a 'strange thing' (*The Jew of Malta* IV.iv.82), worships his nose, and the like. Despite itself, the play seems to have been highly influential in ensuring that the stage Jew remain a physically and ideologically marked type. Too, the Dutch Church libel's author evoked *Tamburlaine* (along with *The Massacre at Paris*) in order to incite seditious riot, but that riot was itself aimed against foreigners. Thus, while Marlowe seems to have been a code word for subversion, the subversiveness of his representations of foreigners seems, in this instance, to have been radically misread.

The counterproductive afterlife of the plays does not necessarily reflect ideological inconsistencies within them. Their internal type-casting of secondary figures, however, does. Although the Turkish Calymath is not markedly different from the other leaders contending for Maltese rule, Ithamore fulfils the stereotype of the Turk as an uncivilised, anti-Christian villain, particularly when he boasts of 'setting Christian villages on fire', cutting throats, and crippling Christians (*The Jew of Malta* II.iii.208–17). The caricatured characterisations of Pilia-Borza and Bellamira, similarly, reinforce the basest conceptions of Italians, just as those of *Faustus*'s very worldly pope and his impotent friars and *The Massacre at Paris*'s militantly anti-Protestant Duke of Guise do of Catholics.

More problematic are Marlowe's representations of women, not because they are one-dimensional and wooden (as critics have often concluded) but because they are two-dimensional and contradictory, because they reinscribe a difference that they simultaneously resist. As Simon Shephard's brief though provocative treatment of Marlovian women suggests, Marlowe shows, rather than merely allows, male control over the staged space and over the definition and agency of the women who share that space. His plays demonstrate how 'the ideology of what women should be ... originates in the man' and how women are fetishised beneath the male gaze.[58] Yet Marlowe also participates in that subjugation and objectification. Although Dido uses and exposes the fetishisation of objects as a mode of self-empowerment, her erotic self-presentation makes her an object of desire. In *Faustus* and *Tamburlaine*, too, Marlowe represents Helen and Zenocrate as objects fetishised by male characters and in so doing fetishises them himself, so effectively, in fact, that 'the face that launch'd a thousand ships' (*Faustus* V.i.92) has become its own suggestive icon, quite detached from Helen, Faustus, or the play.[59]

Even as Marlowe exposes male dominance as male dominance, he presents women who, despite initial acts of resistance, are willingly complicitous in enforcing its terms, and who are unaware of or indifferent to the limitations that we see in their circumscribed situations. Although Zenocrate first resists her captivity at the hands of Tamburlaine, after her 'offensive rape' she is ready (with Desdemona-like devotion) to 'live and die with [him]', 'as his exceeding favours have deserv'd' (*Tamburlaine* III.ii.6,24,10). She is not the only one taken in by the conqueror's 'working words' and deeds; yet, unlike his (her) male competitors and like other

Marlovian women, she follows the leader's lead without a competing agenda, and at the expense of self, home, and heritage. When Tamburlaine threatens to attack Egypt, she begs him to 'have some pity' for her father, her country, and her 'sake' (IV.ii.123), but she remains beside him even when he refuses. In Part 2, as she offers herself up to her sons as what they should 'resemble' 'in death' (2:II.iv.75) and presents their father as what they should emulate in their lives, she embraces the position that Marlowe and Tamburlaine script for her – as an image that gives life and meaning solely to the world of men.

The Jew of Malta's Abigail eventually rebels against her father, but she escapes to a nunnery (which figures as unfavourably in Marlowe as it does in Shakespeare), to a new position of subjugation beneath those who, if the friars are right, are as corrupt as her father, though in a different (sexual) way. Despite her claims that she can 'see the difference of things' (III.iii.68) from that position, she becomes a figure of difference, opting for a circumscribed identity and embracing a religion as other to her as to the audience. After her death, as Barabas continues to murder and deceive, she gets lost in the shuffle as little more than 'the rich Jew's daughter' (I.ii.378), appropriated for his plots and Marlowe's.

While the limitations Marlowe imposes on his Catholic, underclass, and female characters stand at odds with his otherwise liberating agenda, they do not finally disrupt it. Rather, they set off by contrast those instances in which prejudicial expectations are defied. Importantly too, they caution us to recognise that though Marlowe's politics were to some degree ahead of his time, they were also constrained by it. Though the plays stand in radical opposition to dominating discourses, they are also inevitably subject to those constraints. It is Marlovian drama's liminal position between the inside and the outside that finally makes its subversive vision so disturbing, convincing, and compelling.

From Emily C. Bartels, *Spectacles of Strangeness: Imperialism, Alienation, and Marlowe* (Philadelphia, 1993), pp. 4–26.

Notes

[Emily Bartels' reading of Marlowe is primarily historical: it is designed to lend historical and cultural meaning to his preoccupation with spectacles of strangeness and alienation in an age of nascent English Imperialism. Marlowe is obsessed with strangers of various kinds – ethnic, religious, moral, and sexual – all of whom he transforms from marginality to central figures embodying the predominant issues of the plays. In his subversion of Elizabethan prevailing notions he discerns the presence of the other within an allegedly unified world picture. Ed.]

1. I am referring to an often cited mass exodus at a performance of *Doctor Faustus*. Steven Mullaney suggests '*the* vernacular', which the learned regarded as 'barbarous' in comparison to Latin, as estranged within popular culture because of its accommodation of a plurality of dialects and its continual assimilation of foreign terms; see Mullaney, *The Place of the Stage: License, Play, and Power in Renaissance England* (Chicago, 1988), pp. 76–85.

2. I borrow the phrase from Mullaney, who borrows it from Ben Johnson's description of the antimasque in the *Masque of Queens (Place of the Stage*, p. 64).

3. For an informative discussion of England's economic profile in the mid-sixteenth century, see J. A. Sharpe, *Early Modern England: A Social History 1550–1760* (London, 1987), esp. pp. 127–51. Kenneth R. Andrews, *Trade, Plunder, and Settlement: Maritime Enterprise and the Genesis of the British Empire, 1480–1630* (Cambridge, 1984), provides an excellent study of England's early imperialism. See also A. L. Rowse, *The Expansion of Elizabethan England* (London, 1955); James A. Williamson, *The Age of Drake*, 2nd edn (London, 1946); and J. H. Parry, *The Age of Reconnaissance* (Berkley, CA, 1963).

4. The publication history of this text is offered in Margaret T. Hodgen, *Early Anthropology in the Sixteenth and Seventeenth Centuries* (Philadelphia, 1964), pp. 132–3, which also provides a useful survey of other cross-cultural texts.

5. John Leo Africanus, *The History and Description of Africa and the Notable Things Therein Contained*, trans. John Pory, ed. Robert Brown (London, 1896), p. 935.

6. Rowse, *Elizabethan England*, p. 159. Richard Helgerson, *Forms of Nationhood: The Elizabethan Writings of England* (Chicago, 1992), pp. 151–91, offers an excellent discussion of Hakluyt and his construction of English nationhood.

7. See Hodgen, *Early Anthropology*, pp. 144–61, on Renaissance collecting.

8. See Mary B. Campbell, *The Witness and the Other World: Exotic European Travel Writing, 400–1600* (Ithaca, NY, 1988), for a discussion of the ways these myths play into literary traditions.

9. Compare Tzvetan Todorov, *The Conquest of America: The Question of the Other* (New York, 1984), pp. 49–50, on the ways in which European colonialist texts both 'revealed and rejected' cultural difference.

10. See Mullaney, *Place of the Stage*, pp. 26–47.

11. Edward Said, *Orientalism* (New York, 1978), p. 54. See also, Paul Brown, ' "This thing of darkness I acknowledge mine": *The Tempest* and the Discourse of Colonialism', in *Political Shakespeare: New Essays in Cultural Materialism*, ed. Jonathan Dollimore and Alan Sinfield (Ithaca, NY, 1985), pp. 48–71; and Stephen Greenblatt, 'Invisible Bullets: Renaissance Authority and its Subversion, *Henry IV* and *Henry V*', also in *Political Shakespeare*, pp. 18–47.

12. Robert Young, *White Mythologies: Writing History and the West* (London, 1990), provides a useful critique of Said (along with Homi Bhabha, Gayatri Spivak, and others), suggesting that there are really two Orientalisms, one in which the Orient is the imaginary object of colonialist discourse and the other in which it is a real subject of colonialism, see pp. 119–40.

13. Christopher Miller, *Blank Darkness: Africanist Discourse in French* (Chicago, 1985), pp.14–23. Miller argues that Africa emerges in European discourse as the Other's other, a third term which has no meaning of its own and is inscribed like a blank slate from without.

14. Homi K. Bhabha, 'The Other Question: The Stereotype and Colonial Discourse', *Screen*, 24 (1983), 18–36. M. M. Bakhtin also offers a useful critique of monologic discourse; his essay on 'Discourse in the Novel' in particular has informed my own theoretical position (*The Dialogic Imagination*, trans. Caryl Emerson and Michael Holquist, ed. Michael Holquist [Austin, TX, 1981], pp. 259–422).

15. Bhabha, 'The Other Question', pp. 23 (quoting Said), 18.

16. See, for example, Raphael Holinshed, *Chronicles of England, Scotland and Ireland* (London, 1807), 2:92, 419. Simon Shepherd, *Marlowe and the Politics of Elizabethan Theatre* (Sussex, 1986), pp.142–5, gives a useful overview of the conflicted image of the Turk.

17. Miller, *Blank Darkness*, p. 64.

18. Compare Janet Adelman, *Suffocating Mothers: Fantasies of Maternal Origin in Shakespeare's Plays, Hamlet to The Tempest* (New York, 1992), pp. 176–92, who suggests that Antony is inscribed as absence and Cleopatra as presence.

19. For example, see Michael Neill, 'Unproper Beds: Race, Adultery, and the Hideous in *Othello*', in *Shakespeare Quarterly*, 40 (1989), 382–412, who prefers the term 'racialism'. See also Winthrop D. Jordan, *The*

White Man's Burden: Historical Origins of Racism in the United States (New York, 1974) and *White Over Black: American Attitudes Toward the Negro, 1550–1812* (New York, 1968).

20. See the Wakefield *Noah* in *The Wakefield Mystery Plays*, ed. Martial Rose (New York, 1961), pp. 88–106; or the *York Flood, Herod and the Magi, The Slaughter of the Innocents*, and *Christ Before Herod* in *York Mystery Plays: A Selection in Modern Spelling*, ed. Richard Beadle and Pamela M. King (Oxford, 1984).

21. From the epilogue, ll. David M. Bevington, *Tudor Drama and Politics: A Critical Approach to Topical Meaning* (Cambridge, MA, 1968), pp. 156–7.

22. For an excellent study of the theatre's social place and the ways other cultures were 'rehearsed' within it, see Mullaney, *Place of the Stage*. Jean-Christophe Agnew, *Worlds Apart: The Market and the Theatre in Anglo-American Thought, 1550–1750* (Cambridge, 1987), also gives an excellent discussion of the early theatre's place in society. See also Michael Bristol, *Carnival and Theatre: Plebian Culture and the Structure of Authority in Renaissance England* (New York, 1985).

23. Muly Hamet appears in *The Famous History of the Life and Death of Captain Thomas Stuckeley*. See the discussion in Anthony Gerard Barthelemy, *Black Face, Maligned Race: The Representation of Blacks in English Drama from Shakespeare to Southerne* (Baton Rouge, LA, 1987), pp. 86–91.

24. I refer to the by now well-known allegation that in one performance an extra devil was conjured up; see John M. Bakeless, *The Tragicall History of Christopher Marlowe* (Cambridge, MA, 1942), I: 299–300.

25. For an intriguing discussion of the set speech, see Thomas Cartelli, 'Ideology and Subversion in the Shakespearean Set Piece', *English Literary History*, 53 (1986), 1–25.

26. Johannes Birringer, *Marlowe's 'Dr. Faustus' and 'Tamburlaine': Theological and Theatrical Perspectives* (New York, 1984), p. 105. Harry Levin's claim for hyperbole as Marlowe's dominating mode has influenced other critics – such as Frank Fieler, C. L. Barber, and William Blackburn – to see the plays as expressing either attainable or unattainable hyperbolic possibilities. See Levin, *The Overreacher: A Study of Christopher Marlowe* (Cambridge, MA, 1952). Even critics who adopt a darker view of the Elizabethan and Marlovian 'world picture' emphasise the hyperbolic dimensions of Marlovian drama.

27. For discussion of Marlowe's association with the School of Night (or, as it was also called, of atheism), see William Urry, *Christopher Marlowe and Canterbury*, ed. Andrew Butcher (London, 1988), pp. 69–71.

28. Kyd's letters to Sir John Puckering and the Baines note are cited in C. F. Tucker Brooke, *The Life of Marlowe* and the '*Tragedy of Dido,*

Queen of Carthage' (New York, 1930), pp. 98–108. See also Urry, *Marlowe and Canterbury*, pp. 71–9.

29. Brooke, *Life of Marlowe*, p. 101; David Riggs, 'Authorship, Atheism and Tamburlaine', a paper presented at the annual Shakespeare Association of America Convention, Vancouver, British Columbia, 23 March 1991.

30. Jonathan Goldberg, 'Sodomy and Society: The Case of Christopher Marlowe', *Southwest Review*, 69 (1984), 377.

31. See Leah S. Marcus, 'Textual Indeterminacy and Ideological Difference: The Case of *Doctor Faustus*', *Renaissance Drama*, 20 (1989), 16, who quotes the libel.

32. From the 'glosse' on the 'Sonet' appended to the *New Letter of Notable Contents* (1593), reproduced in Brooke, *Life of Marlowe*, pp. 111–12. The point of these poems is not very clear; Brooke declares them 'cloudy drivel' (p. 112).

33. Urry surveys these 'facts', the documents which record them, and the theories built around them (*Marlowe and Canterbury*, pp. 80–98).

34. Ibid, p. 98.

35. Sometime before 1633, Thomas Heywood added a prologue to *The Jew of Malta*, 'crav[ing]pardon' for 'so boldly dar[ing]' to reanimate a figure and a play which 'hath pass'd so many censures'; from the 'Prologue Spoken at Court', in E. D. Pendry's edition of Marlowe's *Complete Plays and Poems* (London, 1976), p. 5. In an introduction to *The Jew of Malta*, N. W. Bawcutt (ed.), (Baltimore, 1978), p. 2, reads this as an apology for the play's old-fashionedness. The accompanying epilogue, however, with its disclaimer that 'if aught here offend ... / We only act and speak what others write', suggests more subversive reasons for rebuke.

36. Stephen Greenblatt, *Renaissance Self-Fashioning: From More to Shakespeare* (Chicago, 1980), p. 194. See also Shepherd, who tries 'to lose Marlowe's works within a wider context' of 'the politics of Elizabethan theatre', situates the plays amidst a variety of cultural documents and dramatic traditions, and begins to explore the relation between the audience, dominant Elizabethan ideologies, and 'the questioning/affirming strategies of the individual text' (*Marlowe and the Politics of Elizabethan Theatre*, pp. xvii–xviii). In covering such a vast ideologic and dramatic terrain, his study, though useful, does indeed 'lose' Marlowe's works and at times the full impact of the contexts in which they are situated. Jonathan Dollimore's chapter on *Faustus in Radical Tragedy: Religion, Ideology and Power in the Drama of Shakespeare and his Contemporaries* (New York and London, 1989), has also contributed to the rehistoricising of Marlowe [reprinted in this volume – Ed.].

37. Greenblatt, *Renaissance Self-Fashioning*, pp. 212, 197, 203.

38. These terms come from Keir Elam, *The Semiotics of Theatre and Drama* (London, 1980), pp. 17–18, who argues that 'when theatrical semiosis is alienated, made "strange" rather than automatic, the spectator is encouraged to take note of the semiotic *means*, to become aware of the sign-vehicle and its operations'.

39. Other critics have also suggested that the plays 'encourag[e]the spectators to compare what they see with what the characters see', but without respect to external codes and to different ends than I propose here (Judith Weil, *Christopher Marlowe: Merlin's Prophet* [Cambridge, 1977], p. 19).

40. A. M. Nagler, *Shakespeare's Stage*, enlarged edn (New Haven, CT, 1981), pp. 32–7; Alan Dessen, *Elizabethan Stage Conventions and Modern Interpreters* (Cambridge, 1984), pp. 84–104; Michael Hattaway, *Elizabethan Popular Theatre: Plays in Performance* (London, 1982), pp. 34–40.

41. Elam, citing the Russian formalist and folklorist Petr Bogatyrev, argues that 'even in the most determinedly realistic of dramatic representations', theatrical signs 'point beyond the denotation to some ulterior cultural signification' (*Semiotics of Theatre*, p. 10).

42. Greenblatt, *Renaissance Self-Fashioning*, pp. 195–6.

43. Bevington discusses this group of plays and their use of setting in *Tudor Drama and Politics*, pp. 156–57, cited in note 21. Marlowe's *Tamburlaine* plays follow in the tyrant play tradition.

44. Simon Shepherd, *Amazons and Warrior Women: Varieties of Feminism in Seventeenth Century Drama* (New York, 1981), p. 13.

45. Marlowe's texts have invited comparisons to Spenser before; see, for example, Roy Battenhouse, *Marlowe's Tamburlaine: A Study in Renaissance Moral Philosophy* (Nashville, TN, 1941), pp. 178–92.

46. Hattaway presents convincing – though, as he admits, not conclusive – evidence that the dragon may have been brought onstage with Mephostophilis, as an ominous sign of 'the powers which [Faustus] has unleashed' but, ironically, does not see or does not fear (*Elizabethan Popular Theatre*, p. 171).

47. Muriel C. Bradbrook, 'The Jew of Malta and Edward II', in *Marlowe: A Collection of Critical Essays*, ed. Clifford Leech (Englewood Cliffs, NJ, 1964), p. 127. For example, Levin, who sees the historicity of the material as a constraint upon the playwright's 'artistic conception', argues that Edward is 'more deeply grounded within the psychological range of his creator' and that his 'sensations are relayed to us more fully and faithfully' (*The Overreacher*, pp. 86–7). J. B. Steane sets the

play apart for its 'unelaborated prosaic manner' (*Marlowe: A Critical Study* [Cambridge, 1964], p. 213), and Claude J. Summers for 'examin[ing] the very centre of Tudor political concerns ... with an immediacy which his plays set in the Orient and Malta necessarily lack' (*Christopher Marlowe and the Politics of Power* [Salzburg, 1974], p. 155).

48. See, for example, Constance Kuriyama, *Hammer or Anvil: Psychological Patterns in Christopher Marlowe's Plays* (New Brunswick, NJ, 1980), p. 195.

49. This is the costume recorded on the Henslowe property list; see Hattaway, *Elizabethan Popular Drama*, p. 86.

50. Miller, *Blank Darkness*, p. 131.

51. Dollimore, too, suggests Marlovian drama as an important antecedent to Jacobean tragedy (*Radical Tragedy*, p. 119).

52. Jacques Derrida, *Dissemination*, trans. Barbara Johnson (Chicago, 1981), p. 25.

53. I am evoking Lancaster's assertion that 'in no respect can contraries be true' (*Edward II* 1.4.251).

54. Marjorie Garber discusses the implications of audience complicity in ' "Vassal Actors": The Role of Audience in Shakespearean Tragedy', in *Renaissance Drama*, 9 (1978), 71–89.

55. Marlowe's plays stand, in this regard (among others), in contrast to Shakespeare's later tragedies in which, as Richard Hapgood has suggested, the 'dramatic life is so generally distributed' that the plays encourage a variety of identifications or experiences ('Shakespeare and the Included Spectator', in *Reinterpretations of Elizabethan Drama*, ed. Norman Rabkin [New York, 1969], p. 126).

56. Michael Goldman, 'Marlowe and the Histrionics of Ravishment', in *Two Renaissance Mythmakers: Christopher Marlowe and Ben Jonson*, ed. Alvin Kernan (Baltimore, 1977), p. 24.

57. My approach clearly departs from that of Spivak and the 'subaltern studies' group, who are interested in recuperating that voice. See Gayatri Chakravorty Spivak, *In Other Worlds: Essays in Cultural Politics* (New York, 1988) and *The Post-Colonial Critic: Interviews, Strategies, Dialogues*, ed. Sarah Harasym (New York, 1990).

58. Shepherd, *Marlowe and the Politics of Elizabethan Theatre*, p. 182; see also pp. 178–97.

59. See, for example, the recent Indigo Girls' song, 'Ghost', *Rites of Passage* (Sony Music Entertainment, 1992).

2

Christopher Marlowe: Ideology and Subversion

MICHAEL HATTAWAY

Subversion and representation

To begin from a moment in *1 Tamburlaine* when Tamburlaine spectacularly violates an Egyptian and, presumably, an Elizabethan cultural practice or ideological code. A Messenger describes to the Soldan of Egypt the quaint and very theatrical device of Tamburlaine's white, red, and black tents. The Soldan retorts:

> Merciless villain, peasant ignorant
> Of lawful arms or martial discipline!
> Pillage and murder are his usual trades –
> The slave usurps the glorious name of war.
> (*1 Tamburlaine*, IV.i.64–7)[1]

His outburst seems to be in excess of the facts until we reflect that, by constituting a new set of martial signals and abrogating to himself the meaning of language (usurping the 'name of war'), Tamburlaine is in fact re-constituting the state, what the Elizabethans termed the 'nation'.[2] This immodest, audacious upstart is enhancing his absolute military authority over Asia by a process of totalisation, and the Soldan is offering a description not only of sedition but of subjection.[3]

From the obverse perspective, it is also a moment of social realism: the Soldan may be regarded as an analogue of the nobility of England, and Tamburlaine as a nightmare figure, one of the Elizabethan bogy-men, this one emblematised in the cruel Turk or Tartar.[4] The old order dominated by the nobility has been subverted or problematised[5] by what is not only a physical but a cultural invasion by Tamburlaine. Codes of war had once been chivalric honour codes, but more lately, of course, they had been used (as in Elizabeth's Accession Day Tilts[6]) to sustain an aristocratic group which, as the quotation suggests, were no longer self-evidently the only hegemonic class. Tamburlaine's new signs proclaim, in fact, a crisis for aristocracy, a triumph of absolutism over constitutionalism, the destruction of hereditary monarchy, and the destabilising of a stratified order of privilege by a new order of status based upon the personality or charisma of a buccaneer.

The moment is related to a sequence near the beginning of the play, the famous stage image, or 'Gestus' as Brecht termed such a device, wherein Tamburlaine laid down his shepherd's weeds:

> Lie here, ye weeds that I disdain to wear!
> This complete armour and this curtle-axe
> Are adjuncts more beseeming Tamburlaine.
> (1 Tamburlaine, I.i.41–3)

That too is an image not just of bravado but of political challenge: by his self-fashioning the shepherd Tamburlaine defies the sumptuary laws which maintained what Shakespeare called 'degree' and we would call a status-system.[7] That was the theory. The fact that these laws existed at all suggests how much the reach of the Elizabethan state exceeded its grasp. Repeated attempts by the Tudors to control the dress of their subjects suggest some degree of phobia on part of the political elite.[8] Well might they fear: some of the most notorious transgressors of the sumptuary code were the players themselves, their own licensed servants.[9] Tamburlaine's dressing up draws attention to the ease and dangers of self-fashioning and social climbing, for both of which the stage provided a model. Moreover, he dreams of and creates an order where monarchical authority is sustained by no title, mystic corporation, or king's 'second body', but solely by sagacity and material power: the nation and the prince become one.[10] 'But what are kings, when regiment is gone, But perfect shadows in a sunshine day' (Edward II, V.i.26–7).

Tamburlaine, in fact, displays within the playhouse what had been carefully kept off-stage elsewhere, in that theatre of power that we know as the Elizabethan court, where elaborate rituals were deployed in order to imply that far more than might was needed to create right.[11] Marlowe, as we know, is rudely demystificatory: even Tamburlaine's lieutenant Theridamus can, with no ceremony, take the crown from the regal Zabina and hand it to Zenocrate: 'Here, madam, you are empress; she is none' (III.iii.227). Crowns are no longer sacral 'ceremonies' (objects) but, like the papier mâché circlets that rounded the temples of the common players, merely indices of power.[12]

It might, however, be claimed that Tamburlaine's eponymous role as scourge or flail of God,[13] *flagellum dei, does* make him, like Shakespeare's kings, 'twin-born with greatness'. However, a theatre audience, denied a coronation sequence, would be keenly aware that he makes his way to power not by undergoing ritual sanctification or by the divine right of the pope[14] but simply by killing kings. Therein lies a political challenge.

Not only tyrants were associated with flails: theatre clowns probably bore them too, as we see in various engravings of the time. Marlowe himself was a man possessed of a dark *élan*, a savage jester who, as his table-talk reveals, scourged his auditors with outrageous aphorisms; in the texts he wrote, he was a mannerist who, in his prologues, drew attention to his outlandish and astounding rhetorical play. He adopts a position of sardonic detachment – bordering on contempt – from his creations, a stance which is like the position of a jester vis-à-vis his subjects:[15] his co-author, Thomas Nashe, certainly occupied that role. In another play, *The Jew of Malta*, Barabas also functions as both jester and scourge.[16] His role is as much that of the playhouse clown as the moral vice, wearing a bottle nose and red beard,[17] confiding in his audience, adopting outrageous roles, plaguing and exposing the hypocrisy of the Christians. Like all scourges of God, Barabas must die at the end, but in a manner that is both frightening and ghoulishly amusing. Indeed many of the most serious moments in the plays seem to be rendered within the conventions of clownery. At the beginning of *Doctor Faustus*, after the climax of the Latin spell – '*nunc surgat nobis dicatus Mephistophilis!*' – a devil appears, only to be rudely dismissed by Faustus:

> I charge thee to return and change thy shape,
> Thou art too ugly to attend on me.

Go, and return an old Franciscan friar,
That holy shape becomes a devil best.
(I.iii.23–6)

The hero and the devils seem to be playing out a clowns' double-
act. Returning to the earlier play, we reflect that Tamburlaine's role
shares some characteristics with that of Barabas. The Scythian
shepherd is not only Herculean[18] but Gargantuan, and by this I
refer not only to his stature but his wit. For him, seizing the crown
from Cosroe is 'a pretty jest' (*1 Tamburlaine*, II.v.90), and there is
something of Groucho Marx in his most serious moments: after
wooing Zenocrate with a great *suasio*, Techelles retorts 'What now!
In love?' To which Tamburlaine replies:

Techelles, women must be flatterèd:
But this is she with whom I am in love.
(I.ii.106–8)

Moreover, just as the theatre clown or stage vice could, by speaking
more than was set down for him or upsetting decorum, usurp the
authority of both player-king and author, so, by the simplest of
tricks or by main force, might the determined man with what
Barabas calls 'a reaching thought' (I.ii.220) displace the monarch
and *his* authority. Comedy is no laughing matter, and understanding this comic detachment is crucial to the understanding of
Christopher Marlowe.

Marlowe's political plays, *Tamburlaine, Edward II, The Jew of
Malta*, and *The Massacre at Paris*, are therefore, as I have inferred,
pointedly secular. They generally demand the use of only one level
of the Elizabethan playhouse,[19] suggest no necessary pattern of
divine retribution, and, as in Machiavelli, their imagery is often
drawn from struggles for survival in the animal kingdom.[20] The fate
of Greek tragedy, Napoleon told Goethe, had been replaced by
politics. Marlowe anticipated this world and wrote plays whose
theme is the gaining, maintaining, and losing of power. This power
is, as Barabas boasts, gained by policy (V.ii.26–47) and is never a
function of moral or divine supremacy. Politicians cultivate fear
rather than love (*Edward II*, V.iv.52), operate by martial rather
than by civil law (*Edward II*, V.iv.88), and win or lose not so much
by main strength as by politic contrivance: the very stuff of the
theatrical improvisation of which I have just spoken. Indeed this

combination of the themes of theatricality and absolutism,[21] 'the-atrocracy', is one of the main topics of this essay.

These two moments from *Tamburlaine*, in short, serve two functions: Tamburlaine is insinuating into the Elizabethan consciousness the nightmare of class war, demonstrating that a peasant's revolt[22] could turn into rebellion or even revolution. As they watched the creation of this type of Asiatic absolutism, Marlowe's audiences were being offered an ironic analysis of the culture they themselves inhabited. A shepherd has, as it were, stepped out of the pages of a pastoral romance into the political arena.[23] By setting aside the old rules of war, he exposes the realities – social and moral realities as I shall demonstrate – of the Elizabethan political order. War, it turns out, belongs not in the realm of theodicy, as a writer like Spenser would have us believe, but in the realm of strategy, an awareness which reached its apogee with the writings of Karl von Clausewitz in the nineteenth century. The Soldan's lines serve as a defamiliarising device, which may lead us to ruminate, with St Augustine, that war is also a form of piracy: 'Set justice aside then', reflected Augustine, 'and what are kingdoms but fair thievish purchases [pursuits]? For what are thieves' purchases but little kingdoms? For in thefts, the hands of the underlings are directed by the commander, the confederacy of them is sworn together, and the pillage is shared by the law amongst them'.[24] Piracy, cynically legitimised by Cecil[25] and the monarchy, was, for the Elizabethans, in reality the most notable form of war.

But we must pay attention not only to what is represented or signified here but to the manner of theatrical representation. We leap forward to another related moment, at the end of Part 1 when, having heard again of Tamburlaine's tents, the virgins of Damascus remind the Governor how selfish have been his tactics. The amazing thing that we then hear is that Tamburlaine's blackness signifies not just 'slaughtering terror' (*1 Tamburlaine*, V.i.72) but melancholy. In fact the scourge of God seems to be tilting towards madness as he threatens the Damascenes with his 'servant Death' (V.i.117)

A complete analysis of these three related moments must there-fore include their mode of representation – spectacle is not just a way of making violence aesthetically intriguing, but serves both as a register of cultural change and an index of Tamburlaine's mind, an elaborate way of representing mood or fancy.

Shakespeare and the truth of fancy

It has long been realised that Marlowe's mode of characterisation resembles that of Spenser. His personages are iconic, both real and ideal: in the case of all the plays, except perhaps *Edward II*, we speak of flesh and blood heroes only at our peril. The texts call for an acting style in which there is as much alienation as identification between player and role. They are strangely intellectual, and Marlowe's location of the discourse of religion within the discourse of power, for example, reveals that, like Machiavelli and others, he understood the workings of what we have come to call ideology.[26] It follows that his characters, their actions and utterances, are more culturally than psychologically significant. Indeed their power derives from their ideological locations more than their actions: Tamburlaine may be less of a 'Herculean hero' than the *type* of one who puts resistance theory into practice and then creates a tyranny as powerful as that which he overthrew. The emphasis is not really on the kind of physical action we find in Shakespeare's Henry VI plays and heroic romances like *Orlando Furioso* by Greene and others: in *Tamburlaine*, for example, battles tend to take place off-stage, being generally signified in theatrical shorthand by drummers and trumpeters.[27] The hero seems to conquer by simple actions that transgress decorum rather than by main strength: picking up a crown, changing his costume, using an emperor for a footstool, serving a banquet of crowns. The 'tragical discourses', as the printer termed them, are essays not on acts of conquest but on the processes of subjection. They constitute a 'Mirror for magistrates' that goes far beyond the kinds of moralising analysis provided by the 1563 collection of that name[28] in that Marlowe displaces the attention from the moral relationships between princes and the deity to the political relationships between princes and their states.

Shakespeare, in fact, gives us an epitome of Marlowe's art in the Pyrrhus speech in *Hamlet* (II.ii.453–505).[29] Marlowe's drama, he reminds us, is drama of the mind's eye; Pyrrhus is an 'antic' or grotesque, both an old-fashioned avenger out of classical drama and a monster, an obsessive image, a horrendous version of what a man who turns executioner – or obeys his father – might become. He, like Tamburlaine and Barabas, revels in excess; his violation of decorum, political and aesthetic, indicates that he is not bound by the rules of art – and must, paradoxically, be a creature from the 'real' world. 'Extravagance is a privilege of the real', as Gérard

Genette wrote.[30] Shakespeare and Marlowe are exploring the 'truth' of fancy in a manner similar to that of François Rabelais. It was Rabelais who wrote of 'this imitation of the ancient Herculeses, Alexanders, Hannibals, Scipios ... and that which heretofore the Barbars and Saracens called prowess and valour we now do call robbing, thievery, and wickedness'.[31] Conversely, in his *School of Abuse* (1579), Stephen Gosson concedes that the players have 'purged their comedies of wanton speeches', but then proceeds to inveigh against the abuses of plays which 'cannot be shown because they pass the degrees of the instrument, reach of the plummet, sight of the mind'[32] – implying that the liminal fancies that the theatre unfolds usurp the place of right reason. Plays are both demystificatory and the seedbeds for unimagined thoughts.

It is also the case that Pyrrhus lies on the undiscovered borders of Hamlet's consciousness: Tamburlaine operates at the threshold of Europe. *1 Tamburlaine* is contained within Asia; the second part of the play starts near Vienna, and moves through Christendom towards Germany and then towards Jerusalem and Babylon. Conversely, as Stephen Greenblatt notes, Marlowe's heroes are themselves outsiders and see the worlds they inhabit with the observant eyes of aliens.[33]

This engagement with ideology and the creation of characters in this particular archetypal mode seem to me to constitute the manner of Marlowe's sedition: his texts do not depict 'life' but life as it is constructed in ideology or belief, conscious or unconscious. Characters in Marlowe are 'figures' in the technical hermeneutic sense, *figurae*, not likenesses of truth, plastic forms, but embodiments of ideas.[34] He is not just the creator of outsize or outrageous. I would go so far as to claim that the critical argument about whether Marlowe's heroes are Promethean rebels – or whether Marlowe himself is in fact reactionary, giving us a series of retellings of the myth of Icarus – is ultimately an arid one, for his plays do not really admit of simple moral readings. They deal rather with the power and the weakness of fancy. It can even be claimed that there is a measure of solipsism to be found throughout Marlowe: there is, I think, an analogy between Marlowe's art and a moment when Tamburlaine vaunts that he can subdue the world. To Zenocrate he addresses a witty conceit which expands the proverb 'Gentility sprang from the pen or pike'[35]

> I will confute those blind geographers
> That make a triple region in the world,

Excluding regions which I mean to trace,[36]
And with this pen reduce them to a map,
Calling the provinces, cities, and towns
After my name and thine, Zenocrate.
(*1 Tamburlaine*, IV.iv.71–6)

The pen is a grim joke for Tamburlaine's sword. The whole is a
figure of what can be conceived but may not be realised. (This does
not, however, prevent a kind of theatrical realism: Hands's Royal
Shakespeare Tamburlaine was memorable not just as a Herculean
monster but, late in the play, as a portly, uxorious, almost suburban
figure, obsessed by the power that was available to him.) Machiavel,
the prologue to *The Jew of Malta*, presents himself as an idea:
doubling the part with that of Barabas, as is frequently done in the
playhouse, makes the hero both an individual and a type.

Ideology, fancy, myth: these are the arenas in which this free-
thinker operates. Marlowe does not engage directly with the
realities of court politics or the formation of class consciousness in
the way Shakespeare does in his history plays, and his handling, in
Doctor Faustus and *The Jew of Malta*, of the relationship between
the accumulation of wealth and actual structures of authority, the
subject Ben Jonson made his own, is an incidental theme and not
embedded in a world that offers *l'effet du réel*.[37] Wealth for
Marlowe is generally what comes from the rape of nature;[38] it is not
displayed, as in Jonson, as an index of political change.

Ideology and representation are the focuses of recent theory-led
criticism, and this has served, I think, to rehabilitate Marlowe. He
suffers if we read him within the traditions of the nineteenth
century: his 'characters', fancies as they are, will be found wanting
compared with the 'rounded' personalities post-romantic criticism
grafted on to Shakespeare, and his ideals – even if they can be determined – do not match those of a post-revolutionary period. The
nineteenth century constituted the 'Renaissance' as a revolution.
But of the three great Burckhardtian concepts, the state as a work
of art, a new subjectivity, and a new secularism (the rending apart
of the veil of faith), only the first seems true of a cultural moment
we now want to call not 'the Renaissance' but 'the early modern
period'. Marlowe's texts do not dramatise a 'great refusal':[39] they
do, however, offer a critique that is arguably pre-revolutionary.

Marlowe is, therefore, obviously a writer in what Gabriel
Harvey, writing in 1592, calls 'the fantastical mould',[40] in which

category he casts Robert Greene, Pietro Aretino, and François Rabelais.[41] It is an interesting group, and I want to argue that Marlowe belongs firmly within it, alongside Greene, who was a fellow 'university wit'. In order so to do, I want to leap to a very different play by a third university wit, George Peele's *Old Wives Tale* of 1593, another kind of heroic romance, in order to complete my attempt to define the Marlovian mode. This play has an induction which Peele used to make his method clear. There we find three pages: Antic, Frolic, and Fantastic – all, incidentally, deconstructions of the subject. I have dealt with the antic and the fantastic. 'Frolic' is another key word in Marlowe:[42] in *Dido* Iarbas, makes sacrifice to Jove – Jove is generally a figure of subversion in Marlowe – 'Father of gladness and all frolic thoughts' (*Dido*, IV.ii.5), and Machiavel comes from France 'to frolic with his friends' (*The Jew of Malta*, Prologue, 4). Queen Isabella says of her husband Edward II:

> I will endure a melancholy life,
> And let him frolic with his minions
> (I.ii.66–7)

'Frolic': the word gives us a way of talking about sex in Marlowe. It is not just an obsessional topic in his texts. His depiction of the frolicsome suggests Marlowe's delight – *jouissance* – in the ludic, the way he and his characters are, as we have seen, clowns who follow their desires and explore and subvert élite groups within their societies. In *Edward II*, Gaveston's masque of the mind depicts the sports of love that might be deployed to draw the pliant king, and Tamburlaine plays the games of rhetoric[43] to win Theridamus over to his cause. He delivers a great and thundering speech, vaunting that he holds Fate bound fast in iron chains, to which Theridamus replies:

> Not Hermes, prolocutor to the gods,
> Could use persuasions more pathetical
> (*1 Tamburlaine*, I.ii.210–11)

At Stratford in 1992 we watched the sports of politics when Antony Sher took one of Tamburlaine's tirades ('Now clear the triple region of the air', *1 Tamburlaine*, IV.ii.30ff.) as a circus performer, doing acrobatics up a rope. Indeed Marlowe's whole *aesthetic* is frolicsome – like Oscar Wilde's – at once indecorous, sensuous, outra-

geous, and serious. There may have been originally more jokes – or
political scenes when the wily turn the powerful into gulls by acts of
bravura outfacing. We remember how the printer of *Tamburlaine*
cut out 'fond and frivolous jestures' (*sic*), a word that resonates, in
the Marlovian context, with the Brechtian notion of the 'Gestus'.
Marlowe is also like our contemporary Joe Orton: from one
perspective his crazy but well-knit plots seem like farce, from
another like tragedy. (Remember how Eliot called *The Jew of Malta*
a tragic farce.)

It was easy for scholars of sixty years ago to describe what made
Marlowe 'primitive': his use of the patterns of the morality play
and his deployment of what has variously been called 'kitchen
humour', 'eldritch laughter', or 'sacral parody'[44] – of the kind we
find in pieces like the *Secunda Pastorum*. Like so many of his
contemporaries, he minds 'true things by what their mock'ries be'
(*Henry V*, IV.i.52–3). But Marlowe also wanted to 'make it new',
and to do this he operated a transgressive aesthetic, was a violator
of decorum, valuing for little what the academic dramatists praised
by Sidney and others were doing. His art of inversion, as at the
moment when Faustus subverts the authority of the devil, questions
values and social structures which we and his contemporaries might
take as basic and secure.

This can make interpretation or theatrical realisation difficult in
that there often seems to be no locating tone. The prologues: are
they serious or sardonic? As Bruce Smith wrote, 'we can never quite
tell whether Marlowe is *playing* the satirist or *taunting* the
satirists'.[45] Audiences laughed at the slaughter of nuns in the 1964
Royal Shakespeare Company production of *The Jew of Malta*.
Tamburlaine may have seemed to certain members of the audience
as a threat and therefore as a horrifying monster. What about the
supernatural machinery in *Faustus*, the mysterious 'dragon' that
appeared, it would seem, in the middle of Faustus' great speech of
conjuring? Was it carnivalised, equipped with squibs, as in *Friar
Bacon and Friar Bungay* where a tree appears '*with the dragon
shooting fire*'?[46] In *Doctor Faustus* Mephistophilis enters '*with a
devil dressed like a woman, with fireworks*'. The moment is
'Rabelaisian' since the fireworks signify both Lucifer's hell and the
female vagina,[47] as Faustus' retort, 'A plague on her for a hot
whore' (II.i.144SD–146), makes us aware. It is significant that the
theatrical history of *Doctor Faustus* registers a decline into clownery and pantomime:[48] there is no need to assume that Marlowe

upheld decorum, the Renaissance hierarchy of genres which forced categorical differences on comedy and tragedy.

There is no such thing as society, said Mrs Thatcher: Marlowe's demolition, by his ludic artistry, of what she and her conservatising forbears called a natural order, demonstrates that there is no such thing as nature. As in Rabelais we rejoice as the lowborn, be they shepherds, scholars, or Jews, lord it over the respectable and over-throw the traditional. Marlowe was using fancies or fantasies to displace myths, question traditional values.

Tacitus and the political moment

Post-romantic critical orthodoxy demands that we skip over the bi-ography, the unorthodox opinions, and certainly do not identify the man with his heroes. And yet that table-talk – if Baines and Kyd are to be believed – is unforgettable, and matches if not the sentiments at least the tone of bits of *The Jew of Malta, Dido*, and *Massacre*. What Hazlitt wrote of Wordsworth might be applied to Marlowe: his 'genius is a pure emanation of the spirit of the age. Had he lived in any other period of the world, he would never have been heard of ... The political changes of the day were the models on which he formed and conducted his poetical experiments'.[49] I do feel that Marlowe had something to say, that he occupies a distinctive mar-ginal position that serves to experiment with and question much of the cultural practice of his time. Marlowe was obviously a man who was author of himself: in turn *we* need to fashion a Marlowe who was not just a picturesque 'individualist' but a keen and sardonic analyst of the forms and pressures of his time. It follows that we should not just consider his heroes as free spirits, authors of their destinies, but as personages brought into being by the hetero-cosms they inhabit. Their trade in violence was not inimical to their cultures but part of it. The nature of their being can be described in a phrase used by Marx when he wrote, concerning a stereotype that his century inherited from the age of Marlowe, 'It is from its own entrails that civil society ceaselessly engenders the Jew.'[50]

There are none of Hazlitt's major significant political changes or *events* during Marlowe's creative period, but there was a political *moment*: Marlowe's blasphemies and iconoclasm are in fact typical of his time. Just before Marlowe went up to Corpus Christi College, Gabriel Harvey noted that, in Cambridge, 'You cannot step into a scholar's study but (ten to one) you shall lightly find open either

Bodin *De Republica* or Le Roy's exposition upon Aristotle's *Politics* or some other like French or Italian politic discourse'.[51] No exact dating is possible, but there is common ground occupied by, say, Kyd's *Spanish Tragedy*, Shakespeare's *Henry VI* trilogy, and Marlowe's *Massacre at Paris*. Let us date it the moment of politic history and locate it about the time of the composition of Marlowe's translation of Lucan's *Pharsalia* and the publication of Sir Henry Savile's translation of Tacitus' *Histories* in 1591[52] with an epistle that, according to Jonson, was written by the Earl of Essex himself.[53] Marlowe himself translated Lucan who, of course, took a very sceptical view of Julius Caesar's imperial ambitions, and Tacitus' view of history was likewise quizzical and secular: his emperors were, unlike some of Shakespeare's monarchs, scarcely possessed of a mystic as well as a natural body, and his great themes were ancient liberty,[54] what his translator, almost certainly invoking *Tamburlaine*, called 'higher aspiring minds',[55] and modern servitude.[56] Jonson was to get into trouble by writing Tacitean history plays in the next century and during the next reign. But Tacitean matter – it is not just a question of style – can be discerned earlier. Tacitus delighted in exposing the hypocrisy of courtiers: his target was absolutism and its handmaid, theatricality. His tone was sardonic and his characters could be theatricalised and fantastical.[57] Marlowe's politics, I believe, are in this mould: unlike Tacitus, however, he was constrained by the literary genres of comedy, romance, and tragedy. Perhaps deliberately he chose the outdated form of the morality play for his narrative of Faustus – 'We must perform / The *form* of Faustus' fortunes good or bad' says the Chorus, almost as a complaint. In the case of *The Jew of Malta* he may have written a Christianised and grotesque variation of the revenge theme put into circulation by Thomas Kyd in *The Spanish Tragedy*. Overall, with the exception of *Edward II*, the emblematic endings of the plays – the Jew in his cauldron, the discovery of the mangled limbs of Faustus – have a sterile, antique, and unresonant quality to them.

Delinquency and deviance

The question is, how far did Marlowe's political and moral scepticism go? In order to answer it I want to explore notions of delinquency and deviance or dissidence. I owe the resonance of these words to Foucault and Jonathan Dollimore, although I am not in agreement with all of what the latter has to say, and am in fact using the words to designate different categories.[58]

Dissidents are those who reject a whole political or theological order, delinquents those who violate its codes and, despite their appearance of being outsiders, have probably *internalised* its codes. Prisons produce, in the words of Foucault, pathologised subjects.[59] Dissidents, or the modern ones we think of, tend to want relief from some totalising political or metaphysical system. This definition of dissidence is encapsulated in 1 Samuel 15.23: 'For rebellion is as the sin of witchcraft, and transgression is wickedness and idolatry.' Definitions of crime are legitimated by invocations of sin – and vice versa. In order to explain what I mean by internalisation I wish to turn to a famous formula of Ovid: *video meliora proboque, deteriora sequor (Metamorphoses*, VII, 21). Medea was thinking about her father's commands and part of her thought was translated thus by Golding:

> But now an uncouth malady perforce against my will
> Doth hale me. Love persuades me one, another thing my skill.
> The best I see and like: the worst I follow headlong still.
>
> (VII, 24–25)

Ovid's phrase became proverbial in the early modern period[60] and, when combined with aspects of Pauline moral theology, almost encapsulated Christian tragedy. Sidney gives us the combined formula when he writes of the way 'our erected wit maketh us know what perfection is, and yet our infected will keepeth us from reaching unto it'.[61]

What might make Marlowe a dissident? He circulated what makes Machiavelli so dangerous, not just his maxims but his *Ideologiekritik*. From the 'Baines libel' we remember 'The first beginning of religion was only to keep men in awe'[62] and this is paraphrased in the plays: 'I count religion but a childish toy, And hold there is no sin but ignorance' (*The Jew of Malta*, Prologue, 14–15) and, from the mouth of the Guise, 'My policy hath fram'd religion' (*The Massacre at Paris*, II.65).[63] More subtly, Tamburlaine's 'sweet felicity of an earthly crown' (*1 Tamburlaine*, II.vi.29) is not just 'Scythian bathos' as Una Ellis-Fermor, in moralising vein, termed it, but a demonstration of the bad faith of the philosophising tyrant. With respect to *The Jew of Malta*, we recognise that on Malta the cash nexus has displaced any mystic sinew – that conceit is John

Donne's – between ruler and ruled. And in the domain of private desire he seems to 'make strange' the metaphoric traffic between sexual and economic transactions in *Doctor Faustus*.

A vulgar Marxist or biographically oriented critic might place Marlowe along with his Faustus among categories of alienated intellectuals deprived of power (Faustus was born to parents base of stock) and alienated from the energies of demotic life.[64] This reading was rendered into stage terms by playing Faustus as a melancholic in a wonderful production by John Barton with Ian McKellen as Faustus (1976). Or, if you consider that Faustus displays the imperfections rather than the perfection of his learning, you may think that Faustus has failed to grasp the new philosophy and new discoveries of the period (Mephistophilis is more informed than he) and plumps for *material* wealth instead. Marlowe, however, had the power he needed – in the playhouse.

For he is, I think, more radical. If we are prepared to concede the category of the homosexual character in the period and associate Marlowe with it we might want to see him looking quizzically at gender roles and ideas of manliness. Indeed I find enough in Marlowe to question the current orthodox opinion that in the early modern period – or at least in literary texts – there was homosexual activity without the emergence of homosexual identity.[65] In Part 2 of *Tamburlaine* the hero has become a monster as he describes the unwarlike appearance of his sons:

> Their hair as white as milk and soft as down,
> Which should be like the quills of porcupines,
> As black as jet, and hard as iron or steel
> (2 *Tamburlaine*, I.iii.25–7)

Calyphas, the third, a bit like Cordelia, resists his father and is slain.

In *Edward II* we witness a particular concatenation of the political and the sexual. Gaveston and Spencer are doubly marginal: by virtue of both sexual and social difference. The barons claim to hate them because they are upstarts and then demonise them. (From a contrary point of view, Edward II is seen through the eyes of Gaveston and Baldock who manipulate the desire of the king in order to manipulate themselves into power.) They are socially mobile:

> My name is Baldock, and my gentry
> I fetched from Oxford, not from heraldry.
> (III.ii.242–3)

The sight of Edward and Gaveston on the throne together generates immediate hatred which is difficult not to construe as partly based on homophobia – as with Tamburlaine. The proximate is constructed as the 'other',[66] which in turn generates the male bonding among the barons that is used to consolidate political authority.

The execution of Edward is peculiarly and horribly sexual: disturbing in that, by making his executioner Lightborn, the barons have legitimised their murder of a political enemy. Only a devil will do. What is noble about the king is that Edward refuses the role of the abject so often filled by the homosexual. There is no confession of guilt of the sort made by Richard II. However, he does not seem to be able to admit, even to himself, that his sexuality makes him different from other men.

Dissidence or ideological subversion is not just associated with particular personalities but is located within texts, particularly in Brechtian 'gests'. Let us look at one more obvious example. It comes from the opening of *The Tragedy of Dido* (1585–6?) where we see Jupiter dandling Ganymede on his knee. Jupiter is prepared to overturn the order of heavens for Ganymede's love. Marlowe was not attempting to evoke disgust at a pathological condition by showing that Jupiter with his minion: it is not a matter of morals. Marlowe asks, by implication, whether any political question is a moral matter. Ganymede will wreak as much havoc in heaven as the feuds of Gods did on earth – that's the point of Act I, scene i.

I should like to propose a model: Marlovian texts are infused with dissident *ideologies* but, perhaps because of the ironic perspective that he adopted upon the genres within which he chose to write, his *characters* constitute a gallery of delinquents. Charles Nicoll has made the challenging but controversial proposal that Marlowe was an intelligencer or even a spy:[67] maybe his point of view as an author was like that of one who chronicles the tawdry lives of the great. Characters in Marlowe, have, it turns out, internalised the dominant ideology. Tamburlaine may claim that 'Will and Shall best fitteth Tamburlaine' (*1 Tamburlaine*, III.iii.41), but he crowns Zenocrate in a way that makes the scene a pastiche of the coronation of the Virgin, and at the end we see him, in Greene's phrase, compulsively 'daring God out of heaven'.[68] Maybe Marlowe's own hegemony as a mocking author makes it inevitable that his characters will be enclosed by the forms and pressures of their literary milieux. (This is certainly something we notice in Marlowe's jesting refusal to maintain one tone in *Hero and*

Leander). Like Ben Jonson he may have loved and loathed the stage in equal measure, enjoyed its capacity to evoke wonder while despising the cheap tricks of the illusionist and the way that mere properties were metamorphosed into 'ceremonies' and objects of desire.

I prefer this theory to the new historicist orthodoxy that 'Marlowe and his heroes ... live in the recognition of the void, in the realisation that rebellion never manages to find its own space, but always acts in the space that society has created for it'.[69] The trouble with this sort of thing is that it derives from a method of reading that concentrates on endings – Aristotelian, Brecht termed it – and does not allow for variant theatrical realisations, dramatic tone, or even humour.

Yet, in another general sense his characters are mere delinquents, because they want some *thing*, they are consumers, their desires are reified, generally something more than they have been assigned, be it love, power, or wealth. As Greenblatt has demonstrated, their aspirations are fostered by nascent capitalism.[70] They do not seek an authentic self: that is Hamlet's problem, the greatest delinquent who failed to be a dissident. Rather, they wish to supplement their being: it should be complete, but the fact of desire demonstrates its incompleteness. This Derridean impasse is hauntingly phrased in *Massacre* when the Guise speaks of his wish 'To bring the will of our desires to end' (II.84). It all seems to be summed up in another formulation of Gabriel Harvey who wrote of: 'The whole brood of venerous libertines that know no reason but appetite, no law but lust'.[71]

Marlowe and liberty

But this catalogue of moral observations upon his characters makes Marlowe unexciting. I think this author is 'larger' than his characters and I want to take further my comparison with Rabelais and place him in the category of the libertine. That is another difficult word: obviously I want to rescue it from being a mere term of abuse, and to conflate its non-pejorative meaning 'free-thinker' with that of the sexual dissident. I am implying that this writer may stand for liberty in a larger sense, for something more than relief from political oppression, something that need not be defeated by a morally triumphalist ending to a mere play. I thought I would end

by thinking about Marlowe and liberty – and relating these specula-
tions to the theatre.

After Foucault, it has become orthodoxy to argue that delinquency and possibly deviance are not only repressed by the dominant order but produced by it, 'consolidating the powers which it
ostensibly challenges'.[72] 'Liberty', of course, was, in the early
modern period, a key word, one that was changing its meaning. It
may not have been an absolute categorical imperative but something to be granted, a privilege, charter, or franchise. In Rabelais,
the Thelemites, whose motto was 'Do what thou wilt',[73] inhabit a
place contained, an abbey founded by Gargantua. In the world of
Hobbes, the liberty of the subject was praetermitted by the sovereign power.[74] The playhouses were contained within the 'Liberties'
of London. It is for reasons like this that cultural theorists have
displaced the designation 'Renaissance', which implies a brave new
world, for the designation 'early modern period'.

Now Jacques in *As You Like It* is described as a libertine. Here
he is on liberty:

> I must have liberty
> Withal, as large a charter as the wind,
> To blow on whom I please:
> (II.vii.47–9)

Liberty, in other words, is possible only within a designated,
contained space.[75] Doctor Faustus gains his liberty only by signing a
compact with a devil, who, when you think about it, is much more
like a politician than a supernatural being. Faustus' stage punishment of dismemberment (seen in the B text only) is corporal: what
we see accorded to a sinner by the devils was what Elizabethan
hangmen accorded to criminals.

However, I want to quote here another passage from Gabriel
Harvey, writing, in 1592, an invective letter – marked, however,
with understanding and compassion – against Robert Greene. It is
an interesting text, full of references to Greene as clown, one given
to 'Tarltonising' – a descendant of the stage clown Richard Tarlton
– and as a disciple of Aretine, whose reputation in the early modern
period was as a sexual and political libertine, a true dissident.

> But ... Zoilus [a fourth century BC pedantic critic of Homer]in his
> spiteful vein will so long flirt [scoff] at Homer, and Thersites in his
> peevish mood so long fling at Agamemnon that they will become

extremely odious and intolerable to all good learning and civil government; and, in attempting to pull down or disgrace other without order, must needs finally overthrow themselves without relief. Orators have challenged a special liberty, and poets claimed an absolute licence – but no liberty without bounds nor any licence without limitation.[76]

Are these phrases of Harvey just the reflex utterances of the good safe university man, or does this last phrase say something about the 'Renaissance'? This text seems to call into question that element of new historicism known as containment theory. Harvey is conceding that poets, wits, and dramatists *were* able to think the unthinkable, move so far beyond the borders of delinquency that they were truly seditious. No limit is comprehensible unless it is capable of being exceeded or transgressed.[77] Now, if Marlowe was a dissident, what positives does he claim, to what ends does he subvert? Is it liberty that he seeks? Nashe wrote of Aretine, 'His life he contemned in comparison of the liberty of speech.'[78]

Liberty, in fact, is an early aim of Tamburlaine: in the first scene in which he appears he claims that he loves 'to live at liberty' (I.ii.26) and that he seizes wealth to maintain his life 'exempt from servitude' (I.ii.31).

A play like *Edward II* makes obvious points about court corruption and, by implication, political and personal liberty. *The Massacre at Paris*, the *Ubu Roi* of its age, a pantomime version of the politics of the French wars of religion – the French wars of religion provided a seed-bed for ideas about liberty – goes further and invokes notion of liberty of conscience. (The phrase is first cited in *OED* in passages from John Knox's *History of the Reformation* of 1572):

> **King Charles** ... my heart relents that noble men,
>   Only corrupted in religion,
>   Ladies of honour, knights, and gentlemen,
>   Should for their conscience taste such ruthless ends.
>   (IV.9–12)[79]

François Hotman, probably the author of Marlowe's source,[80] *A True and Plain Report of the Furious Outages of France*, 1573, allows himself a reflective digression upon the Massacre of St Bartholomew which aligns itself with the play: 'Why was not orderly enquiry and judicial proceeding used according to the custom and laws and general right of nations, and witness produced according to the form of law? But be it that the Admiral and a few other of his confederates and followers had conspired, why yet proceeded the outrageous cruelty upon the rest that were innocent ...'[81] This accords with the report in the Baines libel about St Paul's advice to the primitive Christians (Romans 13.1–7): 'That all the apostles were fishermen and base fellows neither of wit nor worth, that Paul only had wit, but he was a timorous fellow in bidding men to be subject to magistrates against his conscience'.[82] Marlowe from this, it may be judged, was an advocate of political liberty, an advocate of what is termed resistance theory.

To put this in a historical perspective, we might invoke Kierkegaard, writing about the differences between ancient and modern tragedy. In the ancient world, 'even if the individual moved freely, he still rested in the substantial categories of state, family, and destiny. This substantial category is exactly the fatalistic category in Greek tragedy, and its exact peculiarity. The hero's destruction is, therefore, not only a result of his own deeds, but is also a suffering, whereas in modern tragedy, the hero's destruction is not really suffering but is action ... Our age has lost all the substantial categories of family, state, and race. It must leave the individual entirely to himself, so that in a stricter sense he becomes his own creator.'[83]

Two versions of *Doctor Faustus*

The difficult text, of course, is *Doctor Faustus*. Marlowe, it seems to me, may well have been a true but tentative atheist[84] – the kind who is going to need to blaspheme – standing above and beyond that desolate battlefield between good and evil that defines the religious life in *Doctor Faustus*. From the Olympian position of an author, he chose to tell the story of a man who was unable to escape from the prison-house of Manichean ideology in which he was confined: Marlowe, in other words, may be detached not just from his hero but from what, to adapt Plato, we might call the cave of ideology. He has something to say about a *kind of tale* rather than a *kind of hero*. This hero, it now seems to me, is scarcely autonomous; rather he is constructed by what 'heavenly *power* permits' (Epilogue, 8, emphasis added) and social constraints like that described by Mephistophilis as the 'ceremonial toy' of marriage (II.i.147).[85] Faustus' engagement with the rituals of both worship and demonism may have seemed as comic to his author as the antics of Tamburlaine and Barabas. Faustus is not only wicked but he is, disappointingly to some critics, very naughty: he has recourse to necromancy, what the Baines libel dismisses as 'juggling', and is possibly guilty of 'demoniality', sexual congress with demons.[86] These actions are narrated in a way little different from that when we hear of how his rough magic confronts the Pope[87] – although there we hardly think of liberty of conscience.

If Marlowe had lived, he may have been amused by the tales that accreted to his text: the report that Alleyn played the role in a surplice with a cross upon his chest, and the tale of an extra devil on the stage at a performance of the play in Exeter. This detachment, of course, does not prevent Marlowe creating a tragedy. He is perhaps dramatising his own doubt but also showing the magnificent dithering of his hero, vacillating as he does between brave scepticism about the fables by which he lives and moments when he seems to recognise both divine presence and the validity of religious codes. The problem is, does Marlowe allow his delinquent to grow into a dissident, or does he simply offer a parable in which Christian orthodoxy both generates and contains the actions of his hero?

As always, answers to problems like this are best to be found in the theatre. I want to restore an element of agency to Marlowe, but, at the end of the day, am forced to concede that he is unavailable, that I cannot reach him. I have to abandon not only the answers but the questions of the new historicism and become a cultural materialist, using evidence about staging that derives, unfortunately, from texts printed eleven and twenty-seven years after his death respectively.

Yet I want to conclude by proposing a provisional and tentative answer to these questions concerning the extent of Marlowe's subversion by considering briefly the variant *stage directions* in the A (1604) and B (1616) texts of *Doctor Faustus*.[88] The B text, which partly records performances in professional London playhouses, is, I submit, a text of containment in that devils aloft frame Faustus' actions, ironise his intentions. This turns him into a mere delinquent (and may be a 'non-authentic' theatrical interpretation).[89] So we read in the conjuring scene, '*Thunder. Enter* **Lucifer** *and* **Four Devils** [*above*]: *Faustus to them with this speech*' (I.iii.0SD) Later, in middle of his spell, we find that mysterious word *Dragon* (I.iii.19). It is conceivable, of course, that a hell mouth stood on stage throughout the performance, a silent but ironic commentator on the action.

The A Text, in contrast, which records performances by players driven out of London by the plague to play on open one-level stages, reads simply '*Enter Faustus to conjure*'. At the end of the play, before Faustus confesses, B reads '*Thunder. Enter Lucifer, Beelzebub, Mephistophilis above*' (V.ii.0SD). This, and twenty-five lines, beginning

> **Lucifer**   Thus from infernal Dis do we ascend
>   To view subjects of our monarchy ...
>   (V.i.1–2)

do not appear in A. It is obvious that B, by offering a frame of containment, creates a visual, dramatic irony. In A Faustus is man alone, more of a hero, a braver dissident.

This conclusion, of course, must remain provisional. It may well be that this great text, by escaping from the containment of the public playhouses of early modern London and falling first into the hands of strolling players, then into the hands of a twentieth-century reader like myself, someone who is inclined to be 'oppositional', has turned early modern delinquency into contemporary deviance, libertinism to liberty. Marlowe's texts have been, despite our best endeavours, released from history, and my act of reading is inevitably an act of interpretation. It is difficult to avoid the temptations of whiggish history and of appropriating a great mind like Marlowe's to our cause: I might well have turned an early modern and rather sheepish delinquent into a contemporary and almost heroic dissident.

From *Christopher Marlowe and English Renaissance Culture*, ed. Darryll Grantley and Peter Roberts (Aldershot, 1996), pp. 198–217.

Notes

[Michael Hattaway's project here is ideological criticism, namely, reading Marlowe as a political dramatist. He traces elements of ideology and subversion within Marlowe's secular dramatic texts, where politics replace what fate served for Greek tragedy and offer pre-revolutionary critique. And yet politics in the theatre cannot be separated from their mode of representation, and thus the critic must be attentive to the dramatic rituals informing the playwright's theatrical strategy. Ed.]

1. Quotations are taken from *The Plays of Christopher Marlowe*, ed. Roma Gill (Oxford, 1971).

2. As Leonard Tennenhouse writes, plays provided 'a site where the iconography of state power was formulated in tension with various forms of representation that contested the ideology of the Renaissance court'. *Power on Display: the Politics of Shakespeare's Genres* (London, 1986, p. 14).

3. Compare Michel Foucault: 'Rather than ask ourselves how the sovereign appears to us in his lofty isolation, we should try to discover how it is that subjects are gradually, progressively, really and materially constituted through the multiplicity of organisms, forces, energies, materials, desires, thoughts etc. We should try to grasp subjection in its material instance as a constitution of subjects.' Michel Foucault, 'Two Lectures', *Power/Knowledge: Selected Interviews and Other Writings*, ed. Colin Gordon (New York, 1980), pp. 88, 97.

4. As, for example, in a text of 1590, Edward Webbe, *Edward Webbe ... his Troublesome Travels*, ed. Edward Arber (London, 1868); see also Simon Shepherd, *Marlowe and the Politics of Elizabethan Theatre* (New York, 1986), pp. 142–77.

5. Moving laterally to material history, we might remind ourselves of how new military technology – a paraphrase of part of Paul Ive's *Practise of Fortification* (London, 1589) – is rather self-consciously worked into 2 *Tamburlaine* III.ii.54ff.

6. Frances A. Yates, *Astraea: the Imperial Theme in the Sixteenth Century* (London, 1975), pp. 88–111.

7. Gaveston's 'cullions' wear 'proud fantastic liveries', *Edward II*, I.ii.409. Montaigne has an essay on Sumptuary Laws 1.43.

8. N. B. Harte, 'State control of dress and social change in pre-industrial England', in *Trade, Government and Economy in Pre-Industrial England*, ed. D. C. Coleman and A. H. John (1976), pp. 132–65.

9. See Stephen Gosson, *The Schoole of Abuse*, ed. Edward Arber (London, 1868): 'Overlashing in apparel is so common a fault that the very hirelings of some of our players ... jet under gentlemen's noses in suits of silk' (p. 39).

10. Such a constitution is tersely described by Matrevis to Edward II: 'The court is where Lord Mortimer remains' (V.iii.60) and by Machiavel in *The Jew of Malta*: 'Might first made kings, and laws were then most sure / When, like the Draco's, they were writ in blood' (Prologue, 20–1); compare too a line from Marlowe's translation of Lucan's *Pharsalia*, 'Dominion cannot suffer partnership' (93).

11. Recent writings on the relation between ritual and power are surveyed by David Cannadine, 'Introduction: divine rights of kings', in *Rituals*

of Royalty, ed. David Cannadine and Simon Price (Cambridge, 1992), pp. 1–19.

12. Witness a stage image from *1 Tamburlaine*, II.iv.0SD: '*To the battle, and Mycetes comes out alone with his crown in his hand, offering to hide it*'; compare Michael Hattaway, '"For now a time is come to mock at form" – *Henry IV* and ceremony', in *Henry the Fourth, Milton, Gay, pouvoir et musique*, ed. J.-P. Teissedou, Cahiers du Groupe de Recherches et d'Études sur le Théâtre d'Élisabeth I et des Stuarts (Lille, 1990), pp. 147–74.

13. Michael Hattaway, 'Marlowe and Brecht', in *Christopher Marlowe*, ed. B. Morris (London, 1968), pp. 95–112; in the case of Tamburlaine we must remember that he is a figure of the scourge of God – whose claim that he is 'the scourge of the immortal God' (*2 Tamburlaine*, II.iv.80) sounds, because of its grammatical ambiguity, like a symptom of acute hybris.

14. For diatribes against the pope's power to make kings, see *Edward II*, I.iv.96ff, *The Massacre at Paris*, 25–56ff., *Doctor Faustus*, III.i.149–60; for a survey of the doctrine of the divine right of kings, see J. P. Sommerville, *Politics and Ideology in England, 1603–1640* (London, 1986), pp. 9–56.

15. See Judith Weil, *Christopher Marlowe: Merlin's Prophet* (Cambridge, 1977), p. 3.

16. He prays for 'The plagues of Egypt, and the curse of heaven, Earth's barrenness, and all men's hatred' (I.ii.161–2) – and exclaims 'But mark how I am blessed for plaguing them' (II.iii.197).

17. See III.iii.9–10 and IV.ii.99.

18. See Eugene M. Waith, *The Herculean Hero in Marlowe, Chapman, Shakespeare, and Dryden* (London, 1962).

19. Barabas' appearance '*above*' at III.ii.4SD is a device in the intrigue and does not suggest moral authority or dramatic irony.

20. See, for example, *Edward II*, V.i.41–2; V.i.9–13; V.ii.116; V.iii.6–7; V.iii.34–5.

21. For a recent study, see Christopher Pye, *The Regal Phantasm* (London, 1990).

22. For Gaveston as peasant, see *Edward II*, I.iv.218, and for the category of 'peasant' see D. M. Palliser, *The Age of Elizabeth: England under the Later Tudors, 1547–1603* (London, 1983).

23. Compare, for example, Philisides (a figure for Sidney himself) at the tilt in *Arcadia*, II, 21 (Sir Philip Sidney, *The Countess of Pembroke's Arcadia*, ed. Maurice Evans (Harmondsworth, 1977), p. 353.

24. *The City of God*, trans. John Healey (London, 1610), 4.4, Everyman edn, I, 115.

25. See Penry Williams, *The Tudor Regime* (Oxford, 1979), pp. 106–7; Kenneth R. Andrews, *Elizabethan Privateering: English Privateering during the Spanish War, 1585–1603* (Cambridge, 1964).

26. See Jonathan Dollimore, *Radical Tragedy* (London, 1989 edn), pp. 17–28.

27. Pertinent plays are surveyed by Peter Berek, '*Tamburlaine's* weak sons: imitation as interpretation before 1593', *Renaissance Drama*, n.s. 13 (1982), 55–82, who, however, fails to detect the more radical ideology that operates in Marlowe's texts.

28. William Baldwin and others, *The Mirror for Magistrates*, ed. Lily B. Campbell (Cambridge, 1938).

29. Pyrrhus appears in Seneca's *Troades*; Marlowe's own description of Pyrrhus comes in *Dido*, II.i.213ff.; he is also invoked as an archetype of tyranny in Lucan, 30.

30. Gérard Genette, 'Vraisemblance et motivation', *Figures II* (Paris, 1969), p. 74.

31. *The Works of Mr Francis Rabelais ... 1653*, trans. Urquhart and Motteux (London, 1931 edn), I:46.

32. Stephen Gosson, *The Schoole of Abuse*, ed. Edward Arber (London, 1868), pp. 37–8.

33. Stephen Greenblatt, *Renaissance Self-Fashioning* (Chicago, 1980), p. 196.

34. Erich Auerbach, '"Figura"', *Scenes from the Drama of European Literature* (Manchester, 1984 edn), pp. 11–78.

35. M. P. Tilley, *A Dictionary of the Proverbs in England in the Sixteenth and Seventeenth Centuries* (Ann Arbor, 1950), G61.

36. Meaning to 'pass over' as well as to 'draw'.

37. Roland Barthes, 'The reality effect', in *French Literary Theory Today*, ed. T. Todorov, trans. R. Carter (Cambridge, 1982), p. 16.

38. See, for example, *The Jew of Malta*, I.i.106–7: 'What more may heaven do for earthly man / Than thus to pour out plenty in their laps, / Ripping the bowels of the earth for them ... ?'

39. Michel Foucault, *The History of Sexuality: An Introduction*, trans. Robert Hurley (New York, 1978), p. 95.

40. Gabriel Harvey, *Fovre Letters and certeine Sonnets, 1592* (Edinburgh, 1966), p. 67.

41. Weil, *Merlin's Prophet*, compares Marlowe with Rabelais but does not refer to the passage in Harvey.

42. Greenblatt calls his chapter in *Renaissance Self-Fashioning* 'Marlowe and the will to absolute play' (pp. 193–221).

43. In *1 Tamburlaine* he uses the stock phrase 'play the orator' (I.ii.129), also used by Shakespeare's Edward IV (*3 Henry VI*, I.ii.2.

44. Ernst Robert Curtius, *European Literature and the Latin Middle Ages*, trans. Willard R. Trask (London, 1953), pp. 431–5; Muriel Bradbrook, 'Marlowe's *Doctor Faustus* and the Eldritch Tradition', in *Essays ... in Honor of Hardin Crag*, ed. R. H. Hosley (London, 1963), pp. 83–90; Jerzy Grotowski, *Towards a Poor Theatre*, ed. Eugenio Barba (London, 1969), p. 23.

45. Bruce R. Smith, *Homosexual Desire in Shakespeare's England* (Chicago, 1991), p. 206.

46. Robert Greene, *Friar Bacon and Friar Bungay*, ed. J. A. Lavin (London, 1969), 9.83SD; for contexts of a carnival hell see Mikhail Bakhtin, *Rabelais and his World*, trans. Helene Iswolsky (Bloomington, IN, 1984), p. 393.

47. Bakhtin, *Rabolais* p. 377.

48. Michael Hattaway, *Elizabethan Popular Theatre* (London, 1982), pp. 165–7.

49. William Hazlitt, *The Spirit of the Age*, ed. W. Carew Hazlitt (London, 1904), pp. 151, 152.

50. Karl Marx, 'On the Jewish question', cited by Stephen Greenblatt, *Learning to Curse. Essays in Modern Culture* (London, 1990), p. 50.

51. Gabriel Harvey, *Letter-Booke of Gabriel Harvey, AD 1573–1580*, ed. E. J. L. Scott (Westminster, 1884), p. 79; Robert Sidney's heavily annotated copy of Lipsius' 1585 edition of the *Opera* is in the British Library; compare Leonard F. Dean, 'Sir Francis Bacon's theory of civil history-writing', *ELH*, 8 (1941), 161–83; Lisa Jardine and Anthony Grafton, ' "Studied for action": how Gabriel Harvey read his Livy', *Past and Present*, 129 (1990), 30–78.

52. Tacitus, *The End of Nero and Beginning of Galba. Four books of the Histories of Cornelius Tacitus*, trans. Sir Henry Savile ([London], 1591). The *Annals* appeared in 1598. The influence of Tacitus on later drama is set out by Alan T. Bradford, 'Stuart absolutism and the "utility" of Tacitus', *HLQ*, 46 (1983), 127–51; see also J. H. M. Salmon, 'Seneca and Tacitus in Jacobean England', *The Mental World of the Jacobean Court*, ed. Linda Levy Peck (Cambridge, 1991), 169–88.

53. Richard Tuck, *Philosophy and Government 1572–1651* (Cambridge, 1993), p. 105; it may have been written by Anthony Bacon.

54. After narrating how Augustus had refashioned the state, Tacitus wrote 'How many were there which had seen the ancient form of government of the free commonwealth' (Tacitus, *The Annales of Cornelius Tacitus*, trans. R. Greneway ([London], 1598), p. 3.

55. *Annales*, I.4, p. 7; the phrase is used of Asinius Gallus who 'plusquam civilia agitaret', in *Tacitus in Five Volumes, The Loeb Classical Library*, trans. Clifford H. Moore and John Jackson, 5 vols (Cambridge, MA, 1969), III: 268.

56. In the epistle we read 'In these four books ... thou shalt see all the miseries of a torn and declining state: the empire usurped, the princes murdered, the people wavering, the soldiers tumultuous, nothing unlawful to him that hath power, and nothing so unsafe as to be securely innocent ... If thou dost detest their anarchy, acknowledge our own happy government, and thank God for her, under whom England enjoys as many benefits as ever Rome did suffer miseries under the greatest tyrant'. *Histories*, Sig 3^{r-v}.

57. In Book 1 we find a marvellous sentence on one Percennius, leader of the revolt in Pannonia, 'who had been sometimes a ringleader of factious companions on stages and theatres, afterward a common soldier, an impudent and saucy prater, well practised in disturbing assemblies, to show favour unto such actors as he favoured' (*Annales*, I.5, p. 8).

58. See Jonathan Dollimore, *Sexual Dissidence* (Oxford, 1991): 'For Gide transgression is in the name of a desire and identity rooted in the natural, the sincere, and the authentic; Wilde's transgressive aesthetic is the reverse: insincerity, inauthenticity, and unnaturalness become the liberating attributes of decentred identity and desire, and inversion becomes central to Wilde's expression of this aesthetic ...' (p. 14). The author deals with *Doctor Faustus*, but his reading does not seem sufficiently open to the semantics of stage performance.

59. Michel Foucault, *The Foucault Reader*, ed. Paul Rabinow (Harmondsworth, 1984), p. 231.

60. The phrase became proverbial (Tilley B325).

61. Philip Sidney, *An Apology for Poetry*, ed. G. Shepherd (Manchester, 1965), p. 101.

62. Quoted in Judith O'Neill (ed.), *Critics on Marlowe* (London, 1969), p. 10; see Dollimore, *Radical Tragedy*, pp. 11–13.

63. C. Minshull, 'Marlowe's "Sound Machevill" ', *Renaissance Drama*, n.s. 13 (1982), 35–54.

64. 'Marlowe demystifies the power he craves but cannot obtain, a not uncommon strategy of frustrated social ambition on the Elizabethan

political scene' (John D. Cox, *Shakespeare and the Dramaturgy of Power* [Princeton, NJ, 1989], p. 98).

65. This is not the conclusion of, for example, Bruce Smith in *Homosexual Desire*; Smith writes well about the 'master and minion' relationship in *Edward II* (pp. 209–23).

66. Dollimore, *Sexual Dissidence*, p. 33.

67. Charles Nicoll, *The Reckoning* (London, 1992).

68. Robert Greene, *Perimides the Blacksmith* (London, 1588), Sig.A3^r.

69. Jonathan Goldberg, 'Sodomy and society: the case of Christopher Marlowe', *Staging the Renaissance*, ed. David Scott Kastan and Peter Stallybrass (London, 1991), pp. 75–82.

70. Greenblatt, *Self-Fashioning*, pp. 194ff.

71. Pierce's *Supererogation* (London, 1593), p. 45.

72. *Dissidence*, p. 27.

73. Rabelais, I.47, p. 163.

74. Thomas Hobbes, *Leviathan*, ed. Michael Oakeshott (New York, 1962), Chap. 21, p. 161.

75. We can perform a similar semantic exercise on the word 'licentious': it means guilty of the abuse of licence. Baldock boasts to Spenser that he was 'curate-like in mine attire, / Though inwardly licentious enough / And apt for any kind of villainy', *Edward II*, II.i.49–51.

76. Gabriel Harvey, *Foure Letters and certeine Sonnets, 1592* (Edinburgh, 1966), p. 15; compare Gosson, who, in the course of discussion of the effects of plays, wrote: 'I cannot liken our affection better than to an arrow which, getting liberty, with wings is carried beyond our reach; kept in the quiver, it is still at commandment' (p. 44).

77. Compare passages to this effect from Foucault and Montaigne in Dollimore, *Tragedy*, pp. 114–15.

78. Thomas Nashe, *The Unfortunate Traveller and Other Works*, ed. J. B. Steane (Harmondsworth, 1985), p. 310; I see no reason to endorse the conjecture that here and in Harvey 'Aretine' is, in fact, Marlowe – see, for example, Nicoll, *The Reckoning*, p. 55.

79. See *Christopher Marlowe, 'Dido Queen of Carthage' and 'The Massacre at Paris'*, ed. H. J. Oliver (London, 1968), p.180 for Hotman's account of Henri III's revocation of edicts permitting 'liberty of religion'.

80. Ibid. p. lxi.

81. Quoted in ibid, p. 78.

82. Quoted in O'Neill, *Critics on Marlowe*, p. 10.

83. Søren Kierkegaard, *Either/Or*, trans. David F. Swenson and Lillian Marvin Swenson, 2 vols (Princeton, NJ, 1971), I: 141–7.

84. [Joseph Cresswell], *An Advertisement written to a Secretary of my Lord Treasurer's of England by an English Intelligencer as he passed through Germany towards Italy* (n.p., 1592) notes 'Sir Walter Ralegh's school of atheism by the way, and of the conjurer that is master thereof, and of the diligence used to get young gentlemen to this school wherein both Moses and our Saviour, the Old and New Testaments are jested at, and the scholars taught among other things to spell God backward'.

85. Dollimore calls it 'an exploration of subversion through transgression ... Faustus' pact with the devil, because an act of transgression without hope of liberation, is at once rebellious, masochistic, and despairing' (*Radical Tragedy*, pp. 109 and 114).

86. W. W. Greg, 'The damnation of Faustus,' *MLR*, 41 (1946), 97–107.

87. See Frank Kermode on popes as magicians, *Shakespeare, Spenser, Donne* (London, 1971), p. 44.

88. Useful material on historical and ideological implications of the variant readings in the dialogue is to be found in Leah S. Marcus, 'Textual indeterminacy and ideological difference: The case of *Doctor Faustus*', *Renaissance Drama*, n.s. 20 (1990), 1–29; also Janet Clare, '*Art Made Tongue-tied by Authority*': *Elizabethan and Jacobean Dramatic Censorship* (Manchester, 1990), pp. 27–30; Thomas Healy, *New Latitudes: Theory and English Renaissance Literature* (London, 1992), pp. 117–20.

89. Glynne Wickham, however, claims that no London theatre before the late 1590s had the technical capacity to produce the final scenes of the play in the B version: '*Exeunt to the cave*: notes on the staging of Marlowe's plays', *Tulane Drama Review*, 8 (1964), 184–94.

3

Faces of Nation and Barbarism: Prophetic Mimicry and the Politics of *Tamburlaine the Great*

AVRAHAM OZ

I

In the course of depicting the civilizing process Europe was undergoing from the Middle Ages onwards, Norbert Elias locates the fifteenth, sixteenth, or seventeenth centuries as the historical juncture (different in the particular history of each emerging nation-state) where the change in structure of society 'finally gives the central authorities preponderance over all the centrifugal forces, and thus confers on the territories a greater stability'.[1] In his monumental project Elias demonstrates the dialectical relation between the private and collective body, assuming, from the very outset, that had a 'civilized' person of later ages been confronted with the customs of earlier periods, s/he would have been alarmed by their 'barbaric' nature. Christopher Marlowe, a notorious Elizabethan sensationalist, adopts a different, perhaps more creative strategy in his two *Tamburlaine* plays. Taking together tropes of emerging nationhood and civility, and confronting his audience, in a real-time dramatic mirror, with their barbaric past as still threateningly inherent within the political and social structure of the present, he constructs moments such as the following, in which Techelles, looking upon Tamburlaine for the first time, pronounces an oracular statement:

> As princely lions when they rouse themselves,
> Stretching their paws and threat'ning herds of beasts,
> So in his armour looketh Tamburlaine:
> Methinks I see kings kneeling at his feet,
> And he, with frowning brows and fiery looks,
> Spurning their crowns from off their captive heads.
> (*1 Tamburlaine*, I.ii.52–7)

This prophetic vision, expressed by Techelles at the beginning of the play, is soon to materialise on stage. On the face of it, it is nothing but a common speech of praise introducing a heroic figure; yet its special significance depends on the special function of Tamburlaine in the plays, namely, a marginalised Other turned hegemonic tyrant, whose constant dramatic presence retains both attributes side by side, pertaining simultaneously to modes of tragedy and irony.

Techelles' statement involves, in fact, all the major themes I claim here as being Marlowe's major concerns in his early tragic master-piece, namely, nationhood, Empire, and barbarism, as related to their repeated dramatic and performative representation in the most expressive part of the human body, the face, from its most common, daily use:

> look we friendly on them when they come ...
> (*1 Tamburlaine*, I.ii.141)

to its extreme, bigger than life, excessive image:

> Tamburlaine? A Scythian Shepherd so embellishèd
> With nature's pride and richest furniture?
> His looks do menace heaven and dares the gods;
> His fiery eyes are fixed upon the earth
> As if he now devised some stratagem,
> Or meant to pierce Avernus' darksome vaults
> And pull the triple-headed dog from hell.
> (*1 Tamburlaine*, I.ii.154–60)

The ambiguity underlying the performative function of faces, repeated almost obsessively in the *Tamburlaine* plays, is strongly related, I believe, to the concept of mimicry, described by Lacan as a kind of camouflage, which is often invoked in the discourse of nationhood. As Homi Bhabha explains:

> Within that conflictual economy of colonial discourse which Edward Said describes as the tension between the synchronic panoptical vision of domination – the demand for identity, stasis – and the counter-pressure of the diachrony of history – change, difference – mimicry represents an ironic compromise.
>
> (Bhabha, 1994, 85–6)[2]

Mimicry, Bhabha goes on to say, 'is the desire for a reformed, recognisable Other, *as a subject of a difference that is almost the same, but not quite* ... the discourse of mimicry is constructed around an *ambivalence*'; yet it is also the sign of the inappropriate, a difference which 'intensifies surveillance, and poses an immanent threat to both "normalised" knowledge and the disciplinary powers'.[3] Both functions are useful to Marlowe's dramatic strategy as described above.

What may seem a discrepancy here is that Bhabha insists on the comic nature of mimicry, whereas Marlowe, already at the prologue to *1 Tamburlaine*, presents his dramatic enterprise as a 'tragic glass', and as we shall see, justifiably so. It is through the special ambiguity inherent in tragedy that Marlowe intends his audience to be confronted with the special menace in civility, a menace which disrupts the authority of civility through ambivalence and dichotomy, an object Bhabha himself will admit as a major property of mimicry.[4] However, the constant excess in the presentation of Tamburlaine as an extremely heightened tragic hero, as almost the same as current monarchs but not quite, adds a bathetic overtone to Malowe's tragic glass, a kind of bathos which is not absent from later tragedies such as *The Jew of Malta* or *Doctor Faustus*, but also present in *Hamlet* or *King Lear*. The double vision the powerful presence of barbarism within civility exposes the audience to involves both the horror of surveillance revealing the gaze of otherness, and the absurd absence involved in what Bhabha terms as 'the metonymy of presence'.[5] Tamburlaine appears to his early modern audience both as a dream and a nightmare, a desire and an apparition.

Faces, however, may find their territorial equivalents in the expressive function, or the distinctive 'mimicry' inherent in maps. It is in terms of this expressive function, for instance, that

Tamburlaine accounts for Zenocrate's beauty and its worth in lands:

> Brighter than is the silver Rhodope,
> Fairer than whitest snow on Scythian hills,
> Thy person is more worth to Tamburlaine
> Than the possession of the Persian crown ...
> (1 Tamburlaine, I.ii.88–91)

I submit that the *Tamburlaine* plays amount to a complex dramatic project, in which tragic ambiguity provides both subversive perspectives on central authorities seeking to consolidate unified nationhood, and a model of containment affirming Tudor Britain's profound desire to become an Empire. Whereas the latter are discernible in the plays in the triumphant posture of the victorious Emperor, its subversion is suggested by the breach of territorial stability indicated in the inflated image of an amorphous host of conquered kings bowing excessively to the barbarous ruler, a scene more becoming the grossly imagined courts of ancient or feudal Europe (in their affinity to the exuberant images of oriental manners) than the phase of its later, more 'civilized' division into ordered nation states.

However, what complicates the dramatic effect of this moment, as that of the entire double play of *Tamburlaine*, is the fact that both subversion and containment employ 'the frowning brows and fiery looks' of barbarism as their major theatrical vehicle, thus keeping any clear meaning implied by the narrative constantly at bay: making its tragic impact depend on equivocal readings of faces and maps, they yield themselves exclusively to prophetic, hence riddling and often oxymoronic interpretation. Are Tamburlaine's imperial conquests converting the defeated nations into members of the newly hegemonic one? Does Tamburlaine's excessive brutality implicate the whole Imperial project? These unresolved conflicts, and other related ones, make for a constant sense of peripeteian development and loose energies, designed rather to shock and surprise than to ameliorate our dialectic understanding of the constitutive narratives of the civilizing process, in both its private and collective aspects. The original audience of the plays, already settled to the idea of English nationhood, accommodated within their political discourse as partaking in the hegemonic ideology since no less than half a century earlier, was, I believe, much overwhelmed by the transgressive intrusion of the face of barbarism suddenly informing their cherished idea of a stable imagined community.

II

In the attempt to convey that traumatic performative resonance of Marlowe's earliest *Grand Guignol*-like masterpiece, a no lesser image from the recent past comes to mind: the historical narrative represented by the blowing out of the New York twin towers on 11 September 2001, a non-fictional event whose immediate impact, however, has produced responses which transcended the boundaries of reality, prophetically unearthing before Western eyes a special blend of sensational, indeed somewhat excessive tragedy and a thoroughly changed cultural model underlying reality. The relation of that powerful narrative to tragedy lay both in its immediate codification within the discourse of 'Theatre of Terror' (e.g., 'mass murder as performance art'),[6] and its spectacular revelation, in the old Aristotelian sense of *anagnorisis*, of the self-defeating nature of the prematurely valorised victory of the West in the aftermath of the Cold War, rendering 'the unthinkable' as a vividly viable option:[7] both attributes grasping the events as acts of 'Threat'ning the world with high astounding terms / And scourging kingdoms' (*1 Tamburlaine*, prologue, 5–6).

The charged cultural model invoked by the devastating events of September 11 alerted the historical consciousness of the West to the ironically remedial celebration of the other informing the institutional flesh and bones of an overreaching system and committing it to a subversive gaze that displaced its very constitution: an acute reminder how culture itself bears the barbarous seeds of its own doom. For a moment, the global Empire of the capitalist West was tainted by the foreboding face of barbarism resonating in the halls of hegemonic ideology, figuring behind the putative masks inhabiting the palace of insatiable globalisation. Bereft of its local habitation, which had rapidly become an undivided part of the habitual visage of the Capital of capitalism, the cultured architecture of the proud World Trade Center, a unified shrine of balance and symmetry (traumatically displaced by the temporal discrepancy which undermined its outward unity), seems to have given way to its inherent, chaotic otherness, effacing, if temporarily, its structured hegemony and rendering it into an existential riddle, such as suggested by Apollinaire's faceless musician.

And yet this latter image is not entirely serious, its cultural gesture not exclusively informed by grim-face(less)ed serenity. From a different, no less overwhelming perspective, it bears resemblance to mimicry; 2800 individuals have turned into one massive quantity of destruction, and yet, individuality kept prevailing by the doomed victims reaching their loved ones through wireless means of communication, which readorned them with their respective individualities: 'Never had so many had the means to say good-bye'.[8] At the risk of aestheticising the political, one may regard that ambiguous moment of vanishing presence, that picture viewed 'in this tragic glass' (1 Tamburlaine, prologue, 7), as combining the very image of the heights of tragedy with the bathetic abyss of Brechtian gestus. For the 'unthinkable' rendered thinkable contains some awesome jest, a terrifying joke played on humanity, devoid of mirth or laughter, yet so excessive that Brechtian irony is merged in it with Bhabha's metonymy of presence. These lines are revised in the stormy Middle East of 2002, disturbed every few hours by the almost apocalyptic wave of suicide bombers extolling their acts on the living. In its singularity, this phenomenon, a transgression of any manual of civility, is tragic; in its accumulation, a simultaneously overreaching and absurd mimicry of any age-old sacrificial ceremonies, a travestied parody on any pattern of meaning underlying the narratives of Abraham and Isaac, Jesus, Iphigeneia, or Jephtach. As are indeed, in the second and more overwhelmingly absurd part of Tamburlaine the Great, Tamburlaine's killing his own son Calyphas, or the dramatic pageant of Olympia's suicidal jest played on Theridamas.

Hardly on the same scale of those 'unthinkable' events, driving home the barbarous into civility with a vengeance and confined to the limited size of a cultural shock produced within the physical, social and aesthetic contours of a wooden O, Marlowe's Tamburlaine the Great may have effected somewhat of a similar overwhelming impact on its original audience at the Theatre, taking its spectators by surprise when first performed there by the Lord Admiral's Men in 1587 in exposing them to the picture of the Scythian scourge of kingdoms viewed 'in this tragic glass'. Tragedy had dwindled down in a steady pace since the death of Sophocles and Euripides (406 BC) till its total disappearance in the early Middle Ages, and its gradual recovery since Albertino Mussato's Latin Eccerinus (1315) in Italy, to Norton and Sackville's Gorboduc (1561) in London, did not manage as yet to free itself in full from the conventional fetters of the morality tradition. Marlowe's dramatic energies signalled to its audience, in A. D. Nuttall's lively phrasing, 'Not a morality, but this new, exciting thing, a tragedy'.[9] Already C. L. Barber has detected in Marlowe's 'rapid, direct route to tragedy', and *Tamburlaine*'s astonishing contribution to the creation of the genre on the Elizabethan stage, an influential token of 'the theatre becoming a new organ of culture ... an agency of change as well as an expression of it', regarding it as some equivalent of individualistic 'prophesying',[10] that eccentric Elizabethan practice merging charismatic traditions with new modes of rational, individualistic pronouncements, often challenging hegemonic readings of the world's narratives.

Since tragic representation is dependent to a greater extent on its inherent oxymoronic constancy rather than on arbitrary patterns of surprise, typical of other genres such as comedy, tragicomedy or melodrama, it pertains more easily to the prophetic, in its broader, non-futuristic sense.[11] *Tamburlaine*'s innovation in his tragical 'prophesyings' was in the presentation of violence and cruel tyranny as heroic achievements.[12] The subversive enunciation Tamburlaine was disseminating in terms of the nation's growing desire for Empire (to be later echoed by Barabas in terms of Capital) addressed the immoral equivocation of those secular political powers, already negotiating the immanent barbaric menace inherent within us. This perspective rendered the new cultural model already deployed under the Tudor reign as tragically contaminated by parodic elements of self-effacement and reification, as yet contained within the seeds of time. While the growing sense of nationhood under the later Tudor monarchs scrupulously promoted an economy of exclusive individualism, Marlowe's sweeping spectacle of violent otherness destroying any mark of collective solidarity, parodying the profusely emerging social mobility into a *danse macabre* of irreverence and blasphemy, attracted its audience to the mimic pageant of effacing of self and other involved in the double-edged project of early nationalism. Maps, functioning as the territorial face of the nation, became tentative and prone to violent changes when breached:

> having passed Armenian deserts now
> And pitched our tents under the Georgian hills,
> Whose tops are covered with Tartarian thieves
> (*1 Tamburlaine*, II.ii.14–16)

especially in a realm where barbarous kings are challenged to 'subdue the pride of Christendom' (*1 Tamburlaine*, I.i.132). The neatly delineated 'sea wall'd garden' (*Richard II*, III.iv.44) was imaginatively breached by the insatiable desire of a volatile, charismatic shepherd-prince, a land-pirate devouring boundaries and borders in his mangling of provinces, who, beside admiration, could arouse fear, menace, and even monstrous pre-Brechtian *gestus*:

> This country swarms with vile outrageous men
> That live by rapine and by lawless spoil,
> Fit soldiers for the wicked Tamburlaine.
> (*1 Tamburlaine*, II.ii.22–4)

The familiar face of a traditionally local habitation was thus replaced by an ever changing, protean map, prophetically inhabiting a colourful gallery of alien visages. The expressive vehicle of such a complex cultural model, readily provided for prophesying its oxymoronic identity, where culture, like nature, 'means both what is around us and inside us, and the disruptive drives within can easily be equated with anarchic forces without',[13] could not be found either in comedy or in tragicomedy, nor even in the newly devised chronicle play succumbing to a rational chain of historical events. It had to be tragedy, feeding by definition on paradox and ambiguity, and provided, unlike its rival genres, to contain some measure of alarming parody.

III

Getting an identity is like growing a face; and the metaphoric affinity between the human face and the territorial map is known to Maria in *Twelfth Night*, who reports that Malvolio, in his newly assumed identity, 'does smile his face into more lines than is in the new map with the augmentation of the Indies' (III.ii.75–7). It is my contention here that Marlowe was well aware of the more fundamental, less playful interconnection between face, map, and prophecy; barbarism and nation. When he insists on making his audience from the outset, in the prologue to the first play, view in his tragic glass the picture of 'the Scythian Tamburlaine', he chooses his words carefully: his tragic picture combines both map and face. Like the lover, or his associate in lunacy, the poet, who may see 'Helen's beauty in a brow of Egypt' (not only mixing aesthetic values, but substituting map for face), thus the cartographer (as John Gillies rightly reminds us),[14] can be possessed of and by 'such seething brains, / Such shaping fantasies, that apprehend /

More than cool reason ever comprehends' (*Midsummer Night's
Dream*, V.i.4–6, 11). A map is not necessarily a dry, scientific representation of territory: like Bertolt Brecht's deliberately ironic
misrepresentation of the map of America in his *Mahagonny*, thus
Marlowe, who knew his Ortelius well, may use a map as the proclaimed substitute to the face of the monarch's public body:

> And in assurance of desired success
> We here do crown thee Monarch of the East,
> Emperor of Asia and of Persia,
> Great lord of Media and Armenia,
> Duke of Assyria and Albania,
> Mesopotamia and of Parhia,
> East India and the late-discovered isles,
> Chief lord of all the wide vast Exine Sea
> And of the ever-raging Caspian Lake ...
> (*1 Tamburlaine*, I.i.160–8)

Like many of his contemporaries, among them poets and dramatists such as Spenser, Shakespeare or Drayton, Marlowe toiled, in
the last two decades of the sixteenth century, to form a symbolic
face and embodiment to a newly born national identity, proclaimed by Henry VIII barely sixty years beforehand, when he
divorced his monarchy from its religious subordination to the Holy
See in Rome. The execution of Thomas More epitomised the
cutting of one of the last strings still connecting Henry's
proclaimed Empire to the symbolic body of a wider Christian community, overriding its national independence. Without underestimating the difficulty involved in disseminating a fundamentally
new hegemonic ideology among a given community, fostering
nationhood as a substitute for a former religious allegiance was a
relatively easy project. Nation has ever been a useful term for
rulers, being a vague and elusive term, a convenient weapon in the
hand of the central authorities in their strife to subdue, in Elias'
words, 'the centrifugal forces' tending to disintegrate the budding
cohesion of newly formed imagined communities. While creating
an illusion of equality up to a degree, forged by the myths of
collective memory, it has never implicated the alleged common
cause of a given society in any shared social or individual interests,
or breached any set of privileges reserved for the social elite, an act
which could compromise the cherished hierarchies still inherent in
the structure of society since feudalism – nation or no nation.

Rather, ignoring (or failing to address) the arbitrary or contingent formation of the alleged nation, the ruler could postulate instead to the members of the newly formed imagined community a convenient agenda, an expression, a voice. This ventriloquised voice, in its allegedly collective expression, was not supposed to be revealed as part of the king's private body: it had to be capable of a constitutional transformation, as in the case of Elizabeth's famous statement in the Tilbury speech that although she had the body of a feeble woman, her heart and stomach were of a man. The monarch's private body required a real face, in an age where, as Susanne Scholz, following Helen Hackett, tells us, 'new iconographical conventions for the praise of the sovereign developed'.[15] It was given, therefore, a different local habitation, an abstract face, within an invented collective memory or cultural heritage requiring a reified mask, indeed an iconic figure on a cultural map, rather than an individual face.[16]

In this context, the ambivalence inherent in the practice of mimicry, abandoning its comic facet and inverting its route as travelling from hegemony to the marginalised, could play a notable role. This hegemonic agenda was particularly conspicuous in the crisis the English monarchy was undergoing during the final defeat in the Hundred Years War and the loss of Normandy, and likewise during the civil strifes following it, where tropes of nationhood were urgently sought in order to cover legal Acts guarding the interests and perpetuating the privileges of the elite classes. Fostering patriotism often made use of religious symbols and agendas. I have discussed elsewhere a typical Renaissance instance of such an arbitrary agenda, the one dramatised by Shakespeare in having Henry IV call for a crusade at the outset of *1 Henry IV*, thus mimicking (almost affecting in reality, *but not quite*) a metaphorical stretch of the territorial boundaries of the English nation to meet the Holy Land.[17] Similar instances abound throughout the later Middle Ages and the Renaissance, pertaining to different figures than that of Jesus invoked by Shakespeare's Henry IV: since the later Middle Ages, the custodians of St Mary's shrine in Walsingham referred to England as 'Mary's Dowry', and the cult of St George has been associated with England since the dawn of English nationalism.[18] In 1348, long before Shakespeare's King Henry V's famous speech, King Edward III had appropriated the popular cult to institute St George as the patron of the Order of the Garter, reflecting elite values while disseminating the early buds of English nationalism.

IV

In the context of the political turmoil and turbulence inherent in the historical moment within which Elizabethan authors operated, where an emerging nation was in the process of acquiring self-awareness, within a fluid and ever-emerging modern world of growing capitalism and social mobility, religious wars, spreading rationalism and counter-movements, the human face, a notable source of mimicry, may be conceived both as the locus of an eternal stability and a primary signifier of change. Just as a long process leads from the local veneration for a saint to the appropriation of such a cult as a national trope, it takes a long and tortuous process of development from the ancient and medieval mythopoeic yearning for a 'true' image of Christ, like the 'holy faces' still claimed by ancient churches and cathedrals in the Mediterranean and elsewhere (Rome, Genoa, Turin, Laon, Jaén and Alicante),[19] to the complex presence of gaze and face informing the new modern era, where the face of the national subject is ambiguously shaped by the strange image of its otherness. The civilizing process constantly proceeds while shaping and being shaped by the gaze and face of barbarism.

A probable agent in the secret service of Her Majesty, often sent abroad to mix with aliens, Marlowe is well aware of the subversive element underlying the traffic of hegemonic narratives and the dramatic value of ambivalent mimicry. The appropriation of an exotic imperial figure such as fourteenth-century Timur the Mongolian, notorious for his lack of civility, by one of the champions of English nationalism on the Elizabethan stage (following heroic romances by Mexia and Perondino, but also English sources such as Whetstone and Fortescue – the latter, at least, an ardent upholder and disseminator of English nationalism, who does not hide his admiration for the exotic tyrant) to serve a reflection of the English national spirit defying its foes, marks the dialectical corollary of such a process. In *Tamburlaine the Great*, both parts of which were written during the ongoing tension caused by the first test of maturity the English nation was undergoing, between Drake's 1587 raid on the Spanish Armada in Cadiz and the euphoric aftermath of the great Armada battle a year later, Marlowe is undertaking both a surveillance of the new imperial face England is striving to acquire, as well as the faces of the others, surrounding it. And since, as both Marlowe and Shakespeare well know, one cannot look at one's own face until its gaze 'hath travell'd and is married there / Where it may see itself' (*Troilus and Cressida*, III.iii.110–12), these two aspects of face and gaze are intertwined, affecting each other's constraints and meaning.

Marlowe's own death by the piercing of his eye into the brain, though having, of course, no direct bearing on his work, is not irrelevant here. Considered by many as a token of an unaimed, chaotic struggle, that death blow into the face may well not have been so innocent or fortuitous. 'The face,' argues Charles Nicholl, 'and particularly the eye, was regarded as a prime target. The manuals of swordmanship described the thrust alla revolta, whose precise purpose was to skewer your opponent's eye-ball. Nashe transfers this to mental combat: Harvey's style is an unwieldy "two-hand sword", and he cannot "make one straight thrust at his enemy's face".' A 'gash in the face' is also the strike of death which kills Thomas Arden of Faversham.[20]

V

Of all Elizabethan dramatists, Marlowe may be the most explicit in bringing forth the vision of expansionism inherent in the notion of Empire. In doing this, he necessarily gets involved in the face/façade dichotomy of early nationalism. Marlowe, though, may not have been aware of a curious meeting having taken place in 1401, at the siege of Damascus, between his favourite protagonist, Timur i-Lenk ('the limping'), and his contemporary, the great Muslim historian and social thinker Wali ad-Din Abd ar-Rachman Ibn Khaldûn, an early theorist of nationalism in the late Middle Ages. Among other themes discussed in that meeting, was Ibn Khaldûn's central concept of 'asabiyya', namely, group solidarity or a form of nationalism, giving substance, in Ibn Khaldûn's political theory, to sovereignty. In former uses of the term, before the advent of Islam or right after, it used to signify a pejorative form of blind tribal bias. Ibn Khaldûn offers, in his *Muqadimma* ('*Prolegomena*' to the science of history), a saner version of the concept, viewed from various pertinent perimeters (such as raw or cultured communities, similarity and variety of the individual members of the society, its relation to race, power, purity of lineage or degrees of nobility). However, in spite of the elaborate distinctions he makes in his writings, in the radically popularised version of his theory given to

Timur, Ibn Khaldûn's grasp of the concept is mainly quantitative: 'Sovereignty exists only because of group loyalty', the scholar tells the conqueror, 'and the greater the number in the group, the greater is the extent of sovereignty'. Although Marlowe may not have been familiar with Ibn Khaldûn's complex theory of 'asabiyya', his Mongol hero will often indeed draw his sovereignty from the face-less power of the multitude ('the people are of a number which cannot be counted'; Ibn Khaldûn will later describe Timur's army to the ruler of the Maghrib; 'if you estimate it at one million it would not be too much, nor can you say it is less'; and he goes on to account for them in terms of the space they cover, rather than their human distinction: 'If they pitched their tents together in the land they would fill all vacant spaces'. In Marlowe's work as well, the face may disappear beyond the reified number, whereas the two aspects of the facial embodiment of the nation intertwine.

And while an individual face may move an empire, launch a thousand ships and burn the topless towers of Illium, an exotic Mongolian may lend his foreign face to the very core of the English empire, facing the Spanish enemy in Bajazeth the Turk. Both for Marlowe and for Shakespeare, the image of otherness presented to the nationalist gaze is often that of barbarism, a term which has come to be used indiscriminately, and thus of a blurred meaning, more or less like 'nation' itself. Shakespeare's Prince of Arragon is yet another haughty Spanish fool, regarding barbarism not only as a qualitative, but also a quantitative property: what many men desire must by definition comply with 'common spirits', hence with the multitudes, who are barbarous by nature (*The Merchant of Venice*, II.ix.31–3). For him, the barbarous multitude informs a social rank, or, more clearly, a cultural domain. The Constable of France, however, regards the whole British people, to whom he would not care to relinquish such a token of national pride, subtlety and excellence as 'our vineyards' (*Henry V*, III.5.4), as collectively barbarous, thus deploying the term within the political discourse proper. Both are drawing on a concept as ancient as the Greek notion of 'barbaroi', namely, a lack of proper speech (associated with the face both as the traditional residence of individual expression in general, and more specifically as the part of the human body where speech comes from) and hence some lack of appropriate mental capacities.[21] While Aristotle, however, regards slavery as inevitable, since the barbarians, who lack any practical judgement (as do women and children), are slaves by nature and therefore must for their own good function as 'living instruments', Arragon's social rank and cultural distinction seem to relate to some early notion of the Constable's 'nation'. With the decline of slavery in the Middle Ages, the direct control of free citizens over 'barbarians' was substituted by the Arragons' curious, sometimes prophetic gaze into their otherness, suggesting an alternative model of their own mentality. This was about to change again with the new wave of slavery in the New World, but in Shakespeare even Caliban is not yet fully represented as a barbarian slave (let alone Shylock, Glendower, Fluellen, Othello, Morocco or even Aaron), but rather as an extension of one's self to be accounted with as an inevitable Other, occupying the same mental, and often bodily space as the civilized subject.

Slavoj Žižek rightly reminds us that barbarism and culture are not mutually exclusive: barbarism may function within our own culture, where it contends with civilization,[22] which brings to mind, of course, Walter Benjamin's much quoted dictum (coming out of his fatally personal encounter with modern barbarism): 'There is no document of civilization which is not at the same time a document of barbarism'.[23] A German of Jewish origin, Benjamin must have in mind the barbarians of his own culture, who suddenly proclaimed him as a barbarian other, supporting their ideological claims by an allegedly physical evidence. While discrediting his non-Aryan face and upholding its opposite shape, they mostly admired the mystifying effect of the faceless crowd, united by a chilling version of Ibn Khaldûn's group solidarity. In his letter to the ruler of the Maghrib, Ibn Khaldûn, who praises Timur for his intelligence and prowess, holds an ambiguous, semi-exonerating attitude towards the Mongol's radical practices of pillage, cruelty and massacre: 'After that he marched toward Syria and did there what is well-known – Allah is the Master of His affairs' (and he will soon remind his reader that Timur 'is the one who is favoured by Allah').[24] Also in Marlowe, one gets the feeling that, monstrous as he may be, the totality of Tamburlaine does not exceed a human size – he will not rise to the contours of Antony in Cleopatra's dream – and therefore is not beyond forgiveness.

VI

The potential interchangeability of barbarism between the subject and its great Other through the operation of mimicry is already confusing, baffling and often traumatically realised in early modern drama. It is an age which has already experienced the ambiguity of Lutheran denial of Rome as a reaction to its excessive 'barbarism' while betraying its own latent savagery.[25] There is a sense, the creators of Tamburlaine, Shylock and Othello tell us, in which the 'common spirits' of barbarism had already infiltrated both our bodily and national vineyards long before Arragon and the Constable expressed their caveats. Or have they ever left the Imperial hegemony even while the latter was busy constituting its civilized, subjective identity? Can indeed the documents of barbarism be traced in any document of civilization? It is my attempted project here to briefly carve and delineate the discursive space invested by the barbarous in the world of Marlowe's *Tamburlaine*, in order to explore the tension between barbarism as a cultural concept and the concept of nation as its ironically inherent host as often represented in the English early modern theatre.

Whereas Benedict Anderson, Eric Hobsbawm and others insist on nationalism as a strictly modern phenomenon, Anthony D. Smith, B. C. Shafer and others defend some forms of early nationalism, to which the Tudor brand of collective identity clearly pertains. Describing what distinguishes the English sense of nationalism emerging in the sixteenth century (rather progressive, compared to its later development with the progress of both capitalism and imperialism), Liah Greenfeld notes:

> The concept of the nation presupposed a sense of respect toward the individual, an emphasis on the dignity of the human being. One was entitled to nationality (membership in a nation) by right of one's humanity. Essentially, the nation was a community of people realising their nationality; the association of such a community with particular geo-political boundaries was secondary. The love of nation – national patriotism, or nationalism – in this framework meant first and foremost a principled individualism.[26]

On the face of it, there is an oxymoronic facet to the anchoring of one's recently discovered individuality within a collective identity. In early Christianity, when the individual was supposed to invest in the body of Christ, individualism was not an ideologically viable or desired factor in the constitution of humanity. In the preindustrial phase of capitalism, the fusion of institutional and personal identity had not yet been entirely effaced. The institutionalised conception of man as the representation of the second figure in the Trinity had lost its grip by the sixteenth century, but no clear cognitive patterns rendered that heroic gesture called by Stephen Greenblatt 'Renaissance self-fashioning' a common practice yet among the general public.[27] In the domain of 'expressive culture'[28] no major changes had occurred before the scientific revolution of the late seventeenth century, of which marked villains such as Iago or Edmund are notable harbingers. The collision between the early modern urge to dispense with obsolete cognitive patterns and the still coercive power of institutionalised self-images called, however, for liberation through artistic representation, which may partly account for the popularity of Elizabethan theatre, in which self-fashioning became a prominent feature and theme.

Thus a major sense in which both Marlowe and Shakespeare's practice of dramatic representation yields itself to a new discourse of self-fashioning lies in their frequent habit of breaking patterns of subjectivity by interchanging, appropriating, transgressing and tampering with, human identities. Rather than merely imitating external tendencies of growing individualism by insisting on circumscribing holistic, complex psychological constructs, both contemporaries often regard their characters as transcending the boundaries of a totalised subject, making them constantly fashioned by themselves or the gaze of others. Since Elizabethan theatre preceded the Cartesian discourse which was to dominate centuries of liberal humanism, one cannot possibly relate that practice to the later practices of postmodern deconstruction. And yet the free fashioning of identities represented in many of the plays of Marlowe and Shakespeare (whether as an impulse assigned to a given dramatic subject or as an overt or implicit dramaturgic strategy) may be construed as a prophetic resistance to an already corrupting (though recent) process of essentialist individualisation (inherent in the process of civility) which the sharp political sensors of both contemporaries detected, each after his own dramaturgic fashion, in the passage of Western culture into the phase later to be known as early modern discourse. In subverting this too neat development of essentialist nationhood, they let barbarous figures invade the subjects of Imperial European hegemony, prophetically to confuse perspectives on, and problematise the origins of, civility.

In the world of the comedies, where mimicry feels more at home, the resistance against totalisation often breeds early prefigurations of postmodern parody, anticipating the deliberately disenchanting denouements of the later mature and problem comedies: such parodic patterns may be traced in the Phoebe–Ganymede affair in *As You Like It*, where courtly Rosalind's civilizing practices are directed not at her equally civilized Orlando, but at the 'native' residents of the wild forest, whose posture of civility is almost the same as hers, *but not quite*, thus reminding the spectators (on stage and in the theatre) of the fragility of their own claim to civility. Disguise, impersonation and bodily manipulation play a big part in this dramatic strategy. It is hardly surprising to see the King and the rest of the lords disguised as Muscovite 'barbarians' in the fifth Act of *Love's Labour's Lost*. In *The Merchant of Venice*, however, a major use of the 'barbarians' pervades both branches of the plot. The Prince of Morocco seems to serve as a living proof to Arragon's complaint against the barbarous multitude, in choosing 'what many men desire'. Shylock, in his barbarian gaberdine, devilish practice of usury, and currish lack of music in himself, is approached by the Venetian mercantile community as an indispensable factor in its economy, is recognised as a special case (for good and bad) in the Venetian book of law, and finally manages to bring the Venetian justice system, in his very defeat in Court, to adopt his own terms of justice rather than subscribe to their self-proclaimed quality of mercy.[29]

However, in the realm of serious drama, and especially the tragedies, the juxtaposition and interchangeability between civility and barbarism plays a more significant part. In the two parts of *Tamburlaine*, Marlowe carries out his ambitious epic study of heroic human enterprise and the expansionist agenda of the new empire entirely within the home base of barbarism. In it, prophetic riddles drawing on the human face and looks serve as dynamic tools to qualify, extend and shrink subjective identity. In Marlowe's tragedies, as Greenblatt is not alone in arguing, the grotesquely comic constantly exists 'as the mechanical imposed upon the living'; Marlowe's chief barbarian figure, Tamburlaine, may be parodically conceived as 'a machine, a desiring machine that produces violence and death'.[30] Respectively, the mechanical transportation of the shepherd into an ever mightier dominating position almost paradoxically simplifies a major parameter of theatrical characterisation such as class distinction, while Tamburlaine himself is mythically accounted for (e.g., in Menaphon's above-mentioned description of him in *1 Tamburlaine*, II.i, portraying in great detail 'The face and patronage of a wondrous man'), and whereas a certain amount of crude individuation is still retained among the variety of kingly figures victimised by Tamburlaine and made to kneel at his feet throughout his picaresque voyage along the courses of victory (after all, the King of Spain is recognised as an individual who may even lay claim on England through the right of Mary Tudor), anyone ranking below their princely position is reduced to a digit within a mechanical enumeration of reified 'humanoids'. On this level, the chief property of the barbarian is explored as a social phenomenon.

VII

One distinctive feature of this dramatic strategy, in which reification partakes in the operative mode of 'barbaric mimicry', is Marlowe's excessive representation of cavalry as an impersonal war machine, a compound military mechanism, whose human components are metonymically referred to, if at all, by the name of the beast they are riding. Accounting for the army at the outset as 'a horse' ('Theridamas, / Charg'd with a thousand horse' [1 *Tamburlaine*, I.i.46–7]; 'To send my thousand horse incontinent / To apprehend that paltry Scythian' [ll. 52–3]), the horses then assume their expected natural shape at the expense of their potential masters, appropriating, and transforming after their own fashion, what should have been logically conceived as their riders' attitudes toward their foe:

> Thou shalt be leader of this thousand horse,
> Whose foaming gall with rage and high disdain
> Have sworn the death of wicked Tamburlaine
> (ll. 62–4)

It is only the commander of the thousand horses, commissioned to conquer all his foes 'with [his] looks' (l. 75), who is charged to 'go frowning forth, but come … smiling home / As did Sir Paris with the Grecian dame' (ll. 65–6), whose own beauty, as both the authors of *Doctor Faustus* and *A Midsummer Night's Dream* know well, lies chiefly in her face and gaze. The riders themselves, however, have by now vanished entirely from our view, as if melted into thin air, leaving behind them just bestial icons on an abstract map of war:

> That I may view these milk-white steeds of mine
> All loaden with the heads of killed men,
> And from their knees even to their hoofs below

Besmear'd with blood; that makes a dainty show.
(ll. 77–80)

It is significant that when the cavalry is referred to by a lower
ranked character, a nameless spy who accounts in his report for his
fellow men, it is depicted as 'An hundred horsemen of my company'
(II.ii.39). 'Common soldiers', indeed, may be addressed, when
needed, as 'noble soldiers' (ll. 63, 59) or even 'my masters' (l. 74);
and they are able to humanly 'conceive more joy' (I.i.152), which
may amount even to reversing their reified status into appointing an
Emperor who vows in return not only 'to reign sole king' by their
'desires of discipline in arms', but 'Cause the soldiers that thus
honor [him] / To triumph over many provinces' (ll. 172–5).
However, once the shadow of war returns to haunt the discourse,
human beings would be again referred to by the horses they ride
('there are in readiness / Ten thousand horse to carry you from
hence / In spite of all suspected enemies' [ll. 184–6]). As soon as
Tamburlaine appears on the scene, with whom the blind, stormy
war machine is to take over and dominate representation, humans
are regularly invested in beasts, or, by the same token, depicted by
the instruments they operate in battle, their virginity, or, on a
higher, yet not high enough level, by the crowns allocated to them
for their loyalty to the victor:

> Two thousand horse shall forage up and down
> That no relief or succor come by land,
> And all the sea my galleys countermand.
> Then shall our footmen lie within the trench.
> (*1 Tamburlaine*, III.i.61–4)

>   the great commander of the world
> Besides fifteen contributary kings,
> Hath now in arms ten thousand janissaries,
> Mounted on lusty Mauritanian steeds,
> Brought to the war by men of Tripoli;
> Two hundred thousand footmen that have serv'd
> In the two battles fought in Graecia;
> (III.iii.13–19)

The members of an ethnic or national group are thus consistently
conceived throughout both *Tamburlaine* plays as an extension of
the power of their current leader, or, from another perspective, the

reflection of the empire's agenda. And if this practice may be partly ascribed to the alienated vision of the orient on the part of a Christian author, given almost obsessively to the portrayal of the strangeness of others,[31] it is equally applied here to allegedly non-barbarian, Christian nations (albeit catholics, and thus alienated from the protestant empire of England):

> Besides, King Sigismund hath brought from Christendom
> More than his camp of stout Hungarians:
> Slavonians, Almains, Rutters, Muffs, and Danes ...
> Vast Gruntland, compass'd with the frozen sea,
> Inhabited with tall and sturdy men,
> Giants as big as hugy Polypheme,
> Millions of soldiers cut the arctic line.
>
> *(2 Tamburlaine*, I.i.20–2, 26–9)

The only instance in which this pattern is broken is Zenocrate's words of compassion (*1 Tamburlaine*, V.i.319ff), where suffering provides for some degree of individuality. It is she who encounters the true experience of a tragic cleavage to be resolved solely by a decisive solution. It is she who has to learn to be 'wounded in conceit' (l. 415), and be content with her father's overthrow, 'else should [she] much forget [her]self' (l. 500).

The real tragic hero of the plays, however, is Tamburlaine himself, who not fortuitously knows how to compare her at that very moment of resolution to double-faced Juno (l. 510). Significantly, it is only when he sees Zenocrate for the first time, that Tamburlaine is made to discern the most distinctive mark of individuality, namely a face. Faces, eyes and looks as mirrors of individuality and coded prophetic riddles are reserved in the *Tamburlaine* plays solely for the very few figures whose desire excessively soars above the flow of human fate on which the historical narrative runs. Like her closest soul and guide so far, Agydas, who attempts rather simplistically to read Zenocrate's 'heart's sorrow' in her 'heavenly face' (*1 Tamburlaine*, III.ii.4–5), does Tamburlaine prophetically peruse fate and her worth in her 'fair face and heavenly hue'; though in his vision even this most intimate touch of gentle feeling toward the one woman with whom he is in love – toward she whose 'person is more worth to [him] / Than the possession of the Persian crown' significantly promised to him at his birth by a benevolent prophecy (*1 Tamburlaine*, I.ii.90–2) – is phrased in a crude language of possession and intermingled with terror:

> this fair face and heavenly hue
> Must grace his bed that conquers Asia
> And means to be a terror to the world.
>   (I.ii.36–8)

Later on, their love is sealed and symbolised by their children, more precious in his eyes than all the kingdoms he subdued, 'Plac'd by her side, look on their mother's face' (*2 Tamburlaine*, I.iii.18–20); and yet even at this high point of individuality, his familial intimacy gives way to the barbaric discourse of his masculinity: their own looks, he feels, are not martian enough, which makes for another riddle of identity interpreted differently by him and Zenocrate. It is an old riddle in the play: Agydas, a rather flat reader of looks and faces, is not sophisticated enough to decipher Tamburlaine's marital bliss beyond the 'martial stratagem' displayed by his 'looks so fierce' (*1 Tamburlaine*, III.i.40–1).

The only channel of genuine human tenderness in the world of Tamburlaine, his love for Zenocrate, is indeed the sole outlet capable of producing human individuation for the victims of history. But this acknowledgement of their individuality will not bring any conciliation to the sufferers in Tamburlaine's world of undiscriminating, barbarous iniquity. Zenocrate, constant in her alleged inconstancy; who, though changed from her 'first conceiv'd disdain' for him, and, moved by that same complex desire born of the conscientious marriage of intellect and passion, can read in Tamburlaine's looks his more tender merits and true love for her, nevertheless prophetically senses that invincible iniquity, and propounds her helpless knowledge through her wan and pale face:

> since, a farther passion feeds my thoughts,
> With ceaseless and disconsolate conceits,
> Which dyes my looks so lifeless as they are
> And might, if my extremes had full events,
> Make me the ghastly counterfeit of death.
>   (III.ii.12–17)

VIII

Is Marlowe passing judgement on a world so presented? The critical debate regarding the play is well known: some critics argue that he studies the world of an 'Herculean hero', some will assign him didactic intentions, and some would regard Marlowe to be morally indifferent. Power is inextricably intertwined with knowledge in typical Foucauldian patterns: Tamburlaine prizes himself not just for overpowering human foes, but, rather excessively, for holding 'the Fates bound fast in iron chains, / And with [his] hand turn Fortune's wheel about' (1 Tamburlaine, I.ii.174–5). Significantly, oracular expressions are crucial to the structure and characterisation of the two Tamburlaine plays, whose central figure runs throughout its epic narrative a course started by a prophecy given him by the stars at birth. Prophetic messages abound and are directly conveyed in both parts through the use of fully realised riddles. Sometimes the significance of their use scarcely transcends the level of dramatic effectiveness. Tamburlaine, for whom an utmost expression of contempt would be 'a knot of kings, / Sitting as if they were a-telling riddles' (2 Tamburlaine, III.v.58–9), is himself constantly fascinated by his ability to exert his power on human destinies by way of propounding prophetic riddles, bearing divine validity:

> Nor are Apollo's oracles more true
> Than thou shall find my vaunts substantial.
> (1 Tamburlaine, I.ii.211–12)

For the initiate, it is his very individuality, expressed in his face, which 'bears figures of renown and miracle' or, alternatively, 'figure[s] death' (1 Tamburlaine, II.i.4, 21). Unlike Bajazeth, invoking his supposedly awesome looks vainly but in vain (1 Tamburlaine, III.i.49), Tamburlaine's looks, 'the face and personage of a wondrous man', portrayed in epic detail by Menaphon (1 Tamburlaine, II.i.32), both challenge the universe and offer the ready answer for his prophetic riddle. Indeed, Theridamas, immediately taken by 'his looks [which] menace heaven and dare the gods', instantly peruses the prophetic message challenging him to 'judge the inward man' by his 'outward habit', and admits to being 'won with [his] words and conquered with [his] looks' (1 Tamburlaine, I.ii.157, 163, 228). Tamburlaine, by the same token, is capable of reading in Theridamas' 'martial face and stout aspect' the folly of his emperor (ll. 165–70) whom he is soon to poke fun at in a comic riddling session ('a pretty jest', or 'sport', as he lightly refers to his most presumptuous enterprises [II.v.90, 101]) which baffles Mycetes' poor wit entirely (II.iv.22–41). To Cosroe, Theridamas' newly self-appointed emperor designate, who, more wisely than his grotesque brother, would take the Scythian's doom for satisfaction 'even as from assured oracle' (a metaphor Tamburlaine often uses himself), Tamburlaine replies with an oracular statement:

> For fates and oracles of heaven have sworn
> To royalize the deeds of Tamburlaine
> (*1 Tamburlaine*, II.iii.7–8)

which Cosroe totally misconstrues. He learns his answer too late: to his complaint about Tamburlaine's depriving him of his crown and life, Tamburlaine could easily bring Cosroe's own case of usurping his brother's throne as a precedent, but, overtaking human enterprise, he invokes directly 'What better precedent than mighty Jove?' (*1 Tamburlaine*, II.vii.17).

Later on, however, Tamburlaine's almost playful art of riddling becomes more and more explicit. The murder of Agydas is designed and staged by him as the confirmation, by means of a visual riddle, of his victim's prophetic fears identifying the Tyrant's will and the inevitability of fate:

> (*Enter* **Techelles** *with a naked dagger* [*and* **Usumcasane**].)
> **Techelles**   See you, Agydas, how the king salutes you.
>   He bids you prophesy what it imports.
> **Agydas**   I prophesied before and now I prove
>   The killing frowns of jealousy and love.
>   He needed not with words confirm my fear,
>   For words are vain where working tools present
>   The naked action of my threat'ned end.
>   It says, 'Agydas, thou shalt surely die,
>   And of extremities elect the least;
>   More honour and less pain it may procure,
>   To die by this resolved hand of thine
>   Than stay the torments he and heaven have sworn'.
>   (*1 Tamburlaine*, III.ii.88–99)

And the very tension between the different uses of 'prophesy' by Techelles and Agydas (the one meaning 'expound', the other, 'foretell') results here in a verbal riddle, complementary of the visual one. At the very moment where frowns are turned into action (ll. 92–4), foreknowledge is 'proved' in the complex insight of true prophecy and its bearer ranked with the initiate. Having put into effect his interpretation of the Tyrant's prophetic riddle, the dead Agydas is hailed as a sage and as an honourable interpreter:

> **Techelles**   Usumcasane, see how right the man
>   Hath hit the meaning of my lord the king.
> **Usumcasane**   Faith, and Techelles, it was manly done;
>   And since he was so wise and honourable,
>   Let us afford him now the bearing hence,
>   And crave his triple-worthy burial.
>
> (ll. 107–12)

The same identification of his will with fate, as exercised in the case of Agydas, is translated by Tamburlaine into a prophetic challenge when delegating his own frowns and looks to his ready soldiers, still conceived as a collective identity, a silent extension of the tyrant's own power and knowledge:

> View well my camp and speak indifferently:
> Do not my captains and my soldiers look
> As if they meant to conquer Africa?
> (*1 Tamburlaine*, III.iii.8–10)

Which Basso misses, since, though appreciating the valour of Tamburlaine's soldiers, he reads them as a separate entity from their leader's prophetic sense of will and fate united, and tells them by their number (as will later the King of Arabia, turned fortune-teller following Capolin's quantitative report). That lack of commitment to looking before and after and perusing the moment prophetically is soon manifested in Basso's emperor, Bajazeth and his wife Zabina, who both will not acknowledge the complex, multi-layered identity of Tamburlaine and Zenocrate, respectively, and unlike Tamburlaine, whose 'words are oracles' (l. 102) since he is capable of reading the complexity of the moment, judge them simplistically by prejudice. Having missed his time to be attentive to his conscience, Bajazeth will later make a fool of himself when trying, after his defeat, still to command 'dread god of hell' (*1 Tamburlaine*, IV.ii.27) or the furies (IV.iv.17; V.i.217).

The same concept displayed in the death of Agydas' scene is once again conveyed and exercised by Tamburlaine in a dramatic riddle form when encountering the virgins of Damascus, a game whose excessive cruelty brings out perhaps the most extreme gesture of 'inverted mimicry' in the play, in which the mimic Other is the perpetrator empowered by the Imperial privilege:

> Tamburlaine   Virgins, in vain ye labour to prevent
>   That which mine honour swears shall be perform'd.
>   Behold my sword; what see you at the point?
> 1 Virgin   Nothing but fear and fatal steel, my lord.
> Tamburlaine   Your fearful minds are thick and misty, then,
>   For there sits death; there sits imperious Death,
>   Keeping his circuit by the slicing edge.
>   (1 Tamburlaine, V.i.106–12)

The act of murder which ensues, overwhelming as it is in its brutality, produces, as a side effect of the mimic aspect, the same mirthless, laughless jest we talked about above, where the civilized subject discovers her/his barbaric counterpart in the mirror of mimicry held up to human nature.

IX

In 1 Tamburlaine, Tamburlaine's prophetic insight into fate matches the structure of the play's action. Marlowe, who has made him the living spirit of the empire's expansionist project, presents him here, ironically, as the judicious reader of the map/face of the world. 'What would have been even in the mouth of Achilles or Caesar the rant of overweening pride, has metaphysical justification for Tamburlaine.'[32] It is only in 2 Tamburlaine, however, where many of the tensions of the first part are resolved, that the Tyrant's prophecy is proved false once his own fate is concerned, and when he fails to separate his 'two bodies': the individual and the reflection of the national agenda. At the outset, Orcanes' insistence on separating Tamburlaine from 'Fortune that hath made him great' (2 Tamburlaine, I.i.60), as well as Sigismund's quantitative appraisal of his power (l. 106ff), seem still to suggest the continued pattern of false prophecy as practised by Tamburlaine's foes in the first play. However, the differentiation between Tamburlaine's and Zenocrate's opposite readings of their sons' faces marks the futility of Tamberlaine's sterilised masculine, militarist ideology, when not directed any more to turning the world upside down as the emblem of the empire, but mercilessly to preserving his own power at all costs. Here Marlowe brings in the dividing line between the emperor's two bodies in terms of the idea of succession, so central in the Tudor narrative in general and at the time Tamburlaine the Great was written in particular. Satisfied by flattering, shallow reiterations of the former emblem of his prophetic abilities:

> mighty Tamburlaine, our earthly god,
> Whose looks make this inferior world to quake
> (*2 Tamburlaine*, I.iii.138-9)

– now mobilised for the sake of unqualified fear and terror alone, Tamburlaine responds in kind by 'surfeit[ing]in conceiving joy' just by their sycophantic sight (ll. 152–6), and then burst with them in an ecstatic fit of expansionist celebration, sanguinely banqueting on geography. Zenocrate's death, to which Tamburlaine responds by vowing to be 'raving, impatient, desperate, and mad' (II.iv.112), drags him further into binding his prophetic practice to futile 'fiery meteors ... presag[ing]/ Death and destruction' (III.ii.4–5), interpreting the picture of Zenocrate wrongly, her living face no more in sight to qualify his will, after his own fashion as 'Bellona, goddess of the war' (l. 40). From now on he is the rival of true prophecy. After Olympia foreshadows the peripeteia in reversing Tamburlaine's riddle, making Theridamas believe that Death does not sit at the point of the sword (*2 Tamburlaine*, IV.ii) – Tamburlaine is himself deceived by his own riddle, when shaking his sword against heavenly majesty (V.i.194) makes him yield his life to 'his servant Death'. And yet, even in his fatal sickness, recognising and stoically reconciled to the presence of death in him, he is determined and courageous enough to stick to his original agenda:

> In spite of Death I will go show my face!
> (V.iii.115)

And his wish to see the map of the world, which is still to be conquered, even though not by him alone but through the dynamics of succession, reinstates him as the complex tragic hero, not the villain of the play.

Whereas Tamburlaine the emblem of the new Empire is the heroic figure of the awakening national consciousness, his mimic mirror-image in Tamburlaine the barbarian is an awesome parable of distracted humanity. But what is the signified in this ambiguous dramatic statement? In spite of what seems a neatly woven master narrative, leading the second play especially along a route of rise and fall, does indeed Tamburlaine's failure to read properly the world's prophetic riddles necessarily bear on his former success to construe them? Should we necessarily read Tamburlaine's inevitable fall at the end of 2 *Tamburlaine* as a judgement passed by Marlowe on the character of Tamburlaine as a unified subject of the newly proclaimed national aspirations? Is it the fall of the barbarian monster, who still retains, Macbeth-like, his heroic prowess, or does he represent the complexity within the newly defined national project? Defending Paul de Man's attraction to the Nazi ('National-Socialist') ideology at the early stage of the war, Shoshana Felman quotes a text of his uncle, Hendrik de Man, who must have been a great influence on his nephew's ideas:

> the [Nazi] system, despite everything in it that strikes our mentality as alien, had lessened class differences much more efficaciously than the self-styled democracies, where capital continued to lay down the law. Since then everyone has been able to see that the superior morale of the German army is due in large part to the greater social unity of the nation and to the resulting prestige of its authorities. In contrast, the plutocracies offer us the spectacle of authorities deserting their stations and the rich crossing the border by car without worrying about what happens to the masses.[33]

Is one's blindness to the catch in the barbarous flattening of social interdependency necessarily criminal? Bad it certainly is, but could it perhaps be interpreted sometimes in terms of tragic blindness? Does Marlowe demand of his hero to be totally and constantly alert to an absolute code of 'civilized' morality (as C. P. Taylor, for example, not unjustifiably demands of his main character in *Good*)? Or is there some political significance in Marlowe's ruthless, barbarian tyrant's crude belief in shattering by force the iniquity of corrupt, existing hierarchies

> for all my birth,
> That virtue solely is the sum of glory,
> And fashions men with true nobility
> (*1 Tamburlaine*, V.i.125–7)

which he passes accordingly to his fellow rebels?

> Deserve these titles I endow you with
> By valour and by magnanimity
> Your births shall be no blemish to your fame,

For virtue is the fount whence honour springs,
And they are worthy she investeth kings.
                                (IV.iv.188–90)

And is their crude attraction to his ideology necessarily corrupt? At best, Marlowe leaves these questions open, an act which his dramatic strategy of mimicry enables him to do. In *Tamburlaine*, like in Shakespeare's *Cymbeline* years later,[34] self and nation are both ideologically deployed, reconciled to the laws of tragedy and romance, informed by proper measures of civility and respect, and yet charged by an open-ended prophecy, a desire for an unattainable epic lucidity and proportion threatened by ominous ambiguity; a dream of wholesome nation and measurable self, wiping out the barbarous within the 'civilized' Empire, but indeed qualifying reality and yet too vast to be contained by it.

From *Strands Afar Remote: Israeli Perspectives on Shakespeare*, ed. Avraham Oz (Newark, DE, 1998), pp.151–76 (revised).

Notes

[My approach to *Tamburlaine* is part of a larger project whereby I attempt to view rising proto-nationalist consciousness as reflected in early modern English drama in the light of scrutinising the other, both as the menace threatening the subject of nationhood from the outside, and the barbarian force stirring it from within. Both forces qualify the civilizing process, leading the early modern European subject toward establishing its body politic as primarily pertaining to nationhood rather than to religious faith. Using the notion of mimicry, as defined by Homi Bhabha, I attempt to show how Marlowe's Tamburlaine thus functions both as the barbaric threat to the newly defined British subject, as well as the very symbol and embodiment of its desired Empire. Ed.]

1. Norbert Elias, *The Civilizing Process*, trans. Edmund Jephcott (Oxford, 1994), p. 275.

2. Homi K. Bhabha, *The Location of Culture* (London and New York, 1994), pp. 85–6.

3. Ibid., p. 86.

4. Ibid., p. 88.

5. Ibid., p. 89.

6. Strobe Talbott and Nayan Chanda (eds), *The Age of Terror: America and the World After September 11* (New York, 2001), p. xiii.

7. Ibid., pp. 173–4.

8. Ibid., p. vii.

9. A. D. Nuttall, *The Alternative Trinity: Gnostic Heresy in Marlowe, Milton and Blake* (Oxford, 1998), p. 23.

10. C. L. Barber, *Creating Elizabethan Tragedy*, ed. Richard P. Wheeler (Chicago, 1988), pp. 45, 47.

11. See Avraham Oz, *The Yoke of Love: Prophetic Riddles in 'The Merchant of Venice'* (Newark, DE, 1995).

12. Cf. Barber, *Creating Elizabethan Tragedy*, p. 51.

13. Terry Eagleton, *The Idea of Culture* (Oxford, 2000), p. 5.

14. John Gillies, *Shakespeare and the Geography of Difference* (Cambridge, 1994), p. 63.

15. Suzanne Scholz, *Body Narratives: Writing the Nation and Fashioning the Subject in Early Modern England* (Basingstoke, 2000), pp. 85–6.

16. In the varied discussions of nationalism such an approach will pertain to the definition offered by Hobsbawm (E. J. Hobsbawm, *Nations and Nationalism since 1780: Programme, Myth, Reality* [Cambridge, 1992]), except that the latter will not be willing to discuss it as a sixteenth-century phenomenon.

17. See my 'Color our Nation', in Avraham Oz (ed.), *Strands Afar Remote: Israeli Perspectives on Shakespeare* (Newark, DE, 1998).

18. See, for instance, Jonathan B. Bengstone, 'Saint George and the Development of English Nationalism in the Late Middle Ages' (unpublished M.Phil. Thesis, Oxford University, 1994).

19. See Ian Wilson, *Holy Faces, Secret Places* (London, 1992).

20. Charles Nicholl, *The Reckoning: The Murder of Christopher Marlowe* (London, 1992), pp. 85–6.

21. The word suggests nonsense, especially in language. The modern Hebrew colloquial verb 'barber', for example, denotes 'talk much with no substance'. See Anthony Pagden, *Lords of all the World: Ideologies of Empire in Spain, Britain and France c.1500–c.1800* (New Haven & London, 1995), p. 21.

22. Slavoj Žižek, *For They Know Not What They Do: Enjoyment as a Political Factor* (London & New York, 1991), p. 225.

23. Walter Benjamin, 'Theses on the Philosophy of History', in *Illuminations*, ed. Hannah Arendt, trans. Harry Zohn (New York, 1969), p. 256.

24. Walter J. Fischel (ed.), *Ibn Khaldûn and Tamerlane : their historic meeting in Damascus, 1401 A.D. (803 A.H.) : a study based on Arabic manuscripts of Ibn Khaldûn's 'Autobiography'* (Berkeley, CA, 1952), pp. 46–7.

25. See Žižek, *For They Know Not*, p. 225.

26. Liah Greenfeld, *Nationalism: Five Roads to Modernity* (Cambridge, MA, 1992), p. 31.

27. Stephen Greenblatt, *Renaissance Self-Fashioning* (Chicago, 1980).

28. Defined as the personal and collective identity models and meanings, symbolic templates for shared social consciousness, and religious interpretations, evaluations, and rituals. See John H. Marx, 'The Ideological Construction of Postmodern Identity Models in Contemporary Cultural Movements', in Roland Robertson and Burkart Holzner (eds), *Identity and Authority: Explorations in the Theory of Society* (Oxford, 1980), p. 155.

29. See Oz, *The Yoke of Love*.

30. Greenblatt, *Renaissance*, p. 195. See also Clifford Leech, 'Power and Suffering in Edward the Second', *Critical Quarterly*, 1 (1959), 181–96.

31. See Emily C. Bartels, *Spectacles of Strangeness: Imperialism, Alienation, and Marlowe* (Philadelphia, 1993) [part reprinted in this volume, essay 1 – Ed.].

32. Lawrence Kelsall, *Christopher Marlowe* (Leiden, 1981), p.73.

33. Shoshana Felman and Dori Laub, *Testimony: Crises of Witnessing in Literature, Psychoanalysis, and History* (New York and London, 1992), pp. 125–6.

34. See Oz, 'Extending Within: Placing Self and Nation in the Epic of *Cymbeline' JTD*, 4 (1998), 81–97.

4

Marlowe, Marx, and Anti-Semitism

STEPHEN GREENBLATT

A fantasy: Barabas, the Jew of Malta, had two children. The eldest, Abigail, sickened by the revelation that her father had murdered her Christian suitor, converted and entered a nunnery. The other child, a son, likewise apostatised; indeed he wrote a violently anti-Semitic pamphlet denouncing the essence of his father's religion as huckstering, its basis self-interest, its jealous god money. The pamphlet concluded with a call for the emancipation of mankind from Judaism, but, curiously, the son did not convert to Christianity and try to assimilate. On the contrary, he insisted that his father's hated religion was simply the practical essence of Christianity, the thing itself stripped of its spiritual mystifications. The Christians who prided themselves on their superiority to Jews were themselves practising Judaism in their daily lives, worshipping money, serving egoistic need, buying and selling men as commodities, as so many pounds of flesh. The son's name, of course, was Karl Marx.

The purpose of this paper is to read Marlowe's *The Jew of Malta* in the light of Marx's 'On the Jewish Question'.[1] Fantasy aside, this is neither an obvious nor a particularly promising enterprise. There was no 'Jewish Question' in Marlowe's England; there were scarcely any Jews.[2] Civil society, the rights of man, the political state, the concept of citizenship – Marx's basic terms – would have been quite incomprehensible to an Elizabethan. Marx's central theme, that political emancipation is not the same as human emancipation, would likewise have been incomprehensible in an age in

96

which there was scarcely a conception of politics, in the modern sense, let alone a dream that man might some day be emancipated from both state and religion. Marx's discourse is informed by the Enlightenment, the American and French Revolutions, Feuerbach's analysis of religion, and the growth of capitalism; its occasion, a critique of Bruno Bauer's *Die Judenfrage* and 'Die Fähigkeit der heutigen Juden und Christen, frei zu werden', depends upon the particular, historically determined situation of the Ashkenazi Jews of nineteenth-century Germany; its rhetoric is coloured both by the virulent modern strain of popular anti-Semitism and by the author's own troubled relationship to the religion of his fathers.[3]

Nevertheless, Marx's essay has a profound bearing upon *The Jew of Malta*; their conjunction enriches our understanding of the author's relation to ideology and, more generally, raises fruitful questions about a Marxist reading of literature. The fact that both works use the figure of the perfidious Jew provides a powerful interpretive link between Renaissance and modern thought, for despite the great differences to which I have just pointed, this shared reference is not an accident or a mirage. 'On the Jewish Question' represents the nineteenth-century development of a late sixteenth-century idea or, more accurately, a late sixteenth-century trope. Marlowe and Marx seize upon the Jew as a kind of powerful rhetorical device, a way of marshalling deep popular hatred and clarifying its object. The Jew is charged not with racial deviance or religious impiety but with economic and social crime, crime that is committed not only *against* the dominant Christian society but, in less 'pure' form, by that society. Both writers hope to focus attention upon activity that is seen as at once alien and yet central to the life of the community and to direct against the activity the anti-Semitic feeling of the audience. The Jews themselves in their real historical situation are finally incidental in these works, Marx's as well as Marlowe's, except insofar as they excite the fear and loathing of the great mass of Christians. It is this privileged access to mass psychology by means of a semi-mythical figure linked in the popular imagination with usury, sharp dealing, and ruthless cunning that attracts both the sixteenth-century playwright and the nineteenth-century polemicist.[4]

Twentieth-century history has demonstrated with numbing force how tragically misguided this rhetorical strategy was, how utterly it underestimated the irrationality, the fixation upon its object, and the persistence of anti-Semitism. The Christian hatred of the Jew,

nurtured by popular superstition, middle-class *ressentiment*, the frequent complicity of Church and state, the place of the Jews in the
European economy, and the complex religious and cultural barriers,
would not be so easily turned against a particular structure of
economic or social relations or a cast of mind that crossed racial
and religious boundaries but would light with murderous force
upon the whole Jewish community. It is folly to attempt to use a
people as a rhetorical device or to exploit popular prejudice as a
force for constructive change, let alone moral enlightenment. Even
granting that historical hindsight gives us an unearned wisdom,
even granting all of the mitigating intentions with which the
authors evidently used the figure of the Jew, we are obliged to acknowledge that there is something unsavoury, inexcusable, about
both works. Their nature is subdued to what it works in, like the
dyer's hand; they are, I would insist, defiled by the dark forces they
are trying to exploit, used by what they are trying to use. But this
acknowledgement, necessary if we are to keep our moral bearings
and look unflinchingly at the horrors of our history, is not identical
with understanding. The latter will come only by patiently exploring what I have called the shared rhetorical strategy *of The Jew of
Malta* and 'On the Jewish Question'.

I will begin by looking briefly at a famous use of the Jewish
stereotype that contrasts sharply with Marlowe's and Marx's. *The
Merchant of Venice* is built around a series of decisive structural
conflicts – Old Law vs New Law, Justice vs Mercy, Revenge vs
Love, Calculation vs Recklessness, Thrift vs Prodigality – all of
which are focused upon the central dramatic conflict of Jew and
Gentile or, more precisely, of Jewish fiscalism and Gentile mercantilism.[5] The great economic utility of Shylock – and of the Jew in
this period – is his possession of liquid assets, assets which he is
committed, for his very existence, to employ actively.[6] In general, in
the northern Italian city-states, when the Christian merchants were
weaker, the Jewish moneylenders were stronger; in Venice, as Brian
Pullan has shown, there was a vigorous attempt by the merchant
class to undermine the power of Jewish moneylenders through the
establishment of the Monte di Carità, Christian lending institutions
that would disrupt the Jews' 'bargains' by providing interest-free
loans.[7] All of this seems to be reflected in the hatred Shylock and
Antonio have for each other, hatred Antonio attributes to the fact
that he has 'oft deliver'd from his forfeitures / Many that have at
times made moan to me' (III.iii.22–3).[8]

If Shylock is set against Antonio on grounds of fiscalism vs mercantilism, he is set against Portia on grounds equally based upon the economic position of Jews in early modern Europe. As Jacob Katz observes, the constant application of capital, to which the Jews were committed, precluded investment in immovable property. The law did not permit the Jew to acquire land, and the Jew, for his part, did not attempt to secure such permission:

> He could not hope to perpetuate his wealth in that locality, nor did he seek a niche in the dominant social and economic hierarchy. The economic nexus linking the Jew with his environment was purely instrumental.[9]

In Shakespeare's play this economic nexus is suggested above all by Shylock's usury, but it is also symbolised by his non-participation in Venetian society, his cold, empty house, and such subtle indicators of value as his hostility to masquing – 'the vile squealing of the wry-neck'd fife' (II.v.30). All of this is in sharp contrast to Portia, who has plenty of liquid assets; she can offer at a moment's notice enough gold to pay Antonio's 3000-ducat debt 'twenty times over' (III.ii.306). But her special values in the play are bound up with her house at Belmont and all it represents: its starlit garden, enchanting music, hospitality, social prestige. That is, the economic nexus linking Portia with her environment is precisely *not* instrumental; her world is not a field in which she operates for profit, but a living web of noble values and moral orderliness.

Shylock is the antithesis of this world, as he is of the Christian mercantilism of Venice. He is the 'alien', the 'stranger cur', 'a kind of devil', in short, the 'faithless Jew'. Even the language he shares with the Christian Venetians does not provide a bridge between them: he may use the same words, but he uses them in a wholly different sense:

Shylock Antonio is a good man.
Bassanio Have you heard any imputation to the contrary?
Shylock Ho no, no, no, no: my meaning in saying he is a good man, is to have you understand that he is sufficient.

(I.iii.10–15)

Shylock needs to explain his use of the apparently innocuous 'good man', as he will later be pressed to explain why he insists, against all reason and self-interest, upon his bond: linguistically, psychologically, ethically, as well as religiously, he is different. To be sure, he appeals at moments to his sameness – 'Hath not a Jew eyes?' – and this sameness runs like a dark current through the play, intimating secret bonds that no one, not even the audience, can fully acknowledge. For if Shakespeare subtly suggests obscure links between Jew and Gentile, he compels the audience to transform its disturbing perception of sameness into a reassuring perception of difference. Indeed the Jew seems to embody the abstract principle of *difference* itself, the principle to which he appeals when the Duke demands an explanation for his malice:

> Some men there are love not a gaping pig!
> Some that are mad if they behold a cat!
> And others when the bagpipe sings i'th'nose,
> Cannot contain their urine ...
>
> (IV.i.46–9)

The examples would be whimsical – evoking a motive no grander than allegory – were they not spoken by Shylock, knife in hand; instead, they bespeak impulses utterly inaccessible to reason and persuasion; they embody what the rational mind, intent upon establishing an absolute category of difference, terms *madness*.

The Jew of Malta opens with an apparent gesture toward the same principle of differentiation that governs *The Merchant of Venice*. Marlowe's Jew is introduced in the prologue by Machevill as one 'Who smiles to see how full his bags are cramm'd'; he enters, then, already trailing clouds of ignomiiny, already a 'marked case'. But while never relinquishing the anti-Semitic stereotype, Marlowe quickly suggests that the Jew is not the exception to but rather the true representative of his society. Though he begins with a paean to liquid assets, Barabas is not primarily a usurer, set off by his hated occupation from the rest of the community, but a great merchant, sending his argosies around the world exactly as Shakespeare's much-loved Antonio does. His pursuit of wealth does not mark him out but rather establishes him – if anything, rather respectably – in the midst of all the other forces in the play: the Turks exacting tribute from the Christians: the Christians expropriating money from the Jews: the convent profiting from these expropriations; religious orders competing for wealthy converts: the prostitute plying her trade and the blackmailer his. When the governor of Malta asks the Turkish 'Bashaw', 'What wind drives you thus into *Malta*-road?' the latter replies with perfect frankness, 'The wind that bloweth all the world besides, / Desire of gold' (III.1421–3). Barabas' own desire of gold, so eloquently voiced at the start and vividly enacted in the scene in which he hugs his money bags, is the glowing core of that passion which fires all the characters. To be sure, other values are expressed – love, faith, and honour – but as private values, these are revealed to be hopelessly fragile, while as public values, they are revealed to be mere screens for powerful economic forces. Thus, on the one hand, Abigail, Don Mathias, and the nuns are killed off with remarkable ease and, in effect, with the complicity of the laughing audience. On the other hand, the public invocation of Christian ethics or knightly honour is always linked by Marlowe to baser motives. The knights concern themselves with Barabas' 'inherent sinne' only at the moment when they are about to preach him out of his possessions, while the decision to resist the 'barbarous mis-beleeuing *Turkes*' facilitates all too easily the sale into slavery of a shipload of Turkish captives. The religious and political ideology that seems at first to govern Christian attitudes toward infidels in fact does nothing of the sort: this ideology is clearly subordinated to considerations of profit. In Marx's terms, both religion and the political state are shown to rest upon the foundation of civil society which is entirely governed by the relentless pursuit of money.

Because of the primacy of money, Barabas, for all the contempt heaped upon him, is seen as the dominant spirit of the play, its most energetic and inventive force. A victim at the level of religion and political power, he is, in effect, emancipated at the level of civil society, emancipated in Marx's contemptuous use of the word:

> The Jew has emancipated himself in a Jewish manner, not only by acquiring the power of money, but also because *money* had become, through him and also apart from him, a world power, while the practical Jewish spirit has become the practical spirit of the Christian nations. The Jews have emancipated themselves in so far as the Christians have become Jews.
>
> (p. 35)

Barabas' avarice, egotism, duplicity, and murderous cunning do not signal his exclusion from the world of Malta but rather his central place within it. His 'Judaism' is, again in Marx's words, 'a universal *antisocial* element of the *present time*' (p. 34).

For neither Marlowe nor Marx does this recognition signal a turning away from Jew-baiting; if anything, Jew-baiting is intensified even as the hostility it excites is directed as well against Christian society. Thus Marlowe never discredits anti-Semitism, but he does discredit early in the play a 'Christian' social concern that might otherwise have been used to counter a specifically Jewish antisocial element. When the governor of Malta seizes the wealth of the Jews on the grounds that it is 'better one want for a common good, / Then many perish for a priuate man' (I.331–2), an audience at all familiar with the New Testament will hear in these words echoes not of Christ but of Caiaphas and, a few lines further on, of Pilate.[10] There are, to be sure, moments of social solidarity – as when the Jews gather around Barabas to comfort him or when Ferneze and Katherine together mourn the death of their sons – but they are brief and ineffectual. The true emblem of the society of the play is the slave market where 'Euery ones price is written on his backe' (II.764).[11] Here in the market-place men are literally turned, in Marx's phrase, 'into *alienable*, saleable objects, in thrall to egoistic need and huckstering' (p. 39). And at this level of society, the religious and political barriers fall away: the Jew buys a Turk at the Christian slave market. Such is the triumph of civil society.

For Marlowe as for Marx, the dominant mode of perceiving the world, in a society ridden by the power of money and given over to the slave market, is *contempt*, contempt aroused in the beholders of such a society and, as important, governing the behaviour of those who bring it into being and function within it. This is Barabas' constant attitude, virtually his signature; his withering scorn lights not only on the Christian rulers of Malta ('thus slaues will learne', he sneers, when the defeated governor is forced into submission [V.2150]), but on his daughter's suitor ('the slaue looks like a hog's cheek new sing'd' [II.803]), his daughter ('An *Hebrew* borne, and would become a Christian. / *Cazzo, diabolo*' [IV.1527–8]), his slave Ithamore ('Thus euery villaine ambles after wealth / Although he ne're be richer then in hope' [III.1354–5]), the Turks ('How the slaue jeeres at him', observes the governor of Barabas greeting Calymath [V.2339]), the pimp, Pilia-Borza ('a shaggy, totter'd staring slaue' [IV.1858]), his fellow Jews ('See the simplicitie of these base slaues' [I.448]), and even, when he has blundered by making the poison too weak, himself ('What a damn'd slaue was I' [V.2025]). Barabas' frequent asides assure us that he is feeling contempt even when he is not openly expressing it, and the reiteration of the derogatory epithet 'slaue' firmly anchors this contempt in the structure of relations that governs the play. Barabas' liberality in bestowing this epithet – from the governor to the pimp – reflects the extraordinary unity of the structure, its intricate series of mirror images: Pilia-Borza's extortion racket is repeated at the 'national' level in the extortion of the Jewish community's wealth and at the international level in the Turkish extortion of the Christian tribute. It is as if the play were anticipating the historian Frederic Lane's notion of Renaissance international relations as a kind of glorified gangsterism, a vast 'protection' racket.[12]

At all levels of society in Marlowe's play and behind each version of the racket (and making it possible) is violence or the threat of violence, and so here too Barabas' murderousness is presented both as a characteristic of his accursed tribe and as the expression of a universal phenomenon. This expression, to be sure, is extravagant – he is responsible, directly or indirectly, for the deaths of Mathias, Lodowick, Abigail, Pilia-Borza, Bellamira, Ithamore, Friar Jacamo, Friar Barnadine, and innumerable poisoned nuns and massacred soldiers – but then everything about Barabas is extravagant: he is more contemptuous than anyone else, more resourceful, cynical, egotistical, and avaricious. The difference, however, in each of these cases is of degree rather than of kind; Barabas expresses in extreme, unmediated form the motives that have been partially disguised by the spiritual humbug of Christianity. Barabas cannot *in the last analysis* be assimilated to his world – Marlowe ultimately veers away from so entirely sociological a conception – but it is important to grasp the great extent to which the Jew is *brought into being* by the Christian society around him. His extraordinary energy does not alter the fact of his passivity throughout the play; his actions are always *responses* to the initiatives of others. Not only is the plot of the whole play set in motion by the governor's expropriation of Barabas' wealth, but each of Barabas' particular plots is a reaction to what he perceives as a provocation or a threat. Only his final stratagem – the betrayal of the Turks – seems an exception, since the Jew is for once in power, but even this fatal blunder is a response to his perfectly sound perception that '*Malta* hates me, and in hating me / My life's in danger' (V.2131–2).

Barabas' passivity sits strangely with his entire domination of the spirit of the play, and, once again, we may turn to Marx for an explication:

Judaism could not create a new world. It could only bring the new creations and conditions of the world within its own sphere of activity, because practical need, the spirit of which is self-interest, is always passive, cannot expand at will, but *finds* itself extended as a result of the continued development of society.

(p. 38)

Though the Jew is identified here with the spirit of egotism and selfish need, his success is credited to the triumph of Christianity which 'objectifies' and hence alienates all national, natural, moral, and theoretical relationships, dissolving 'the human world into a world of atomistic, antagonistic individuals' (p. 39). The concrete emblem of this alienation in Marlowe's play is the slave market: its ideological expression is the religious chauvinism that sees Jews as inherently sinful, Turks as barbarous misbelievers.

The Jew of Malta ends on a powerfully ironic note of this 'spiritual egoism' (to use Marx's phrase) when the governor celebrates the treacherous destruction of Barabas and the Turks by giving due praise 'Neither to Fate nor Fortune, but to Heauen' (V.2410). But we do not have to wait until the closing moments of the play to witness the Christian practice of alienation. It is, as I have suggested, present throughout and nowhere more powerfully than in the figure of Barabas himself. For not only are Barabas' actions called forth by Christian actions, but his identity itself is to a great extent the product of the Christian conception of a Jew's identity. This is not entirely the case: Marlowe invokes an 'indigenous' Judaism in the wicked parody of the materialism of Job and in Barabas' repeated invocation of Hebraic exclusivism ('These swine-eating Christians', etc.). Nevertheless, Barabas' sense of himself, his characteristic response to the world, and his self-presentation are very largely constructed out of the materials of the dominant, Christian culture. This is nowhere more evident than in his speech which is virtually composed of hard little aphorisms, cynical adages, worldly maxims – all the neatly packaged nastiness of his society. Where Shylock, as we have seen, is differentiated from the Christians even in his use of the common language, Barabas is inscribed at the centre of the society of the play, a society whose speech is a tissue of aphorisms. Whole speeches are little more than strings of sayings: maxims are exchanged, inverted, employed as weapons; the characters enact and even deliberately 'stage'. When Barabas, intent upon poisoning the nuns, calls for the pot of rice porridge, Ithamore carries it to him along with a ladle, explaining that since 'the prouerb saies, he that eats with the deuil had need for a long spoone, I haue brought you a ladle' (III.1360–2).[13] And when Barabas and Ithamore together strangle Friar Barnadine, to whom Abigail has revealed their crimes in confession, the Jew explains, 'Blame not vs but the prouerb, Confes & be hang'd' (IV.1655).

Proverbs in *The Jew of Malta* are a kind of currency, the compressed ideological wealth of the society. Their terseness corresponds to that concentration of material wealth that Barabas celebrates: 'Infinite riches in a little roome'. Barabas' own store of these ideological riches comprises the most cynical and self-serving portion:

> Who is honour'd now but for his wealth?
> (I.151)

> *Ego mihimet sum semper proximus.*
> (I.228)

> A reaching thought will search his deepest wits,
> And cast with cunning for the time to come.
> (I.455–6)

> ... in extremitie
> We ought to make barre of no policie.
> (I.507–8)

> ... Religion
>
> Hides many mischiefes from suspition.
> (I.519–20)

> Now will I shew my selfe to haue more of the Serpent
> Then the Doue; that is, more knaue than foole.
> (II.797–8)

> Faith is not to be held with Heretickes.
> (II.1076)

> For he that liueth in Authority,
> And neither gets him friends, nor fills his bags,
> Liues like the Asse that AEsope speaketh of,
> That labours with a load of bread and wine,
> And leaues it off to snap on Thistle tops.
> (V.2139–43)

> For so I liue, perish may all the world.
> (V.2292)

This is not the exotic language of the Jews but the product of the whole society, indeed its most familiar and ordinary face. And as the essence of proverbs is their anonymity, the effect of their recurrent use by Barabas is to render him more and more typical, to *de-individualise* him. This is, of course, the opposite of the usual process. Most dramatic characters – Shylock is the appropriate example – accumulate identity in the course of their play; Barabas loses it. He is never again as distinct and unique an individual as he is in the first moments:

> Goe tell 'em the Iew of *Malta* sent thee, man:
> Tush, who amongst 'em knowes not *Barabas?*
> (I.102–3)

Even his account of his past – killing sick people or poisoning wells – tends to make him more vague and unreal, accommodating him to an abstract, anti-Semitic fantasy of a Jew's past. The shift that critics have noted in Barabas' language, from the resonant eloquence of the opening to the terse irony of the close, is part of Marlowe's rhetorical design, it is one of the ways in which he reveals Barabas as the alienated essence of Christian society.

Even the Jew's exclusion from political power does not mark him off decisively from Christian society; rather it enacts, as Marx puts it, 'the contradiction between politics and the power of money'. The relationship between Barabas and the world of the play is almost perfectly expressed by Marx's own aphorisms:

> The Jew, who occupies a distinctive place in civil society, only manifests in a distinctive way the Judaism of civil society.
> Judaism has been preserved, not in spite of history, but by history.
> It is from its own entrails that civil society ceaselessly engenders the Jew.
>
> (p. 36)

With these aphorisms we are close to the heart of *The Jew of Malta*, as close, in any case, as Marx's 'On the Jewish Question' will take us. But precisely at this point we should, I think, feel a certain uneasiness, for where Marx would collapse the Jew into 'the Judaism of civil society', Marlowe insists upon elements of Barabas' character which do sharply and qualitatively distinguish him even from the world that has engendered him and whose spirit he expresses. For his own part, Barabas insistently excludes himself from all groups, Turks, Christians, *and* Jews:

Nay, let 'em combat, conquer, and kill all,
So they spare me, my daughter, and my wealth.
(I.191–2)

By itself this sentiment is not surprising; it is simply the expression of that ruthless egotism fostered by the whole society. But Barabas does seem set apart from everyone in the play, especially in his cold clarity of vision, his apparent freedom from all ideology. 'A counterfeit profession is better / Then vnseene hypocrisie' (I.531–2), he tells his daughter. In the long run, the play challenges this conviction, at least from the point of view of survival; the governor, who is the very embodiment of 'vnseene hypocrisie', eventually triumphs over the Jew's 'counterfeit profession'. But Marlowe uses the distinction to direct the audience's allegiance toward Barabas: to lie and to know that one is lying seems more attractive, more moral even, than to lie and believe that one is telling the truth.

The ethical basis of such a discrimination does not bear scrutiny; what matters is that the audience becomes Barabas' accomplice. And the pact is affirmed over and over again in Barabas' frequent, malevolently comic asides:

> **Lodowick**   Good *Barabas* glance not at our holy Nuns
> **Barabas**   No, but I doe it through a burning zeale,
>   *Hoping ere long to set the house a fire. (Aside)*
>   (II.849–51)

Years ago, in Naples, I watched a deft pickpocket lift a camera from a tourist's shoulder bag and replace it instantaneously with a rock of equal weight. The thief spotted me watching but did not run away – instead he winked, and I was frozen in mute complicity. In *The Jew of Malta*, the audience's conventional silence becomes the silence of the passive accomplice, winked at by his fellow criminal. Such a relationship is, of course, itself conventional. The Jew has, for the audience, something of the attractiveness of the wily, misused slave in Roman comedy who is always on the brink of disaster, always revealed to have a trick or two up his sleeve. The mythic core of this character's endless resourcefulness is comic resurrection, and, though Barabas is destined for a darker end, he is granted at least one such moment: thrown over the city walls and left for dead, he springs up full of scheming energy. At this moment, as elsewhere in the play, the audience waits expectantly for Barabas' recovery, *wills* his continued existence, and hence identifies with him.[14]

Along with this identification, the audience grants Barabas certain traditional rights by allowing him the privileged status of unmasker or satirist. Where in Marx's 'On the Jewish Question' there is an unvoiced but essential boundary between the author, who stands free of the social structure he excoriates, and the Jew, who is the quintessential product of that social structure, in Marlowe's play the boundary is blurred and the Jew linked in subtle ways with the playwright. The result is that even as the audience perceives Barabas as the alienated essence of Christian society, it identifies with Barabas as the scourge of that society.

The most striking indication of a subtle link between Marlowe and his hero, a link that distinguishes the Jew from the world around him and justifies the audience's identification with him, is Barabas' unique capacity for what one must call aesthetic experience. In his opening soliloquy this is manifested as an eloquent appreciation of his wealth:

> Bags of fiery *Opals, Saphires, Amatists,*
> *Iacints,* hard *Topas,* grasse-greene *Emeraulds,*
> Beauteous *Rubyes,* sparkling *Diamonds,*
> And seildsene costly stones...
>
> (I.60–3)

Though the passion for wealth is widely shared, no one else in the play is capable of such a response. And it becomes clear that it is not only wealth that excites Barabas' energy, eloquence, and delight; money is not finally the jealous god of the Jew of Malta. To be sure, Barabas does speak to the end of turning a profit, but wealth is gradually displaced as the *exclusive* object of his concern; his main object through the latter half of the play seems to be revenge, at any cost, upon the Christians. Then, with his attempt to destroy the Turks and restore the Christians to power, it becomes evident that even revenge is not Barabas' exclusive object. At the end he seems to be pursuing deception virtually for its own sake:

> why, is not this
> A kingly kinde of trade to purchase Townes
> By treachery, and sell 'em by deceit?

Now tell me, worldlings, vnderneath the sunne
If greater falsehood euer has bin done.
(V.2329–33)

As Barabas, hammer in hand, constructs the machinery for this climactic falsehood, it is difficult not to equate him with the playwright himself, constructing the plot, and Marlowe appears consciously to encourage this perception: 'Leaue nothing loose, all leueld to my mind', Barabas instructs his carpenters, 'Why now I see that you haue Art indeed' (V.2285–6). Deception here takes on something of the status of literary art: the tragic artist's special power is the power to deceive. Such a conception of art does not preclude its claim to strip away fraud since tragedy 'with its myths and emotions has created a deception such that its successful practitioner is nearer to reality than the unsuccessful, and the man who lets himself be deceived is wiser than he who does not.' This paradox in Plato's *Gorgias* depends upon an epistemology and ontology summed up in his proposition that 'Nothing whatever exists'. And, as I have argued elsewhere, it is precisely this dark vision, this denial of Being, that haunts all of Marlowe's plays.[15]

Barabas devises falsehoods so eagerly because he is himself a falsehood, a fiction composed of the sleaziest materials in his culture. At times he seems almost aware of himself as such: 'we are villaines both' (V.979), he announces to Ithamore after they have run through a catalogue of outrageous, blatantly fictional misdeeds. In celebrating deception, he is celebrating himself – not simply his cunning, his power to impose himself on others, his inventiveness, but his very distance from ontological fullness. Barabas is the Jewish Knight of Non-Being. From this perspective, the language shift, to which I alluded earlier, is a deliberate assault upon that immediacy, that sense of presence, evoked at the beginning in Barabas' rich poetry with its confident sense of realised identity. 'Infinite riches in a little roome' is speech dreaming its plenitude, its *possession* of being.[16] Without that opening soliloquy, so unlike anything Barabas speaks thereafter, we would have no norm by which to measure his *effacement*: he exists subsequently in the failure of the opening rhetoric to return, in the spaces between his words, in his lack of substance. He is a thing of nothing.

This is why the particular objects Barabas sets for himself and passionately pursues seem nonetheless curiously unreal: nothing can desire nothing. But if there is no substance, within or without, there remains in Barabas an intense, playful energy. Marlowe's hero is not defined finally by the particular object he pursues but by the eerie playfulness with which he pursues it. This playfulness manifests itself as cruel humour, murderous practical jokes, a penchant for the outlandish and the absurd, delight in role-playing, entire absorption in the game at hand and consequent indifference to what lies outside the boundaries of the game, radical insensitivity to human complexity and suffering, extreme but disciplined aggression, hostility to transcendence and indeed to the whole metaphysics of presence. There is some evidence for a similar dark playfulness in Marlowe's own career, with the comic (and extremely dangerous) blasphemies, the nearly overt (and equally dangerous) homosexuality, the mysterious stint as double agent, and, of course the cruel, aggressive plays themselves. The will to play flaunts society's cherished orthodoxies, embraces what the culture finds loathsome or frightening, transforms the serious into the joke and then unsettles the category of the joke by taking it seriously. For Barabas, as for Marlowe himself, this is play on the brink of an abyss, *absolute* play.

Nothing could be further from Marx. To be sure, Marx dreamed of play as the very centre of social existence but only in a society transformed by communism. The essential quality of this revolutionary playfulness is the return of man's powers to himself through the abolition of the division of labour and hence a liberated polymorphousness:

> As soon as the distribution of labour comes into being, each man has a particular, exclusive sphere of activity, which is forced upon him and from which he cannot escape. He is a hunter, a fisherman, a shepherd, or a critical critic, and must remain so if he does not want to lose his means of livelihood; while in communist society, where nobody has one exclusive sphere of activity but each can become accomplished in any branch he wishes, society regulates the general production and thus makes it possible for me to do one thing today and another tomorrow, to hunt in the morning, fish in the afternoon, rear cattle in the evening, criticise after dinner, just as I have a mind, without ever becoming hunter, fisherman, shepherd or critic.[17]

This is, in effect, a hypostatisation of the experience of writing or reading literature, a realisation at the level of the body in time and space of what we now only imaginatively experience. Marx then reserves, in the ideal scheme of things, an extraordinarily privileged place for what we think of as the play of art. But precisely by locating this experience in an historical or, if you will, posthistorical moment, Marx cuts literature off from absolute play, from its essence as Marlowe conceives it. Before its concrete, material realisation in a truly communist society, play can never be in and for itself; it is rather a way station, a form of planning, a mode at once of criticism and of prophecy. The vision of the revolutionary society for Marx, like the apocalyptic vision in Christianity, undermines the autonomy of play and renders it a critical reflection upon everything that exists or a model of non-alienated labour.[18] As the former, play may keep man from being locked in the reified structures of his particular society; as the latter, it may keep alive in a dark time certain vital human possibilities. But it is not emancipation itself which must always be pursued beyond the particular moments of liberated artistic play.[19]

It is this passionate, relentless pursuit of emancipation that governs Marx's rhetorical strategy in 'On the Jewish Question', and it is this rhetorical strategy – the quest for a world without 'Jews' or 'Judaism' – that is ultimately blocked in *The Jew of Malta* by Marlowe's absolute play, that is, by his buried identification with Barabas. This identification should not be overstated: Barabas is not, after all, an artist; the trap door and cauldron are not a playwright's plot but a Machiavelli's. The connection between the artist and the Jew is only strong enough to complicate the conclusion, based on our use of Marx's essay, that Barabas is the alienated essence of Christian society. To shore up this conclusion, we could argue that Barabas' passion for deceptive play does not exist for its own sake but rather to serve his instinct for survival: 'For so I liue, perish may all the world' (V.2292). Such an argument would serve to reintegrate Barabas into the now familiar world of rapacious egotism. Yet beneath this egotism, so zestfully proclaimed in his asides, lies a dark, indeed scarcely visible, but potent self-destructiveness.

This self-destructiveness certainly does not exist at the level of conscious motivation, and with a character who manifests as little interiority as Barabas, it is difficult and quite possibly pointless to talk of unconscious motivation. The self-destructiveness rather is built into the very structure of Barabas' identity. He is determined, he says, to survive, determined not to be 'a senseless lumpe of clay / That will with euery water wash to dirt' (I.450–1), determined not to 'vanish ore the earth in ayre, / And leaue no memory that e're I was' (I.499–500). Yet the play as a whole depicts Barabas' own commitment to just such erosion of himself as a complex, integrated subject. Having cut himself off from everyone and everything, neither persecuted outsider nor accepted insider, he is a far more shadowy figure at the close than he was at the start. That he dies in his own trap is no accident, nor is it solely the result of the governor's superior cunning: his career is in its very essence suicidal. He proclaims that he always wants to serve his own self-interest: '*Ego mihimet sum semper proximus*' (I.228); but where exactly is the self whose interests he serves? Even the Latin tag betrays an ominous self-distance: 'I am always my own neighbour', or even, 'I am always *next* to myself'. Beneath the noisy protestations of self-interest, his career is a steady, stealthy dispossession of himself, an extended vanishing, an assault upon the subject.

Once again we might attempt to reintegrate Barabas into his world and find in his self-destructiveness the supreme expression of that 'human self-estrangement' Marx saw embodied in the Jew. But we are prevented from doing so by the uncanny sense that we have an unmistakable complicity in Barbaras' whole career, that Marlowe would have us admire Barabas' progress toward the boiling cauldron as he would have us admire the Jew's cynical clarity of vision and his playfulness. Where Marx depicts human self-estrangement in order to turn his readers toward pursuit of human emancipation, Marlowe depicts something very similar in order to disabuse his audience of certain illusions. And the greatest of these illusions is that human emancipation can be achieved.

Marx can finally envisage the liberation of mankind from what he inexcusably calls 'Judaism'. Marlowe cannot. In fact, Marlowe celebrates his Jew for being clearer, smarter, and more self-destructive than the Christians whose underlying values Barabas travesties and transcends. Self-destructiveness in the play, as elsewhere in Marlowe's work, is a much-admired virtue, for it is the sign that the hero has divested himself of hope and committed himself instead to the anarchic, playful discharge of his energy. Nothing stands in the way of this discharge, not even survival, and certainly not that imaginary construction, that collection of social scraps and offal, that is Barabas' identity. This identity – everything that marks him as at once his society's most-hated enemy and its most characteristic product – is in the last analysis subordinate to his radical will to play, the will that is inseparable from the process that destroys him.

The Jew of Malta diverges most crucially from Marx at the point at which the latter invokes, in effect, what Ernst Bloch calls *Das Prinzip Hoffnung*, the principle of hope. In Marx there is the principle of hope without the will to play: in Marlowe, the will to play without the principle of hope.

From *Critical Inquiry*, 5 (1978), 291–307.

Notes

[Stephen Greenblatt is commonly regarded as the founder and leading figure of the methodology associated with the critical movement known as New Historicism. The practice of the reader within that discipline was related by Greenblatt himself to anthropologist Clifford Geertz's notion, in his influential *Patterns of Culture* (1973), of 'thick description', namely, the practice of reading a literary text or historical anecdote while placing it within 'a network of framing intentions and cultural meanings'. New historicists are concerned with representational aspects of the text, and of intertextual relations of text and discourse. Like Cultural Materialism (samples of which we may meet elsewhere in this volume) to which it was (not quite justifiably) related by opponents of both methodologies, New Historicism was described as neo-formalistic approach, scant in evidence, and attacking artistic unity. However, the imaginary line of continuity Greenblatt is drawing between Barabas and Marx is enlightening and arguably provides us with a 'thick reading' of Marlowe's text. Ed.]

1. All citations to Marlowe's *The Jew of Malta* (*Complete Works*, ed. C. F. Tucker Brooke [Oxford, 1910]) and Marx's 'On the Jewish Question' (*Early Writings*, trans. and ed. T. B. Bottomore [New York, 1963]) will appear in the text.

2. On Jews in Renaissance England, see Cecil Roth, *A History of the Jews in England* (Oxford, 1964): Salo W. Baron, *A Social and Religious History of the Jews*. 2nd edn, vol. 2, *Citizen or Alien Conjurer* (New York, 1967); and C. J. Sisson, 'A Colony of Jews in Shakespeare's London', *Essays and Studies*, 22 (1937), 38–51.

3. On Marx's essay, see Shlomo Avinieri, *The Social and Political Thought of Karl Marx* (Cambridge, 1968), pp. 43–6: Isaiah Berlin, *Karl Marx: His Life and Environment*, 3rd edn (London, 1963), pp. 27, 99–100; Jean-Yves Calvez, *La Pensée de Karl Marx*, 6th edn (Paris, 1956), pp. 64–78; Franz Mehring, *Karl Marx: The Story of His Life*, trans. Edward Fitzgerald (Ann Arbor, MI, 1962), pp. 68–73;

Robert C. Tucker, *Philosophy and Myth in Karl Marx* (Cambridge, 1961), pp. 111–13; and Istvan Meszaros, *Marx's Theory of Alienation* (London, 1970), pp. 28–31, 71–4.

4. Anti-Semitism, it should be emphasised, is never merely a trope to be adopted or discarded by an author as he might choose to employ zeugma or eschew personification. It is charged from the start with irrationality and bad faith and only partly rationalised as a rhetorical strategy. Marlowe depicts his Jew with the compulsive cruelty that characterises virtually all of his work, while Marx's essay obviously has elements of a sharp, even hysterical, denial of his religious background. It is particularly tempting to reduce the latter work to a dark chapter in its author's personal history. The links I am attempting to establish with Marlowe or the more direct link with Feuerbach, however, locate the essay in a far wider context. Still, the extreme violence of the latter half of Marx's work and his utter separation of himself from the people he excoriates undoubtedly owe much to his personal situation. It is interesting that the tone of the attack on the Jews rises to an almost ecstatic disgust at the moment when Marx seems to be locating the Jews most clearly as a product of bourgeois culture; it is as if Marx were eager to prove that he is in no way excusing or forgiving the Jews.

5. All citations to *The Merchant of Venice*, ed. John Russell Brown (Cambridge, MA, 1955), will appear in the text. There is a useful summary of the voluminous criticism of the play by Norman Rabkin, 'Meaning and Shakespeare', in *Shakespeare 1971*, ed. Clifford Leech and J. M. R. Margeson, Proceedings of the World Shakespeare Congress, Vancouver, 1971 (Toronto, 1972, pp. 89–106. Of particular importance are C. L. Barber's chapter on the play in *Shakespeare's Festive Comedy* (Princeton, NJ, 1959) and Barbara Lewalski's 'Biblical Allusion and Allegory in *The Merchant of Venice*', *Shakespeare Quarterly*, 13 (1962), 327–43. On usury and Shakespeare's play, see John W. Draper, 'Usury in *The Merchant of Venice*', *Modern Philology*, 33 (1935), 37–47; E. C. Pettet, '*The Merchant of Venice* and the Problem of Usury', *Essays and Studies*, 31 (1946), 19–33: and Benjamin Nelson, *The Idea of Usury: From Tribal Brotherhood to Universal Otherhood* (Princeton, NJ, 1949). On fiscalism and mercantilism, see Immanuel Wallerstein, *The Modern World-System: Capitalist Agriculture and the Origins of the European World-Economy in the Sixteenth Century* (New York, 1974), pp. 147–51.

6. See Jacob Katz, *Tradition and Crisis: Jewish Society at the End of the Middle Ages* (1st edn, 1958: New York, 1971), pp. 46–7; see also Anthony Molho, 'A Note on Jewish Moneylenders in Tuscany in the Late Trecento and Early Quattrocento', in *Renaissance Studies in Honor of Hans Baron*, ed. Anthony Molho and John A. Tedeschi (Florence, 1971), pp. 101–17.

7. See Brian Pullan, *Rich and Poor in Renaissance Venice: The Social Institutions of a Catholic State, to 1620* (Oxford, 1971).

8. Shylock seems, in part at least, to confirm this notion at III.i.46 ff.

9. Katz, *Tradition and Crisis*, pp. 47–8.

10. See G. K. Hunter, 'The Theology of Marlowe's The Jew of Malta', *Journal of the Warburg and Courtauld Institutes*, 27 (1964), 236.

11. Shylock attempts to make this a similarly central issue in the trial scene, but, as we might expect, the attempt fails (IV.i.90–100).

12. Frederic C. Lane, *Venice and History* (Baltimore, 1966).

13. For the Jew as devil, see Joshua Trachtenberg, *The Devil and the Jews: The Medieval Conception of the Jew and Its Relation to Modern Antisemitism* (New Haven, CT, 1943).

14. See my 'The False Ending in Volpone', *JEPG*, 75 (1976), 93.

15. For Gorgias, see Mario Untersteiner, *The Sophists*, trans. Kathleen Freeman (0xford, 1954), p. 113; Thomas G. Rosenmeyer, 'Gorgias, Aeschylus, and *Apate*', *American Journal of Philology*, 76 (1955), 255–60. For Marlowe's 'Gorgian' aesthetic, see my 'Marlowe and Renaissance Self-Fashioning', in *Two Renaissance Mythmakers*, ed. Alvin B. Kernan, Selected Papers from the English Institute 1975–76 (Baltimore, 1977).

16. For an illuminating discussion of this concept of presence, in Western ontotheology, see Jacques Derrida, *Of Grammatology*, trans. Gayatri Chakravorty Spivak (Baltimore, 1974), pp. 27–73.

17. Marx, *The German Ideology*, pt. 1, in *The Marx–Engels Reader*; ed. Robert C. Tucker (New York, 1972), p. 124.

18. On the problematical status of play in Marx's thought, see Francis Hearn, 'Toward a Critical Theory of Play', *Telos*, 30 (1976–77), 145–60; on art as a model of non-alienated labour, see Hans Robert Jauss, 'The Idealist Embarrassment: Observations on Marxist Aesthetics', *New Literary History*, 7 (1975), 191–208.

19. The most searching exploration in Marxist thought of these 'moments' of emancipation is by Jurgen Habermas: see esp. 'Toward a Theory of Communicative Competence', *Recent Sociology*, no. 2, ed. Hans Peter Dreitzel (New York, 1970), pp. 115–48; and *Knowledge and Human interests*, trans. Jeremy J. Shapiro (Boston, 1971). For an ambitious exploration of the opposition of play and seriousness in Renaissance culture, see Richard A. Lanham, *The Motives of Eloquence: Literary Rhetoric in the Renaissance* (New Haven, CT, 1976).

5

'So neatly plotted, and so well performed': Villain as Playwright in Marlowe's *The Jew of Malta*

SARA MUNSON DEATS and LISA S. STARKS

I

Given the topicality and virulence of the controversy concerning the theatre at the time, it is not surprising to find the dramas of the Elizabethan and Jacobean periods actively participating in this debate, self-reflexively censuring, championing, or simply exploring their own medium – its nature, its purpose, its materials, and its moral validity. Jonas Barish demonstrates the deep ambivalence that many playwrights of the period felt toward their own medium, focusing particularly on the tension between fascination and disapproval in the plays of Shakespeare and Ben Jonson.[1] Anne Righter, in her influential treatment of the play metaphor in Shakespeare, further chronicles what she sees as Shakespeare's transition throughout his writing career from conventional acceptance to mistrust to celebration of dramatic art.[2]

Among these valuable commentaries, however, the plays of Christopher Marlowe have surprisingly been neglected. This oversight is particularly significant since Marlowe's dramas were written before those of Shakespeare and Jonson and unquestionably influenced these plays in many ways. We submit that Marlowe shared with Shakespeare and Jonson a deep ambivalence toward his own medium and that his plays, like those of many of his contemporaries, self-reflexively probe, censure, and celebrate dramatic art. Moreover, Marlowe's ambivalence toward his art and his profession is most vividly embodied in the character of Barabas, the surrogate playwright and villain in Marlowe's *The Jew of Malta*. Indeed, Barabas may well be the first villain as playwright to tread the Renaissance stage, and, as such, the progenitor of an entire clan of villainous interior playwrights. Among these are Iago, Vindici, and Volpone, a trio of Machiavellian-Vice villains for whom 'the play's the thing' for which they sacrifice not only their consciences but sometimes their little kingdoms as well. Yet although the theatrical functions and motivations of Iago, Volpone, and Vindici (*The Revenger's Tragedy*) have been thoroughly explored, the dramaturgical importance of Barabas, the probable progenitor of all three, has been critically overlooked.[3] We will seek to demonstrate here the centrality of the theatrical motif to Marlowe's *The Jew of Malta* as well as the relevance of the play to the antitheatrical debate of the period. We will further attempt to show that *The Jew of Malta* not only reflects but actually participates in this antitheatrical debate, not only introducing the interior director (or adapting him from his medieval ancestor, the morality Vice), but also dramatising some of the issues that would be debated throughout the following decades, both on the page and on the stage.

In situating Marlowe's play not only in relation to the antitheatrical debates of the period but also in relation to the development of the Elizabethan/Jacobean drama, we are merging two critical methodologies – the new historicist and the rhetorical. New historicism not only asserts that cultural forms, including literature, are produced by the economic, political, and social forces of their historical periods, but also holds that these cultural forms, in turn, mould and shape the very material forces that have produced them. This approach thus dissolves the boundaries between historical and literary texts, between social and cultural forms. Conversely, the rhetorical perspective self-reflexively comments on the play as play, focusing on the nature and function of dramatic art itself. In combining these two critical methodologies in a new historical/rhetorical analysis, we seek to explore the significance of *The Jew of Malta* both as an aesthetic object and as a cultural form interacting with its social milieu.

II

Barabas is a Janus-faced figure, looking back to the medieval Vice (himself often a thespian of no mean ability) and forward to the numerous Elizabethan and Jacobean Scoundrels who become intoxicated with the artistry of their own villainy. Although Barabas is often interpreted like Volpone as the embodiment of greed, like Iago as the archetypal Machiavel, or like Vindice as the prototypic revenger, from first to last, he is also an obsessive dramaturge, scripting scenarios and manipulating his cast of victims for his own pleasure and profit. If one views the play from a 'realistic', or what Catherine Belsey terms an 'illusionist', perspective – thereby stressing that dramatic reality is always an illusion[4] – the theatrical motif clarifies Barabas's motivation, which otherwise lacks credibility. For Barabas, we submit, delight in improvisation and impersonation proves paramount, and it is his obsession with 'playing' (not the Machiavel's desire for power nor the usurer's greed) that galvanises his energy throughout much of the play and prompts his final, fatal intrigue against Calymath. Furthermore, if one views the play from an emblematic perspective, interpreting Barabas not as a three-dimensional credible human being but as a rhetorical construct of the antitheatrical debate, Barabas emerges as the surrogate playwright, the mouthpiece through which Marlowe can communicate with his audience, sharing with them the creative process and the sheer joy of playmaking, while also warning them, through Barabas's spectacular fall, of the perils of playmaking. Lastly, the potency of Barabas's plays within Marlowe's play comments on the power of dramatic art to construct reality.

Barabas's race and profession immediately establish him as the stereotypic usurer, while his posture, gesture, and dialogue – the fingering of coins as he chants a hymn to precious stones – mark him as a stage icon for the sin of covetousness.[5] However his scornful rejection of 'paltry silverlings' makes it clear that he values means as well as ends, style as well as substance, implying that his persona as usurer is only one of the many roles in which his creator will cast him. As the play progresses, the thespian Jew consciously assumes an entire repertoire of public roles, spanning the social spectrum of Malta from governor to tycoon to (potential) friar to musician, while his creator conflates dramatic conventions to produce a hybrid private villain – part Jewish usurer, part Machiavel, part revenger, part medieval Vice – who is also a surrogate playwright.

The opening scene of the play reveals Barabas as an inveterate role-player. He first acts the part of the wise Jewish patriarch, pretending prudently to advise his fellow Jews while actually withholding from them crucial information concerning the plans to confiscate their wealth. In the following scene, cast in the role of the despised Jew and Christ-killer by the sanctimonious Christians, Barabas switches the scripts and plays instead the innocent martyr, while Ferneze speaks lines that echo the infamous words of the high-priest Caiaphas to Christ:

> No Jew, we take particularly thine
> To save the ruin of a multitude
> And better one want for a common good.
> Than many perish for a private man.[6]
> (I.ii.95–8)

Here Marlowe achieves a trenchant role-reversal, momentarily casting his playwright-villain-vice in the role of Christ while manoeuvring the governor of Christian Malta temporarily into the role of the arch Christ-killer Caiaphas. After the exit of Ferneze and the Maltese knights, Barabas assumes yet another Biblical alias, that of the much suffering Job, mimicking Job's lines from the Bible while trivialising Job's great spiritual agon into a mundane loss of wealth. However, despite his consistent role-playing, the protean Barabas does not make his debut as interior playwright until he discovers that his house has been confiscated as a nunnery. Desperate to retrieve his treasure, he casts Abigail as a penitent convert and himself as the betrayed father, craftly devising a plot to regain his wealth. His stratagem is successful, and his first financial 'hit' inspires his subsequent revenge tragedy.

After he regains his treasure and dedicates himself to vengeance (II.iii.7–31), Barabas, the ostensible emblem of covetousness, ironically becomes increasingly indifferent to 'the desire for gold', the powerful force propelling the majority of the play's characters, including emperors, governors, knights, friars, and bawds. If we view Barabas as an illusionist character with psychologically credible drives, we must conclude that, as the play progresses, playing and plotting become for Barabas more and more an end in themselves rather than a means to an end. On one occasion, Barabas nonchalantly dismisses a defaulted debt with a snap of the fingers and a cursory aside:

> My factor sends me word a merchant's fled
> That owes me for a hundred tun of wine:

I weigh it thus much; I have wealth enough.
(II.iii.241–3)

He then turns his energies to the manipulation of Lodowick and
Mathias. The Jew of Malta expresses a similar disregard for money
earlier in the same scene during his bravura boasting contest with
Ithamore. Gloating over his purported atrocities, Barabas sarcasti-
cally vaunts that 'now and then, to cherish Christian thieves, / I am
content to lose some of my crowns' (II.iii.175–6). But since this
heroic-boasting contest is probably itself an improvisation – more
an audition for the role of apprentice villain than an accurate
account of actual knaveries – Barabas's testimony (like all his public
dialogue) is highly suspect. Nevertheless, this claim does anticipate
the Jew's later indifference toward wealth and may thus express his
priorities.

Conversely, if we view Barabas as an emblematic character, we
must conclude that, as the play progresses, the Jew begins more and
more to assume the role of the surrogate playwright through whom
Marlowe communicates with his audience. In his second interior
drama, Barabas scripts a play in which he must prompt the characters unknowingly to respond to his cues. Promising his daughter
Abigail to both Lodowick and Mathias, Barabas exploits their competitive desires to orchestrate his plot. He simultaneously pressures
his daughter to play a part very much 'out of character', coercing
her to encourage Lodowick's advances even though she loves
Mathias. As he directs his unsuspecting actors in their parts, he
continually confides his designs to the audience in asides, thus
informing them that he is acting – even as the actor playing Barabas
is acting, and that he is also directing the action – even as the actors
in the play are being directed. Frequently, he also boasts of his skill
as both playwright and director, using the term 'cunning' to
describe his craft:

True, and it shall be cunningly perform'd.
(II.iii.364)

I cannot choose but like thy readiness;
Yet be not rash, but do it cunningly.
(II.iii.375)

So, now will I go in to Lodowick,
And like a cunning spirit feign some lie.
(II.iii.378–9)

Since 'cunning' at this time denoted not only cleverness but also art or skill, the triple repetition of this suggestive term stresses the importance to Barabas of style as well as substance.[7] Furthermore, in putting such words in his villain's mouth, Marlowe draws attention to his own play as play, as a mimesis; for even as Barabas's scene is being performed, the scene that Marlowe has composed is also being cunningly enacted.

Marlowe, through Barabas, also comments on the process of playmaking. Barabas is a playwright at work, contemplating various possible dramatic strategies and resolutions. First, after auditioning Ithamore for the part of tool villain in a kind of 'any evil you can do, I can do better' contest, Barabas directs the slave to deliver the letter that will trigger the fatal duel. In response to Ithamore's query, ' 'Tis poison'd, is it not?' (II.iii.369), Barabas briefly considers that ploy, 'and, yet, it might be done that way' (l.370). Finally, however, Barabas rejects the predictable solution, seeking instead a more cunning tactic whereby he will manoeuvre the two rivals into destroying each other. Through this canny ruse, Barabas displays his adroit craftsmanship, even as Marlowe does himself. While watching his first revenge tragedy performed according to his directions, Barabas/Marlowe applauds himself on his craft:

> O bravely fought! and yet they thrust not home.
> Now Lodowick, no Mathias; so! [*Both fall.*)
> So now they have show'd themselves to be tall fellows.
>
> (II.iii.1–2)

Ithamore, Barabas's alter-ego and 'clack', also praises the brilliance of both Barabas's and Marlowe's production, 'Why, was there even seen such villainy, / So neatly plotted, and so well perform'd?' (III.iii.1–2). Thus through Barabas and Ithamore, Marlowe not only shares with the audience his creative plotting, but he also invites audience admiration for his skilled dramaturgy.

Through Barabas, Marlowe continues to construct one outrageous situation after another. In the episode of the convent murders, Marlowe parodies the tradition of the Italianate villain, allowing Barabas to revel in his ruse of 'time-released' poison, a ploy that he will later use as the French musician. Marlowe now expertly spins the skein of this intrigue into the unfolding pattern, allowing Barabas to manipulate the hypocritical friars through their greed, even as he had earlier manipulated the suitors through their lust. Barabas then plays each against the other to construct, as he gloats, 'such a plot for both their lives, / As never Jew nor Christian knew the like' (IV.i.117–18), a plot whereby the friars, although actually Barabas's victims, appear to have destroyed each other.

In the next episode, Barabas is confronted by two rival interior dramatists. First, Ithamore seeks to write his own script, casting himself as the mythic hero, Bellamira as the epic heroine, Philia-Borza as the Senecan Nuntius, and Barabas as the caricatured Jew. Barabas's furious response derives partially from fear of discovery (IV.iii.60–2), partially from grudging loss of gold (IV.iii.49), but equally, we suspect, from being temporarily out-plotted (and with such insulting dialogue) by his apprentice playwright. However, Bellamira, unwilling to respond to Ithamore's cues, seeks to substitute her own scenario. Finally Barabas, hamming it up as a French musician, usurps both Ithamore's and Bellamira's scripts. Through the stratagems of the poison and the sleeping potion, both traditional theatrical devices, Barabas and Marlowe not only succeed in resolving the blackmail but also provide Barabas with the escape he needs in order for the play to continue.

Undaunted by his narrow escape, Barabas seizes this opportunity to compose a new vignette in which he enacts the ally of the Turk and a traitor to Malta. Barabas's well-executed plot succeeds, and he accepts the role of governor of Malta, only to decide that as governor he must script a new scenario, incorporating Ferneze as co-star while eliminating Calymath and his cohorts from his new cast of characters.

Viewed from an illusionist perspective, Barabas's final intrigue raises serious problems concerning motivation and character consistency. In Act V, scene ii, Barabas shares with the audience in soliloquy his rationale for conspiring with his enemy Ferneze against his benefactor Calymath:

> Thus hast thou gotten, by thy policy,
> No simple place, no small authority:
> I now am Governor of Malta; true,
> But Malta hates me, and in hating me,
> My life's in danger; and what boots it thee,
> Poor Barabas, to be the Governor,
> Whenas thy life shall be at their command?
> No, Barabas, this must be looked into;
> And, since by wrong thou got'st authority,

Maintain it bravely by firm policy,
At least unprofitable lose it not.
                    (ll. 27–37)

As a number of commentators have observed, the Jew's reasoning is not only poor 'policy' but also faulty Machiavellism. For although Machiavelli prudently warned rulers not to make themselves odious to their subjects, he also cautioned against trusting an opponent whom one had offended.[8] In temporarily trusting Ferneze, whom he has certainly wronged and probably intends later to betray (V.ii.108–12), Barabas disregards Machiavelli's caveat and even his own dictum: 'Great injuries are not so soon forgot' (I.ii.207). Such naïve logic from the wily Barabas suggests rationalisation, and critics have offered alternative explanations for the Jew's alliance with his foe, ranging from 'desire for gold' (the bribe collected by the Governor), to naïve trust, to conservative longing for the status quo, to need for love.[9] We would argue, however, that Barabas's primary desideratum is not gold, revenge, stability, or love. For example, despite his vow to 'make a profit' of his policy, Barabas seems surprisingly unconcerned with the thousand pounds offered by the Governor, temporarily rejecting the ransom:

            nay, keep it still,
For if I keep not promise, trust not me.
And Governor, now partake my policy.
                    (V.v.24–6)

He then turns with relish to contemplate his newest wicked charade (just as he earlier disdained to pursue the debt owed him by the merchant, preferring instead to plot ingenious tragedies of blood). Moreover, the thesis that Barabas's primary motivation is revenge, although applicable to much of the drama, fails to explain the Jew's perverse behaviour in his moment of triumph, when he forgoes vengeance upon his deadly enemy to direct his hostility toward his patron. Revenge without play-acting seems to hold little attraction for Barabas. It is also difficult to see Barabas as naïvely trusting his erstwhile ally, whom he apparently plans to double-cross should the opportunity arise, as he tells us in an aside (V.ii.108–12). Finally, the arguments that the conservative merchant seeks a return to stability, or that the alienated Outsider yearns for acceptance and attempts to purchase this approval by saving Malta from the Turk, attractive though these readings may be, find meagre support in the play's dialogue.

Barabas's specious reasoning does reflect the attempt to offer credible, prudent motives for irrational impulses, but Barabas's exultant asides to the audience suggest that these drives are more artistic and directorial than mercenary or emotional. Addicted to histrionics for the sake of histrionics, Barabas, the virtuoso hoaxer and poseur, revels not in the trivia of ordinary commerce but in the 'kingly kind of trade' of purchasing towns by treachery and selling them by deceit (V.v.49–51), with the inventiveness of the deceit more critical than the value of the town. Or, viewed from another perspective, the artistic pleasure of the well-plotted stratagem becomes more important than the monetary reward. Saluting the handiwork of the carpenters in constructing his death machine, Barabas is also lauding his own expertise in dramatic skullduggery:

> Leave nothing loose, all levell'd to my mind,
> Why, now I see that you have art indeed.
> (V.v.4–5)[10]

Like the chronic recidivist who must kill and kill until he is finally apprehended, Barabas must plot and plot until he is finally entangled in his own scenario. It is this mechanical repetition that renders Barabas comic rather than tragic. Initially, the Jew, as master puppeteer, pulled the strings; ultimately, he becomes the marionette of his own obsession.[11]

Viewed from an illusionist perspective, therefore, Barabas's obsession with playing provides a credible motivation for his final bizarre intrigue. However, approached from an emblematic perspective, the final episode of the play can be interpreted very differently. This incident displays Marlowe's dramaturgical skill in escaping from a perplexing situation. How can he dispose of Barabas, who as villain/hero of the tragedy must be annihilated by Act V, since the Jew of Malta is obviously able to write and act his way out of any predicament? By allowing Barabas to become intoxicated by his own artistic techniques and by introducing a new, more adept playwright with a conflicting script, Marlowe again proves his own adroit craftsmanship. Thus, unlike his villain/hero and dramatic alter-ego Barabas, Marlowe maintains his aesthetic detachment and scripts a play that successfully resolves his dilemma. Consequently, when we observe Barabas constructing the set for what seems to be his interior play – acting as stagehand and stage manager as well as playwright, director, and actor – we realise that, ironically, he is building a set for Ferneze's counter-drama. And as Barabas lauds his own artistic intrigues, 'Leave nothing loose, all levell'd to my mind / Why, now I see that you have art indeed' (V.v.4–5), we realise that Marlowe, standing behind his surrogate playwright, is congratulating himself on his own well-made play.

Yet even as he boils, literally 'stewing in his own juice', Barabas brags of his exploits, of his – and of Marlowe's – skill as a drama-tist. Thus, in his death as in his life, Barabas revels in intrigue, offer-ing an emblem for both the pleasures and the dangers of playmaking.

The perils of playwrighting are reflected not only in Barabas's spectacular fall but also in the increasing loss of power and status resulting from his masquerades. This progressive limitation is revealed in Barabas's downward trajectory as he declines socially, histrionically, and tonally. Socially, he descends from the financial magnate of the first act (master of merchants, patriarch to peers, associate of aristocrats, adversary of governors) to the trickster of the latter acts (ally of slaves, opponent of promiscuous nuns, venal friars, and swindling bawds). After completing the circuit of Malta's social estates, Barabas's fortune, like the rotating wheel on which he rides, surprisingly ascends, as he tangles again with rulers before plummeting to disaster. Accompanying this social demotion (and later brief promotion) is a trivialising of the public roles that Barabas selects, or is constrained to perform. The arrogant tycoon, the wise Jewish patriarch, the righteous martyr, and the lamenting Old Testament prophet of the first act become the unctuous mar-riage broker of the second, the aggrieved father of the third, and both the lugubrious convert and the buffoonish French musician of the fourth. In the last act, consonant with the circular movement of the drama, Barabas assumes a number of somewhat more dignified roles, including an antitype of Christ, the ally of the Turk, and the governor of Malta, a prestigious part that, surprisingly, he does not feel qualified to perform. In Malta's theatre of the absurd, there-fore, Barabas plays many parts. As he rollicks through his multiple masquerades, the drama's tone modulates to an accompanying key, alternating from tragicomedy to black comedy to farce.

Ironically, Barabas's obsession with the aesthetics of intrigue leads to an increasing loss of control over his medium, as the Jew becomes less and less the presiding genius and more and more the active participant in his own skits. Although Barabas plots and scripts the manslaughter of the two rival lovers, he is not an active performer in the catastrophe of his New Comedy turned Revenge Tragedy. Similarly, he directs without physically taking part in the massacre of the nuns, although this time he does furnish a central prop – the murder weapon. However, despite Barabas's care in plotting these initial plays-within-the-play, each script erodes Barabas's control of the action by requiring an encore performance: the slaying of the lovers leads to the homicide of Abigail and the nuns, which, in turn, results in the murder of the friars. Moreover, Barabas becomes increasingly involved physically in each successive murder, progressing from *playwright-director*, watching from 'above' the catastrophe of his initial revenge tragedy, to playwright-director-*stage manager*, descending to centre stage to prepare the toxic weapon for his second murder mystery, to playwright-director-stage manager-actor, with the help of Ithamore, physically strangling one of the friars and setting the stage for the framing of the other. Ithamore's unexpected debut as rival dramatist impels Barabas into improvising a fourth interlude, in which he performs all the theatrical functions – playwright, director, stage manager, costume designer, and actor (cast as a triple murderer). Totally underrehearsed and stripped of supporting cast, Barabas gives a clumsy solo performance that almost leads to the closing of his show. Yet always a quick study, with his characteristic resilience the Jew recoups his fortune and turns the French farce of Act IV (a definite flop) into the passion play of Act V (a resounding hit).[12] Although Barabas is ostensibly in control in Act V, his incurable recidivism has progressively stripped him of both his cast and his crew; he even presumably poisons the stagehands who construct his murder machine (V.iv.10). Thus his last scene is reduced to a fatal one-man *grand guignol* production as the direction of the action passes from Barabas to his nemesis and rival interior director, Ferneze.

III

The Jew of Malta focuses centrally on power, as the major power-brokers – Calymath, Ferneze, del Bosco, and Barabas – compete for dominance, and the minor power-brokers – prostitute, pimp, and friars – vie for the wealth that will grant them limited control. However, on one level at least, as this essay has attempted to demonstrate, the drama is also centrally concerned with 'playing'. Within the world of the play, of course, the playwright is the quintessential power-broker, absolutely controlling the dramatic universe while also influencing the external world through the play's impact on the audience. In this reading, therefore, Barabas becomes a portrait not only of the flawed Machiavel, who falls because he becomes too involved in his plotting and is thus overcome by the more skilful Machiavel, but also of the flawed playwright, who fails because he loses his detachment, becomes too involved in his plotting, produces a bad play, and is ousted by the superior actor-playwright.

Barabas's fatal aesthetic obsession is foreshadowed in the play's prologue through Machevill's exemplum of Phalaris as the negligent tyrant, who becomes so preoccupied with 'letters' that he ignores the proper use of force for protection ('strong-built citadels') and thus is overthrown by envious great ones *(Prologue, 22–6)*. Striking similarities unite the Phalaris of legend with the Barabas of the drama. Both prototypes of cruelty and guile, indulging in similar types of atrocities, become so absorbed in the 'arts' (Phalaris with belles lettres, Barabas with play-acting) that they carelessly underestimate their enemies, are overthrown by 'great ones' and burn to death in their own torture machines.[13] Through these analogies, the play dramatises the perils of involvement and the necessity for detachment in both politics and playwrighting, thereby exemplifying not only Machiavelli's political dictums but Marlowe's own aesthetic practice.

In treating the issue of aesthetic detachment. *The Jew of Malta* actively participates in the theatrical debate of the period, since actors' ability to 'lose themselves' in their parts was alternately censured and lauded by detractors and supporters of the theatre. For example, Thomas Heywood, in his *An Apology for Actors*, seeking to praise the actor's ability to 'become the part', rather ineptly cites the legend of the Roman emperor and sometimes amateur actor, Julius Caesar, who became so carried away by passion in his portrayal of Hercules that he actually slew the unfortunate actor playing the role of the messenger Lychas.[14] I. G., in his *Refutation of the Apology for Actors*, adduces the very same episode to castigate the lack of control and detachment he sees as characteristic of the profession of acting, and, by implication, also of playwrighting.[15] Thus both the protheatre and antitheatre factions used the same anecdote to buttress their arguments for or against the stage.

From a metadramatic perspective, therefore, Barabas's dazzling although doomed productions and performances not only stress the simultaneous pleasure and peril of dramatic art, but also illustrate the power of the theatre, showing how drama may not only reflect but also actively construct what is perceived as reality. In so doing, the play anticipates one of the central tenets of both new historicism and cultural materialism. The reciprocal relationship between society and cultural forms is affirmed by Jonathan Dollimore who argues that literature not only represents but actually intervenes in history.[16] Mary Beth Rose further asserts:

> [D]rama not only articulates and represents cultural change, but also participates in it; seeks not only to define, but actively to generate, and in some cases to contain, cultural conflict. Far from acting as a fictional reflection of an imagined external reality that can somehow be grasped as true, the drama is constituent of that reality and inseparable from it.[17]

Stephen Greenblatt refers to the power of literature to 'produce, shape, and reorganise' culture as 'energy'.[18] Barabas, we submit, embodies this type of shaping energy, and many of the episodes in *The Jew of Malta* microcosmically illustrate the potency of the drama in generating and constructing perceived reality.

In *The Jew of Malta*, fictional life often imitates fictional art, with Barabas's various improvisations frequently not only anticipating but also often precipitating the roles and actions that he is later constrained to perform. Initially, Barabas publicly mourns his loss of wealth while secretly gloating on his hidden cache; later, he learns that his fiction has become an actuality and that he has been transformed into the victim that he had earlier played. In the following interior drama, Barabas feigns the part of the aggrieved father, casting Abigail as the penitent convert, and the friars as the eager gulls; later, he, his daughter, and the friars will play these roles in earnest. Soon after, in his hyperbolic vaunting contest with Ithamore, Barabas impersonates the 'monsterous Jew' stereotype into which he will eventually develop, actually creating himself from fragments of anti-semitic literature and legend. finally, Barabas's sham death presages his actual catastrophe, and he becomes the dead man that he had earlier pretended to be. Thus Barabas is continually constructed by the roles that he chooses or is forced to assume.

By demonstrating the power of the theatre to construct perceived reality, *The Jew of Malta* supports the assertions of both the detractors and the supporters of the stage, for both the attackers and the defenders of the theatre affirmed the ability of the drama to influence human behaviour and the way human beings perceive reality. These debaters alternately extolled and vilified the drama for its power to move audiences to emulate the vices and virtues that they saw enacted on the stage and thus through mimicry to create themselves in the images of dramatic fictions. Barabas, functioning simultaneously as playwright, actor, and audience of his own theatrics, both creates fictions and is created by them. Through this reciprocal mimesis, therefore, the play both acknowledges and interrogates the potency of its own medium.

In stressing the relationship of *The Jew of Malta* not only to the antitheatrical debate of the period but also to the later interior playwrights strutting and fretting across the Elizabethan and Jacobean stages, we are claiming for Marlowe's play some of the same generative power that we have credited to Barabas's internal dramas. Marlowe's play, by debating the Vice-Machiavel as playwright, profoundly influenced the development of the English drama, while through its probing exploration of the potential power, pleasure, and peril of the stage, it also introduced into the antitheatrical debate the ambivalence toward its own medium, that would pervade the drama of the following decades. Therefore, just as the Jew's interior plays not only participate in the formation of their protean creator Barabas but also intervene in the politics of Malta, so Marlowe's play not only participates in the formation of the contemporary drama but also intervenes in the theatrical politics of the period. Just as Barabas's many improvisations both shape and are shaped by the actions of Ferneze and the citizens of Malta, so Marlowe's play both generates and is generated by the dramatic conventions and theatrical controversies of its time, simultaneously drawing on and influencing both its literary heritage and its social milieu. Moreover, like Barabas, who delighted Ithamore with the well-crafted plots and skilled performances of his interior dramas, *The Jew of Malta*, part revenge tragedy and part satiric comedy, would provide the pattern for a number of the revenge tragedies and satiric comedies starring the villain as playwright, which throughout the following decades would captivate theatrical audiences and doubtless win the accolades, 'so neatly plotted and so well performed'.

From *Theatre Journal*, 44 (1992), 375–89.

Notes

[Deats and Starks extend the discussion into the area of anti-theatricalism, a phenomenon to which attention was called by Jonas Barish in his *The Antitheatrical Prejudice* (1981). Here Marlowe is read against the conspicuous prejudice, rampant in his days, against theatrical performance. The problematisation of theatricality, inherent in the original texts, sheds light on self-reflexive aspects of the work of Marlowe and some of his fellow playwrights in the days where drama was struggling to break the fetters of medieval orthodoxy and to consciously question and adopt new forms. Ed.]

1. Jonas Barish, *The Antitheatrical Prejudice* (Berkeley, CA, 1981), pp. 127–54. Our discussion of the theatrical debate is deeply indebted to Barish's definitive study. Many of the subsequent references to this work will be included within the text. See also Jonathan Dollimore's discussion of this controversy in 'Two Concepts of Mimesis: Renaissance Literary Theory and *The Revenger's Tragedy*', in *Drama and Mimesis*, ed. James Redmond (New York, 1980), pp. 25–50.

2. Anne Righter, *Shakespeare and the Idea of the Play* (London, 1964). Other studies investigating Shakespeare's relationship to the antitheatrical prejudice of the period include Jean E. Howard, 'Renaissance Antitheatricality and the Politics of Gender and Rank in *Much Ado About Nothing*', in *Shakespeare Reproduced: The Text in History and Ideology*, ed. Jean E. Howard and Marion F. O'Connor (London, 1987), pp. 163–87, and Jyotsna Singh, 'Renaissance Antitheatricality, Antifeminism, and Shakespeare's *Antony and Cleopatra*', *Renaissance Drama*, n.s. 20 (1989), 99–121.

3. Amid the plethora of exegesis on *The Jew of Malta*, only four critics, to our knowledge, have commented on the theatricality of Barabas, and none of the four has developed his often provocative insights into a 'metadramatic' reading of the play nor related Barabas's histrionic/directorial stance to the central critical crux of the play – the Jew's abortive alliance with Ferneze. Among the critics noting the overt theatricality of the play are Charles Masinton, *Christopher Marlowe's Tragic Vision* (Athens, OH, 1972), pp. 58–68; Don Beecher, '*The Jew of Malta* and the Ritual of the Inverted Moral Order', *Cahiers Elisabéthains*, 12 (1977), 50; Michael Goldman, 'Marlowe and the Histrionics of Ravishment', in *Two Renaissance Mythmakers:*

Christopher Marlowe and Ben Jonson, ed. Alvin Kernan (Baltimore, 1977), p. 31; Stephen Greenblatt, 'Marlowe, Marx, and Anti-Semitism', *Critical Inquiry*, 5 (1978), 303–7 [reprinted in this volume – Ed.].

4. Catherine Belsey, *The Subject of Tragedy* (London, 1985), pp. 23–6.

5. Morton Bloomfield, in *The Seven Deadly Sins* (East Lansing, MI, 1969), p. 199, cites a number of iconographic representations to illustrate the linking of covetousness with coffers, bags, and the counting of coins.

6. All quotations from *The Jew of Malta* are taken from Roma Gill's edition of *The Complete Plays* of *Christopher Marlowe* (Oxford, 1971). For a fuller discussion of the Biblical echoes in this scene, see Sara Munson Deats, 'Biblical Parody in Marlowe's *The Jew of Malta: A Reconsideration*', *Christianity and Literature*, 37 (1988), 32–6.

7. The *OED (The Shorter Oxford English Dictionary*, ed. C. T. Onions [Oxford], 3rd edn, 1933) gives the following denotations of 'cunning' as current at this time: 'intelligence; knowledge how to do a thing; ability, skill; a science or art, a craft; skilful deceit, craftiness.'

8. Barabas's violation of several important Machiavellian precepts is discussed by Irving Ribner, 'Marlowe and Machiavelli', *Comparative Literature*, 6 (1954), 352–3, and by Catharine Minshull, 'Marlowe's Sound Machevill', *Renaissance Drama*, n.s. 13 (1982), 40, 47–8.

9. Nan Carpenter ('Infinite Riches: A Note of Marlovian Unity', *Notes and Queries*, o.s. 196 [1951], 50–2) speaks for majority opinion when she defines 'the desire for gold' as the unifying theme of the play, the force initiating both the drama's central action and its subsidiary plots. Although a number of other critics focus on a Machiavellian power drive as the play's dominant motif, most of these commentators would agree that the Jew's fatal league with Ferneze results not from adherence to so much as deviation from the credo of Machiavellian 'policy'. Greenblatt ('Marlowe and Renaissance Self-Fashioning', in *Two Renaissance Mythmakers*, p. 53) gives an example of this faulty Machiavellianism, arguing that Barabas is finally undone by the 'minute shreds of restraint and community that survive in him'. For a valuable survey of this critical crux of the play, see Kenneth Friedenreich, '*The Jew Of Malta* and the Critics: A Paradigm for Marlowe Studies', *Papers in Language and Literature*, 13 (1977), 318–35.

10. N. W. Bawcutt's gloss on the word 'levelled' – 'well made, accurately and symmetrically constructed' – combines with the use of the term 'art' to support our metadramatic reading of this passage (*The Jew of Malta*, The Revel Plays [Baltimore, 1978], p. 185, n. 5.5.3).

11. Greenblatt discusses the *repetition compulsion* of all of Marlowe's heroes, 'Renaissance Self-Fashioning', p. 50).

12. For a fuller discussion of the degree to which Barabas parodies the passion, death and resurrection of Christ see Deats, 'Biblical Parody', p. 31.

13. Phalaris was a Sicilian tyrant of the 6th century BC who gained a notorious immortality by allegedly roasting his enemies in a brazen bull fitted with mechanical pipes through which the victim's agonised groans resounded like the bellowing of an animal. Legend suggests that the sadistic ruler occasionally varied his torture tactics by scalding his adversaries in cauldrons of oil, and other tales involve him in a number of treacherous stratagems, including several massacres occurring during feasts. According to tradition, the tyrant's only ameliorating feature was his interest in belle-lettres, a virtue that Machiavel censures as contributing to his downfall. Accounts differ concerning Phalaris's eventual overthrow – some attribute his fall to a popular uprising while others suggest a coup by a rival oligarchy.

14. Thomas Heywood, *Apology for Actors* (1610), E3; facsimile edition (New York and London, 1973).

15. I. G., *A Refutation of the Apology for Actors*, p. 28. Barish also discusses this incident in *The Antitheatrical Prejudice*, p. 119.

16. Jonathan Dollimore, *Political Shakespeare*, ed. Jonathan Dollimore and Alan Sinfield (Ithaca, NY, 1985), p. 10.

17. Mary Beth Rose, *The Expense of Spirit: Love and Sexuality in English Renaissance Drama* (Ithaca, NY, 1988), p. 2.

18. Stephen Greenblatt, *Shakespearean Negotiations* (Berkeley, CA, 1988), p. 6.

6

Economic and Ideological Exchange in Marlowe's *Jew of Malta*

DAVID H. THURN

The focus among new historians on sovereignty and the mechanisms of power that derive from it – censorship, punishment, surveillance, spectacle, and the enforcement of normative hierarchies in social relations – produced an influential theoretical model for explaining the mediation of royal authority in Tudor and Stuart England.[1] Expressing the notion that institutional and cultural practices in this period worked to represent, and thereby to manage or contain, subversive energies within orthodox discursive forms, the so-called 'containment' model more recently has been questioned by both new historicists and their critics. A frequent objection is that this model posits a concept of power which is more structurally unified, more stably in control, more totalising in intention and achievement than the actual operations of force and authority in the period can justify.[2]

In response, some recent work on early modern England has attempted to supplement the containment model with a model of negotiation or exchange, which makes it easier to theorise complex cultural transactions without implying that they are all ultimately controlled by the strategic intentions of the crown. Not limited to the notion of a single mode of power conceived as an instrumental, totalising exercise of political or juridical authority, the economic model can better accommodate exchanges among relatively autonomous areas within the social structure. An exchange theory can support a more historically precise account of the circulation of force and value within a culture whose practices cannot always be described in the rather grand terms of power, subversion, and containment, and subsumed under the rubric of a monolithic sovereign authority.

For new historians, the exchange model can help explain a fuller range of representational transactions in English Renaissance society by locating them within a *general* economy of culture. For their critics, the notion of exchange has a similar value, but it is part of a larger argument which asserts the primacy of the *strictly* economic sphere in explaining cultural formations: here, the exchange model serves a historical account of the preconditions of capitalism and the emergence of civil society. I am thinking in the first instance of Steven Mullaney's notion of 'cultural speculation' in 'Brothers and Others, or the Art of Alienation', and Stephen Greenblatt's theory of symbolic capital in *Shakespearean Negotiations*; and in the second, of Richard Halpern's genealogy of capital in *The Poetics of Primitive Accumulation*.[3] Halpern argues that a general economy of culture too rapidly absorbs and cancels the concept of capital (understood in a restricted economic sense), and insists that in the transaction between the economic and the cultural, it is the economic which 'plays the leading role both in "funding" a symbolic economy and in specifying what can and cannot enter its circuits of exchange'.[4] I would like to consider Marlowe's *Jew of Malta* in this context, for in revealing and enacting complex interplay within and between the commercial and ideological spheres, the play raises in an exemplary way the vexing question of how best to theorise the mutual determination of the economic and cultural spheres in early modern England. I would like to suggest, first, that Marlowe's treatment of merchant's capital (and the excesses that accompany it) in *The Jew of Malta* may be understood as symptomatic of one phase in the prehistory of capitalism; and secondly, that the context provided by economic history can help reveal the explanatory limits of the containment and exchange models in accounts of the play's ideological effects.

Because it produces apparently contradictory effects of strictly enforced ideological containment on the one hand, and of a nearly unrestricted circulation of semiotic value on the other, *The Jew of Malta* would seem to call for both models, each one representing the theoretical vanishing point of the other. The challenge is to articulate the relation between containment and exchange, to determine how and to what extent the free circulation of symbolic capital is regulated by the play's disposition of its ideological materials, drawn largely from sixteenth-century discourses of the Jew and the Machiavel.

This way of describing the play's peculiar effects may be seen to repeat a longstanding recognition that the violent forces unleashed in the drama seem very nearly to cut loose from their generic vehicle. Critics have struggled to account for a general perception that the aggressive energies of the play, while they are generated in part by the requirements of the form and the prejudicial materials of its subject, nevertheless threaten somehow to disrupt and displace them. In this view, the literary form of the revenge play and the specific ideological content Marlowe gives it become little more than a pretext for destructive free play. It is as if a force of naked aggressivity increasingly erupts through the play's verse, tearing away from the ideological content which serves as its source, producing a sense of violent, nearly entropic dispersal, of uncontrolled disintegration. Thus, Harry Levin sees underlying the play's contradictions the characteristically 'Marlovian notion of containing the uncontainable', a notion which helps to explain why 'the "extreme revenge" of Barabas runs away with the play, egregiously transcending the norms of vindictiveness'.[5] And Wilbur Sanders discovers in reading certain lines that 'the aggressive energies are not *in* the verse but erupting through it, so that one has the impression of a wounded beast lashing about in the dark, a beast for whom Barabas is no more than a vehicle'. For Sanders the plot is 'necessarily the representation of a machine that is running down' in a kind destructive free-fall, the play becoming 'a kind of anti-drama, a theatre of disintegration'.[6]

Stephen Greenblatt's early reading of the play, in 'Marlowe, Marx, and Anti-Semitism', also tries to explain the dramatic logic underlying the apparently conflicting impulses in Marlowe's *Jew*.[7] Greenblatt sees in the play both a programme of ideological containment (the Jew's identity is constructed out of the materials of the dominant, Christian culture) and a movement towards negativity, non-being, and dispossession (a certain self-destructiveness is built into the very structure of the Jew's identity, and manifests itself in a will to absolute play). The will to absolute play, that is, has a kind of de-symbolising effect upon the ideological content of the drama. It is this that gives Barabas his 'apparent freedom from all ideology'.[8]

The idea of absolute play functions, in the rhetoric of Greenblatt's argument, to shift the grounds of analysis from the ideological materials of the Jew's 'identity' to a psychological structure of identification made possible by a perception of shared 'aesthetic experience'.[9] Fascinated by Barabas, the audience increasingly 'identifies' with him, admiring his 'cold clarity of vision', his playfully destructive progress toward the deadly cauldron.[10] In this account, the figure of the Jew is gradually displaced by a figure of radical, anarchic play: ideological analysis tends to be subordinated to aesthetic celebration.

The implications should be clear: the concept of an *absolute* play risks eliding the historical restrictions implied both by a containment model deployed in a taxonomy of sovereign power and by an exchange model serving a dynamic economy of culture. History recedes before the figure of Barabas conceived as a triumph of the will to absolute play. I want to argue that the dark playfulness of Marlowe's Jew is very precisely regulated by ideological imperatives within a dramatic form which itself is bound by the terms of a specific period in economic history.

As merchant and revenger, Barabas stands at the centre of the commercial and representational economies of the *The Jew of Malta*, embodying at the outset a principle of surplus and unrestricted expenditure. The play moves, however, to limit and regulate the Jew's role in both circuits of exchange: first, on the level of plot, as his merchant's capital is made available to the state by force of legal decree; secondly, on the textual level, as Barabas's complexity is reduced to a caricature which underwrites an ideologically tendentious revenge plot. Even as it calls attention to its own arbitrary manoeuvre, the play attaches the excesses of the merchant's trade and of revenge to the Jew, subjecting his assets to literary expropriation, both exposing and drawing upon the fund of symbolic capital – here, the popular conception of the Jew – which was used to sanction and mystify the economic imperatives of the state. The literary genre of the revenge play would seem particularly suited to treat this complex transaction, for revenge is closely associated in the period with the practice of usury.[11] While Barabas is not, as Greenblatt rightly points out, defined primarily as a usurer, the rhetoric of Marlowe's play works to subsume the specific practice of usury under the sign of the stage Jew, who is distinguished above all by his selfish, if playful, aggression.[12] I would like to examine in more detail the intimate link between economic and representational circuits of exchange in *The Jew of Malta*.

The luxurious lines of the opening soliloquy offer a seductive portrait of Barabas 'in his counting house, with heaps of gold before him'. He commands the stage, an opulent overlord amidst stupifyingly concentrated wealth, sovereign in his self-sufficiency, but still capable of the niggling irritation of a businessman who must count his petty cash. Annoyed at the Samnites and men of Uz who pay for his Spanish oils and Grecian wines with 'paltry silverlings', Barabas prefers instead the Arabians who richly pay with wedges of gold, or the Moor who can 'in his house heap pearl like pebble-stones' (I.i.6–23). He emulates those 'men of judgment' who 'frame / Their means of traffic from the vulgar trade, / And as their wealth increaseth, so enclose / Infinite riches in a little room' (I.i.34–7). The enclosure of extravagant wealth frees the merchant from the liabilities and sordid demands of commercial traffic: the calculations of trade are swept away by a ravishment which knows no number. Impatient with coffers 'crammed full' with coin that must be counted, 'wearing the fingers' ends with telling it' (I.i.14–16), Barabas commands resources beyond the reach of vulgar telling.

In Barabas, Marlowe presents a figure of astonishing plenitude who not only understands the wind that drives Calymath's bashaw 'into Malta road' – 'The wind that bloweth all the world besides, / Desire of gold' (III.v.2–4) – but turns it to his profit. The first scene has Barabas ask, 'But how now stands the wind?' (I.i.38), as he consults his vanes in expectation of his Egyptian argosies. The play is positively spruce in bringing on first one merchant, then another in swift answer to the Jew's solicitous questions. As his fortune trolls in 'by land and sea', and he is 'on every side enriched' (I.i.102–3), Barabas's acquisition of wealth appears effortless: the sea is his servant and the very winds of the world's desire drive his substance to surplus. Extravagance has outstripped utility in his 'Bags of fiery opals, sapphires, amethysts' (I.i.25), and his 'Whole chests of gold, in bullion and in coin' (IV.i.65). Barabas first appears as a supremely successful merchant, in confident command of an international economy: in Alexandria, merchandise remains unsold, and he has debts owing 'In Florence, Venice, Antwerp, London, Seville, / Frankfurt, Lubeck, Moscow, and where not' (IV.i.68–73), as well as 'Great sums of money' (IV.i.74) lying in banks the world over.

We glimpse in this portrait of Barabas certain features of the prehistory of capitalism, including the dominance of merchant's capital, the expansion of markets, and the reorganisation of economic relations at more abstract regional, national, and international levels.[13] But when Ferneze seizes the assets of Barabas and the other Jews of Malta, he dramatises an important distinction between merchant's capital and capital in its later historical forms. The distinction may be understood in terms of vertical control and horizontal expansion, or restricted and unrestricted circulation. Unlike the mechanisms of capital in the late modern era, which permit it to proliferate, annex, and expand at an increasing rate, merchant's capital remains closely linked in the period to a legal and political monopoly which safeguards traditional territorial privileges. The movement of merchant's capital is more strictly limited in being subject to the hierarchical obligations imposed by sovereign power.[14] The Governor, forced to raise tribute monies for the Turks in fulfilment of such an obligation, authorises the seizure by a decree based upon theological and ethnic categories. The play may be seen as symptomatic of the structure of economic relations in the early modern era, which depended upon the Jew both because his assets provided fiscal security[15] and because his difference made him readily available as scapegoat for domestic anxieties over the excesses of trade and venture capitalism: he enabled a rather specious legal discrimination between legitimate and illegitimate business practices.

As part of an attempt to control economic abuses by law, sixteenth-century Europe relied upon a medieval distinction which states that only the merchant, in venturing his capital, worked for the common good, while the usurer operated solely out of self-interest.[16] Implicit here is a distinction between justifiable returns on a commercial venture and profits *guaranteed* in a contract of loan. It is significant, however, that ecclesiastical law also recognised a difference, which was known in England, between a 'manifest' usurer, one who has become scandalous for his public practice of usury, and whose crime is therefore highly visible, unconcealable, and the 'occult' or 'mental' usurer, whose practice of usury was hidden by the acceptable formulas of the bankers and international merchants. What distinguished a public usurer was precisely his visibility. While the occult usurer was generally treated with indulgence, the manifest usurer was held subject to rigorous penalty.[17]

Now while Marlowe depicts the Jew as a great merchant who risks his resources in crazed vessels buffeted by chance winds, Barabas also appears in a dazzling surfeit of selfish gain: the movement of the opening sequence quickly produces an impression that these are investments with guaranteed returns, and that these returns, enclosed in a little room by the figure of the greedy Jew, are defined by hostile self-interest, encoded by the law as usury. Barabas occupies a rather precarious position before the law: as a merchant he is sanctioned by the state, while his visible surplus is always subject to arbitary taxation and the penalties of restitution for usurious gain. His assets a primary source of revenue, a 'ready supply of cash and credit',[18] the Jew gave the state in this period the 'guaranteed returns' that the law, in other instances, was designed to prohibit. The law therefore cuts both ways, either proscribing or permitting the 'usurious' acquisition of funds, depending upon whether it applies to the Jew or the state.

The Jew served handily to provide the state with necessary revenue and also with the ideological assets which sanctioned its appropriation. One of the Knights of Malta explains, "Tis not our fault, but thy inherent sin', a view which enrages Barabas: 'What! Bring you scripture to confirm your wrongs? / Preach me not out of my possessions' (I.ii.11–12). The law of Malta converts the Jew's surplus into its own ideological and fiscal currency. And this is what the play does as well: it works increasingly to convert the Jew's 'surplus use-value' into the visible currency of popular tradition, his complexity into a caricature of the Jew as a usurious and scheming figure, given to ruthless cunning and murderous pranks. Because he acquires the abstract coherence of a familiar myth, the excess he personifies is easily given an ideological content. When we see Barabas acting 'like a Jew', working his devilish stratagems in mischievous glee, he becomes available to a system of signs in which the Jew is no more than a composite of scriptural and popular accusations against him: trained in Florence (the home of Machiavelli) in the arts of deception (II.iii.20–9), Barabas is introduced by 'Machevil' himself in the play's prologue as an apt student; his audience with Ferneze quickly establishes the Jew's role in the Christian reading of biblical narrative; and Barabas's famous account of how he has 'spent his time' amply illustrates the popular animus against the Jew. This speech reduces Barabas to ideological currency as it tells of how he has killed sick people, plotted treasonous betrayal, filled jails with bankrupt victims of his usury (ruined by 'extorting, cozening, forfeiting, / And tricks belonging unto brokery'), and of how he has occasionally led one to 'hang himself for grief, / Pinning upon his breast a long great scroll / How I [the Jew] with interest tormented him' (II.iii.176–200).

The play, adrift with pieces of biblical and proverbial folklore, marshals its cultural resources in rendering the Jew according to the terms of popular tradition.[19] Marlowe allows the play to provide an account very much like the 'long great scroll' which so neatly explains how Barabas 'with interest' torments his victims: Barabas becomes a kind of emblem for which the play provides the caption. Rather than becoming less integrated and more mysterious through the course of the play, as Greenblatt sees him, the figure of Barabas seems to become increasingly legible within the categories available in the early modern discourse of the Jew. As he becomes more visibly scandalous, Barabas is made to submit to the law of commerce in Malta and to the rule of an ideologically tendentious plot. The play's economy depends upon converting the Jew's surplus to the utility of an abstract model, to the terms of myth, caricature, and farce. By means of a kind of semiotic reduction, the play offers a language to account for the Jew, in effect pinning to his breast an explanatory scroll.

A similar logic governs Marlowe's handling of the revenge plot: both as merchant and revenger, the figure of Barabas is produced and limited by certain cultural 'scripts' concerning the Jew. If, as merchant, Barabas appears in command of an international economy, as revenger he quickly assumes command of the stage: his power over commercial exchange mirrors his power over dramatic exchange, a consequence of Marlowe's explicit rendering of the play's action in the terms of the marketplace. The world of *The Jew of Malta* depends upon an economy capable of reducing everything to a single financial and semiotic currency – it is the law of the slave market in Act II, by which 'every one's price is written on his back' (II.iii.3). The pursuit of money in the play is directly correlated with the pursuit of revenge in schemes which align the actions of plotting, performing, and purchasing, and aggressively turn every opportunity to profit. After watching the murderous plot against Lodowick and Mathias take shape, Ithamore notes: 'Faith, master, I think by this you purchase both their lives'. 'True,' Barabas responds, 'and it shall be cunningly performed' (II.iii.367–9). Barabas will gain revenge by promising his 'diamond' to both suitors: Abigail is herself the token of exchange in his bloody plot to purchase their lives. After the stratagem has proved successful and the bodies are carried off, Ithamore asks admiringly, 'Why, was there ever seen such villainy, / So neatly plotted and so well performed?' (III.iii.1–2). As both merchant/usurer and revenger, Barabas demands interest, guaranteed returns, and therefore deals in a surplus that violates the law: he always knows more than he can 'tell', and he uses his surplus to selfish advantage both in the Malta road and in the plot.

As a successful revenger, Barabas exercises great care in controlling appearances and exchanges of words within his plots ('Here must no speeches pass', he says in the scene he stages to set Lodowick and Mathias at each other's throats [II.iii.341]). The play stresses Barabas's capacity to manipulate signs by regulating the commerce between silence and speech, between concealment and revelation. And Barabas strives to be alone in knowing 'To what event [his] secret purpose drives', because only in this position can he ensure that his intentions do not become visible and therefore subject to the law or to the manipulation of opposing policy. Before Barabas and Ithamore tighten a noose around Bernardine's neck, the slave voices misgiving: 'I fear me he mistrusts what we intend'. Barabas yields to a moment of circumspection when he asks, 'Yet if he knew our meanings, could he 'scape?', before he recalls that they have anticipated the friar's cries and placed him in an inner chamber, well removed from the street (IV.i.133–8). By keeping his underlying meanings hidden, the Jew can prosecute his secret purpose, making *manifest* only those meanings that will serve his plots. To discover the underlying meanings, on the other hand, is to steal this signifying power. Thus when Pilia-Borza learns from Ithamore the incriminating knowledge that enables the slave to blackmail Barabas, he realises that he can now act alone: 'Let me alone to urge it now I know the meaning' (IV.iv.78). In his casually enigmatic reply, Ithamore gives us the sense, which is borne out by the plot, that hidden and manifest meanings are not easily constrained by policy, but are subject to a strange doubling and reversal: 'The meaning', as he says, 'has a meaning' (IV.iv.79). Meaning is not restricted by a single intention, but always 'has a meaning' that can be appropriated differently and set to work in other contexts, policies, or stratagems.

For this reason, Barabas is always anxious to keep his wealth and his meanings to himself and his accomplices (Abigail, and later, Ithamore), to deny others access to his hidden surplus. Thus he keeps a cache of jewels under his floor planks. When the shag-rag knave Pilia-Borza tells Ithamore that he might simply take his master's wealth, the slave replies: 'If 'twere above ground I could and would have it, but he hides and buries it up as partridges do their eggs, under the earth'. And it is 'by no means possible' to 'find it out' (IV.ii.62–6). In response to this dilemma, the band of scoundrels conspires to blackmail the Jew, writing extortion letters designed, of course, to convert words into gold. Demanding pen, ink, and a ream of paper, Ithamore declares, 'I'll write unto him, we'll have money straight' (IV.ii.73). Soon swollen with a sense of his advantage, Ithamore sets a stiff rate for his labour: 'tell him I scorn to write a line under a hundred crowns' (IV.ii.128–9). To this Pilia-Borza responds with dry irony: 'You'd make a rich poet, sir' (IV.ii.130). Literalising the ready compatibility of linguistic and financial currencies in the play, the extortion scheme hints mordantly of the literary market-place in which Marlowe practised his own trade. The poets' muses, Thomas Dekker will later remark, 'are now turned to Merchants', and the theatre 'is your Poets Royal Exchange'.[20] Like money, words can function as an abstract currency which replaces diverse things with their signs, transcribing heteroge-neous surplus within a system of common signs in order to constitute it as literary, conceptual, or ideological commodity.[21] But the more specific point here is that Marlowe's plot makes correspondence, exchanges of letters, the means both of forcing Barabas to put his wealth into circulation and of undermining his sole direction of the revenge plot.

Each time Barabas's hidden fund of wealth and secrets is betrayed, it is by way of writing: the Governor's decree; Abigail's letter to Barabas informing him of her conversion, and her subse-quent written confession to Bernardine, which is the same confes-sion that the two friars will shortly use to confront and then blackmail the Jew; and the series of extortion letters sent by the band of scoundrels in Act IV. Writing is the instrument by which Barabas loses his control over the plot: it is the means for the disbursement of surplus enclosed in a little room or buried under the earth, and of incriminating secrets of revenge. The stratagems by which Barabas implements his 'meanings' cannot finally frame his means of traffic from the vulgar trade, but are repeatedly subject to counterplot and the chances of a potentially ungovernable spirit of revenge.

So far I have tried to suggest that the play reveals the process by which the Jew's surplus – both his wealth as merchant/usurer, and his secrets as revenger – is converted, whether by legal decree or extortion letter, into common currency subject to the threat of law, but also that the play *performs* a similar process in rendering Barabas a 'manifest' Jew subject to the terms of popular tradition. The Jew, we might say, is betrayed by writing both on the thematic and textual levels of the play. But the Jew's surplus is not wholly contained within either the economic or representational spheres of exchange. For even Ferneze's ruthless confiscation of the Jew's entire estate does not leave Barabas without resources, as we learn that he has hidden away 'Ten thousand portagues, besides great pearls, / Rich costly jewels, and stones infinite' (I.ii.246–7). And from the time Barabas has his small fortune in hand, we wait only one short scene before hearing that he has 'become as wealthy as [he] was' (II.iii.11). Neither does the revenge plot function as a simple movement from surplus to forced expenditure as the Jew is increasingly made to appear the victim of his own secret and deadly purpose. The ideological enclosure or 'containment' of the Jew does not fully restrict the play's semiotic expenditure.

The various schemes of enclosure represented in and by *The Jew of Malta* carry within them the traces of a potential for wild proliferation, which may be the source of the play's savage humour.[22] Marlowe presents in Barabas a figure who submits with ludic abandon to the imperative of profit and acquisition, to a policy which demands that nothing be lost, that even the sheer accidents of plot be appropriated, enclosed, and put into an investment. The play is laughable because even as it draws us into complicity and asks us to admire such resources of cunning, it exposes the absurdity, the baselessness of investment in a plot which multiplies occasions for loss. Barabas fascinates and amuses us precisely because he appears to be blind to the possibility of loss. It is around this blind spot that the play constructs schemes which produce a sense of loss being turned to account. But Barabas also fascinates because he brings us into contact with the forces these schemes are designed to control: representing the paradoxical intersection of acquisition and loss, of surplus and expenditure, Barabas has a more complex and contradictory role than a notion of absolute play would allow.

The odd commerce between acquisition and loss in the economy of the play appears in certain specific features of its theatrical and linguistic style. For here, the same textual strategies work both to satisfy and frustrate the desire for formal resolution. For instance, the simultaneous deaths of Lodowick and Mathias inspire in Katherine and Ferneze an almost operatic exchange which rings with repeated phrases and syntactical structures,[23] concluding in the formal closure provided by two rhymed couplets (III.ii.10–37): it's as if the repetitions are the effect of an attempt to fix the fierce energy of grief in a formal aesthetic structure, in a perception of symmetry. They represent the formal equivalent of a move towards containment on the thematic level, which appears in the parents' mutual commitment to find out 'the causers' of their grief, and Ferneze's decision to inter the victims in 'one sacred monument of stone' (III.ii.27, 30). Paradoxically, however, the reciprocal grief of Ferneze and Katherine very nearly extends the chain of violence as their anguish brings them close to suicide, and while the couplets can produce effects of resolution, the rhymes can also raise the spectre of endless echo.

The smart symmetry of the exchange also marks the staging of the scene in which Barabas and his slave frame Jacomo for killing the already dead Bernardine. Virtually identical characters, the two friars, one alive, one dead, present an image as uproarious as it is compelling in its odd mirroring effect. We take dark pleasure in our knowledge that the simulated life of a dead friar will implicate the other friar in his murder and ensure his own death. The scene generates an uncanny thrill by using even a propped-up corpse as an 'agent' of violent revenge. The subterfuge provides a glimpse of a dangerous automatism that appears at times to drive the dramatic action in the play:[24] a force of repetition very nearly overtakes our sense of the role of human agency in the extravagant sequence of violence that defines the plot.

Time and again, Marlowe stages moments of apparent closure and fulfilment which are nevertheless marked by effects of uncontrollable proliferation, as when Barabas, reunited with his hidden cache, hugs his bags in a transport of joy:

> O my girl,
> My gold, my fortune, my felicity,
> Strength to my soul, death to mine enemy:
> Welcome, the first beginner of my bliss!
> O Abigail, that I had thee here too,
> Then my desires were fully satisfied;
> O girl, O gold, O beauty, O my bliss! *(Hugs his bags.)*
>   (II.i.47–54)

This is the excitement of absolute possession, a state in which the differences between girl, gold, beauty, fortune, and felicity seem to collapse in the satisfaction of complete union with the object of desire. But of course the speech also suggests a desire that requires an endless series of satisfactions.

The double gestures of the dramatic rhetoric also appear in the word play, the puns, the strategies of linguistic compression that animate many of Barabas's exchanges with his victims and that make the language of *The Jew of Malta* so distinctive among Marlowe's major plays. The scene of Barabas's negotiations with Lodowick at the slave market, for example, pivots upon the use of 'diamond' to mean both the precious stone and Abigail herself:

> Lod.   What sparkle does it give without a foil?
> Bar.   The diamond that I talk of ne'er was foiled.
>   *But when he touches it, it will be foiled. (Aside)*
>   Lord, Lodowick, it sparkles bright and fair.
> Lod.   Is it square or pointed? Pray let me know.
> Bar.   Pointed it is, good sir – *but not for you. (Aside)*
>   (II.iii.56–61)

The asides function here, as elsewhere, to highlight the dual registers set in play by the pun: the technical terms of the jeweller's trade support the additional sense of sexual defilement in 'foiled' and of 'appointed' or 'assigned' in 'pointed'. Barabas goes on to say with bitter irony that Lodowick well deserves the diamond since his father had shown so much charity in bringing the Jew 'to religious purity' (II.iii.73) by seizing his goods and converting his house into a nunnery. Lodowick's hypocritical assurance that the Jew's soul 'shall reap the fruit of it' allows Barabas to indulge in more jeering play, this time upon the sexual implications (copulation, pregnancy) of the theological language he uses to indicate his confidence in the prayers of the nuns and friars: 'And seeing they are not idle, but still doing, / 'tis likely they in time may reap some fruit – / I mean in fullness of perfection' (II.iii.84–6).

The simultaneous compression and dispersion of meanings that characterises the pun has other manifestations in the linguistic style of the play. It appears, for example, in the echoing sound of phrases like 'This is the ware wherein consists my wealth' (I.i.33); 'here lives my soul's sole hope' (II.ii.29); 'and was my father furtherer of their deaths?' (III.iii.25); and 'Cellars full of wine, and sollars full of wheat' (IV.i.63). Or in the ravishing density of alliterative and assonant sound in the counting-house soliloquy, which enacts poetically both the dazzling concentration and wild proliferation of the Jew's wealth (see esp. I.i.1–7, 19–28). These are features of what we can call the play's 'verbal usury' – a technical term important to Judaeo-Christian jurisprudence, ethics, and philosophy, where it refers to the linguistic counterpart of usury, to practices that generate an illegal or unnatural supplement to meaning.[25] Just as the Jew uses money to increase principals, so he uses puns, or forms of stylistic excess to supplement the principal meanings of words.

If, then, *The Jew of Malta* restricts its representational transactions under the aegis of ideology, it also appears to provide a glimpse of an unrestricted space of verbal productivity which precedes any discursive or ideological content. Any attempt to theorise either the internal economy of the play or the larger cultural economy in which the play participates would seem to require both a containment and an exchange model. For the simulation of ideological coherence in the play appears always on the verge of dissolution into a linguistic pleasure freed from all direction and purpose, ungoverned by instrumental control. The merchant's capital, which funds both the action of the play and the public theatre in which the play was produced, is itself marked by the conflicting imperatives of these two models: it enters the sphere of free exchange which is the source of its profits, but always remains subject to the hierarchical obligations imposed by sovereign power.

The fantasy of the Jew is precisely constituted by these conflicting economic and representational imperatives. A grotesque projection of social antagonism, Marlowe's Jew is the dramatic embodiment of a strictly chimerical entity, the positive form of a structural negativity. The play both collects interest on the Jew's ideological assets, and disburses it in an ecstasy of thrilling expenditure. But the crucial point here is that the pleasure generated by the play has a structure, the structure of an ideological fantasy of the Jew. It is a fantasy, moreover, that bears the marks of a specific historical context.[26]

In making the relationship between capital and culture part of its thematic content, *The Jew of Malta* allows us to gain some sense of both the complexity of and the restrictions upon their circuits of exchange. A historical account of the role of merchant's capital within the structure of economic relations in the period cannot alone provide the proper context for explaining the ideological effects of literary form. But it can perhaps help to articulate the limits of specific theoretical models in contemporary critical practice. A theory of exchange which seeks to accommodate cultural transactions not covered by the concept of containment allows for more complex, more historically precise critical narratives. The task is to account for a fuller range of representational exchanges in Tudor and Stuart England without relying upon a notion of absolute play, which might better describe the circulation of capital in a later time.

From *Theatre Journal*, 46 (1994), 157–70.

Notes

[Ideologically-inclined criticism (such as Michael Hattaway's essay 2 above) often relies on the 'containment' model, asserting that a single dominant power in a given period is placed in an ultimately privileged position over other voices, which it turns subversive. David Thurn, however, offers to read Marlowe's text in terms of an exchange theory. The perspective of an 'economical model', he suggests, can account with better precision for the early modern period, marked rather by shifting interests and complex historical processes than by a monolithic model of power and subversion. Ed.]

1. I would like to thank Victoria Kahn for her incisive comments on the final draft of this essay.

2. Stephen Greenblatt characterises the problem in these terms in *Shakespearean Negotiations* (Berkeley, CA, 1988), p. 2. See also Richard Helgerson, *Forms of Nationhood: The Elizabethan Writing of England* (Chicago, 1992). p. 304 n. 9, p. 341 n. 80; and Debora Kuller Shuger, *Habits of Thought in the English Renaissance: Religion, Politics, and the Dominant Order* (Berkeley, CA, 1990), pp. 1–16.

3. Steven Mullaney, 'Brothers and Others, or the Art of Alienation', in *Cannibals, Witches and Divorce: Estranging the Renaissance*, Selected papers from the English Institute, 1985 (Baltimore, 1987), pp. 67–89; Stephen Greenblatt, *Shakespearean Negotiations;* Richard Halpern, *The Poetics of Primitive Accumulation: English Renaissance Culture and the Genealogy of Capital* (Ithaca, NY, 1991).

4. Halpern, *Poetics*, p. 15.

5. Harry Levin, *The Overreacher: A Study of Christopher Marlowe* (Cambridge, MA, 1952), pp. 66, 75.

6. Wilbur Sanders, 'Barabas and the Historical Jew of Europe', in *The Dramatist and the Received Idea: Studies in the Plays of Marlowe and Shakespeare* (Cambridge, 1968), pp. 55, 54.

7. Stephen Greenblatt, 'Marlowe, Marx, and Anti-Semitism', *Critical Inquiry*, 5 (1978), 291–307 [reprinted in this volume – Ed.]. I would like to acknowledge here that my thinking about Marlowe's play owes a great deal to this generative essay.

8. Ibid., pp. 302; see also pp. 300 and 306.

9. Ibid., pp. 302–3. Greenblatt does acknowledge the risks of psychologising Barabas: 'This self-destructiveness certainly does not exist at the level of conscious motivation, and with a character who manifests as little interiority as Barabas, it is difficult and quite possibly pointless to talk of unconscious motivation. The self-destructiveness rather is built into the very structure of Barabas's identity' (p. 306). It is perhaps, then, all the more surprising that Greenblatt should continue to attribute a will to Barabas that functions independently of the ideological materials that constitute him. For more on the effect of psychological categories on Greenblatt's analysis of the Marlovian hero, see my 'Sights of Power in *Tamburlaine*', *English Literary Renaissance*, 19 (1989), 4 n. 4.

10. Greenblatt, 'Marlowe, Marx', pp. 302–3.

11. Since St Ambrose in the 5th century, preachers argued that the practice of usury was an act of hostility, an offence against charity towards one's neighbour. See John Bossy, *Christianity in the West: 1400–1700* (Oxford, 1985), p. 77. But anti-usury tracts in early modern England explicitly link the usurer with vices such as revenge: Henry Smith, in *The Examination of Usury* (1591), even claims that without usury, there would be no 'revenging'. See Thomas Moisan, '"Which is the merchant here? and which the Jew?": subversion and recuperation in *The Merchant of Venice*' in *Shakespeare Reproduced: The Text in History and Ideology*, ed. Jean E. Howard and Marion F. O'Connor (New York, 1987), pp. 193, 203 n. 8.

12. See, for instance, the rhetoric of Barabas's famous autobiographical speech, which culminates in a description of his usury and related economic abuses (II.iii.176–202).

13. Halpern, *Poetics*, pp. 69–70.

14. Halpern points out that because it relies upon a political and legal monopoly to protect its means of profit, merchant's capital is still feudal in form, structurally incompatible with a capitalist mode of production (*Poetics of Primitive Accumulation*, pp. 66, 70).

15. See Immanuel Wallerstein, *Capitalist Agriculture and the Origins of the European World-Economy in the Sixteenth Century*, vol. I of *The Modern World-System* (San Diego, CA, 1974), pp. 147–51.

16. On this distinction, see Benjamin N. Nelson, 'The Usurer and the Merchant Prince: Italian Businessmen and the Ecclesiastical Law of

Restitution, 1100–1550', *Journal of Economic History*, Supplement: *The Tasks of Economic History*, 7 (1947), 104–22; also Walter Cohen, 'The Merchant of Venice and the Possibilities of Historical Criticism', *ELH*, 49 (1982), 768. For a general study of usury, see Benjamin Nelson, *The Idea of Usury: From Tribal Brotherhood to Universal Otherhood*, 2nd edn (Chicago, 1969); on usury in Renaissance England, see Norman Jones, *God and the Moneylenders: Usury and Law in Early Modern England* (Oxford, 1989).

17. In England, anxiety over the relentless pursuit of money led to a ban on usury under Edward VI, a ban later voided by Elizabeth in the Act Against Usury of 1571, which, while it was designed to repress usury, had the effect, in practice, of setting a 10% maximum interest rate. But the main point here is that legal attempts to control usury are always marked by a confusion over the difference between the usurer and the merchant, a confusion especially evident in English Parliamentary debates during the later years of Elizabeth's reign. See Francis Bacon's essay on usury, in which he wrestles with the problem by considering separately the 'commodities' and 'discommodities' of usury in order then to propose a way of regulating the practice. Francis Bacon, *The Essays*, ed. John Pitcher (Harmondsworth, 1985), pp. 183–6.

18. Wallerstein, *Capitalist Agriculture*, p. 149.

19. On the theological background, see G. K. Hunter, 'The Theology of Marlowe's *The Jew of Malta*', *Journal of the Warburg and Courtauld Institutes*, 27 (1964), 211–40; on proverbs, see Greenblatt, 'Marlowe, Marx', pp. 300–1. On popular fictions of otherness in the play, see Simon Shepherd, *Marlowe and the Politics of Elizabethan Theatre* (Brighton, 1986), pp. 169–77; see also Emily C. Bartels, 'Malta, the Jew, and the fictions of Difference: Colonialist Discourse in Marlowe's *The Jew of Malta*', *English Literary Renaissance*, 20 (1990), 3–16.

20. Dekker, 'The Guls Horn-Booke', 1609; cited in Moisan, '"Which is the merchant here"', p. 191.

21. For a fuller theoretical account of the comparison, see Jacques Derrida, *Of Grammatology*, trans. Gayatri Spivak (Baltimore, 1974), p. 300; for literary readings that explore the 'new forms of metaphorisation ... that accompanied new forms of economic symbolisation and production', see Marc Shell, *Money, Language, and Thought: Literary and Philosophical Economies from the Medieval to the Modern Era* (Berkeley, CA, 1982).

22. For a general account of the imagery of enclosure in Marlowe, see Marjorie Garber, '"Infinite Riches in a Little Room": Closure and Enclosure in Marlowe', in *Two Renaissance Mythmakers: Christopher Marlowe and Ben Jonson*, ed. Alvin Kernan (Baltimore, 1977), pp. 3–21.

23. 'What sight is this? My Lodowick slain' / 'Who is this? My son
    Mathias slain!'; 'venged thy death' / 'revenge his death'; 'O leave to
    grieve me, I am grieved enough' / 'that grieves me most of all'; 'Lend
    me that weapon that did kill my son' / 'that weapon was my son's'
    (III.ii.10–26).

24. There is even a sardonic suggestion at points in the play that language
    itself, that words in common circulation, must assume the responsibil-
    ity for murderous action: 'Blame not us but the proverb, "confess and
    be hanged"', commands Barabas just as he and Ithamore strangle
    Bernardine (IV.i.146).

25. See Shell, *Money*, pp. 49–50.

26. See Slavoj Žižek's important analysis of the ideological function of the
    Jew in *The Sublime Object of Ideology* (London, 1989): '[F]ar from
    being the positive cause of social antagonism, the "Jew" is just the em-
    bodiment of a certain blockage – of the impossibility which prevents
    the society from achieving its full identity as a closed, homogeneous to-
    tality. Far from being the positive cause of social negativity, *the "Jew"
    is a point at which social negativity as such assumes positive existence*'
    (p. 127). For Žižek, 'the last support of the ideological effect (of the
    way an ideological network of signifiers "holds" us) is [a] non-sensical,
    pre-ideological kernel of enjoyment. ... [B]eyond the field of meaning
    but at the same time internal to it – an ideology implies, manipulates,
    produces a pre-ideological enjoyment structured in fantasy' (pp.
    124–5). For our purposes this formulation has the advantage of being
    able to account for both the strange pleasure associated with
    Marlowe's Jew and the historical determinations of the ideological
    fantasy that structures it.

7

Dr Faustus: Subversion Through Transgression

JONATHAN DOLLIMORE

One problem in particular has exercised critics of *Dr Faustus*: its
structure, inherited from the morality form, apparently negates
what the play experientially affirms – the heroic aspiration of
'Renaissance man'. Behind this discrepancy some have discerned a
tension between, on the one hand, the moral and theological imperatives of a severe Christian orthodoxy and, on the other, an
affirmation of Faustus as 'the epitome of Renaissance aspiration ...
all the divine discontent, the unwearied and unsatisfied striving
after knowledge that marked the age in which Marlowe wrote'.[1]
   Critical opinion has tended to see the tension resolved one way
or another – that is, to read the play as ultimately vindicating
either Faustus or the morality structure. But such resolution is
what *Dr Faustus* as interrogative text[2] resists. It seems always to
represent paradox – religious and tragic – as insecurely and
provocatively ambiguous or, worse, as openly contradictory. Not
surprisingly Max Bluestone, after surveying some eighty recent
studies of *Dr Faustus*, as well as the play itself, remains uncon-
vinced of their more or less equally divided attempts to find in it an
orthodox or heterodox principle of resolution. On the contrary:
'conflict and contradiction inhere everywhere in the world of this
play'.[3] If this is correct then we might see it as an integral aspect of
what *Dr Faustus* is best understood as: not an affirmation of
Divine Law, or conversely of Renaissance Man, but an exploration
of subversion through transgression.

Limit and transgression

Raymond Williams has observed how, in Victorian literature, individuals encounter limits of crucially different kinds. In *Felix Holt* there is the discovery of limits which, in the terms of the novel, are enabling: they vindicate a conservative identification of what it is to be human. In complete contrast *Jude the Obscure* shows its protagonist destroyed in the process – and ultimately because – of encountering limits. This is offered not as punishment for hubris but as 'profoundly subversive of the limiting structure'.[4] *Dr Faustus*, I want to argue, falls into this second category: a discovery of limits which ostensibly forecloses subversive questioning in fact provokes it.[5]

What Erasmus had said many years before against Luther indicates the parameters of *Dr Faustus*' limiting structure:

> Suppose for a moment that it were true in a certain sense, as Augustine says somewhere, that 'God works in us good and evil, and rewards his own good works in us, and punishes his evil works in us' ... Who will be able to bring himself to love God with all his heart when He created hell seething with eternal torments in order to punish His own misdeeds in His victims as though He took delight in human torments?[6]

But Faustus is not *identified* independently of this limiting structure and any attempt to interpret the play as Renaissance man breaking out of medieval chains always founders on this point: Faustus is constituted by the very limiting structure which he transgresses and his transgression is both despite and because of that fact.

Faustus is situated at the centre of a violently divided universe. To the extent that conflict and contradiction are represented as actually of its essence, it appears to be Manichean; thus Faustus asks 'where is the place that men call hell?', and Mephostophilis replies 'Within the bowels of these elements', adding:

> when all the world dissolves
> And every creature shall be purify'd.
> All places shall be hell that is not heaven.
> (v.117, 120, 125–7)

If Greg is correct, and 'purified' means 'no longer mixed, but of one essence, either wholly good or wholly evil',[7] then the division suggested is indeed Manichean.[8] But more important than the question of precise origins is the fact that not only heaven and hell but God and Lucifer, the Good Angel and the Bad Angel, are polar opposites whose axes pass through and constitute human consciousness. Somewhat similarly, for Mephostophilis hell is not a place but a state of consciousness:

> Hell hath no limits, nor is circumscribed
> In one self place, but where we are is hell,
> And where hell is, there must we ever be.
> (v. 122–4)

From Faustus' point of view – one never free-ranging but always coterminous with his position – God and Lucifer seem equally responsible in his final destruction, two supreme agents of power deeply antagonistic to each other[9] yet temporarily co-operating in his demise. Faustus is indeed their subject, the site of their power struggle. For his part God is possessed of tyrannical power – 'heavy wrath' (i.71 and xix.153), while at the beginning of scene xix Lucifer, Beelzebub and Mephostophilis enter syndicate-like 'To view the *subjects* of our monarchy', earlier Faustus had asked why Lucifer wanted his soul; it will, replies Mephostophilis, 'Enlarge his kingdom' (v.40). In Faustus' final soliloquy both God and Lucifer are spatially located as the opposites which, *between them*, destroy him:

> O, I'll leap up to my God! Who pulls me down?

>   see where God
> Stretcheth out his arm and bends his ireful brows

> My God, my God! Look not so fierce on me!

> Ugly hell, gape not! Come not, Lucifer.
> (II.145, 150–1, 187, 189)

Before this the representatives of God and Lucifer have bombarded Faustus with conflicting accounts of his identity, position and destiny. Again, the question of whether in principle Faustus can repent, what is the point of no return, is less important than the fact that he is located on the axes of contradictions which cripple and finally destroy him.

By contrast, when, in Marlowe's earlier play, Tamburlaine speaks of the 'four elements / Warring within our breasts for regiment' he is speaking of a dynamic conflict conducive to the will to power – one which 'Doth teach us all to have aspiring minds' (1.II.vii.18–20) – not the stultifying contradiction which constitutes Faustus and his universe. On this point alone *Tamburlaine* presents a fascinating contrast with *Dr Faustus*. With his indomitable will to power and warrior prowess, Tamburlaine really does approximate to the self-determining hero bent on transcendent autonomy – a kind of fantasy on Pico's theme of aspiring man. But like all fantasies this one excites as much by what it excludes as what it exaggerates. Indeed exclusion may be the basis not just of Tamburlaine as fantasy projection but *Tamburlaine* as transgressive text: it liberates from its Christian and ethical framework the humanist conception of man as essentially free, dynamic and aspiring; more contentiously, this conception of man is not only liberated from a Christian framework but re-established in open defiance of it. But however interpreted, the objective of Tamburlaine's aspiration is very different from Pico's; the secular power in which Tamburlaine revels is part of what Pico wants to transcend in the name of a more ultimate and legitimate power. Tamburlaine defies origin, Pico aspires to it:

> A certain sacred striving should seize the soul so that, not content with the indifferent and middling, we may pant after the highest and so (for we can if we want to) force our way up to it with all our might. Let us despise the terrestrial, be unafraid of the heavenly, and then, neglecting the things of the world, fly towards that court beyond the world nearest to God the Most High.[10]

With *Dr Faustus* almost the reverse is true: transgression is born not of a liberating sense of freedom to deny or retrieve origin, nor from an excess of life breaking repressive bounds. It is rather a transgression rooted in an *impasse* of despair.

Even before he abjures God, Faustus expresses a sense of being isolated and trapped; an insecurity verging on despair pre-exists a damnation which, by a perverse act of free will, he 'chooses'. Arrogant he certainly is, but it is wrong to see Faustus at the outset as secure in the knowledge that existing forms of knowledge are inadequate. Rather, his search for a more complete knowledge is itself a search for security. For Faustus, 'born, of parents base of stock', and now both socially and geographically displaced (Prologue, II.11, 13–19), no teleological integration of identity, self-consciousness and purpose obtains. In the opening scene he attempts to convince himself of the worth of several professions – divinity, medicine, law, and then divinity again – only to reject each in turn; in this he is almost schizoid:

> Having commenc'd, be a divine in show,
> Yet level at the end of every art,
> And live and die in Aristotle's works.
> Sweet Analytics, 'tis thou hast ravish'd me!
>
> When all is done, divinity is best.
>
> Philosophy is odious and obscure,
> Both law and physic are for petty wits,
> Divinity is basest of the three,
> Unpleasant, harsh, contemptible, and vile.
> (i.3–6, 37, 105–8)

As he shakes free of spurious orthodoxy and the role of the conventional scholar, Faustus' insecurity intensifies. A determination to be 'resolved' of all ambiguities, to be 'resolute' and show fortitude (i.32; iii.14; v.6; vi.32, 64) is only a recurring struggle to escape agonised irresolution.

This initial desperation and insecurity, just as much as a subsequent fear of impending damnation, suggests why his search for knowledge so easily lapses into hedonistic recklessness and fatuous, self-forgetful 'delight' (i.52; v.82; vi.170; viii.59–60). Wagner cannot comprehend this psychology of despair:

> I think my master means to die shortly:
> He has made his will and given me his wealth
>
> I wonder what he means. If death were nigh,
> He would not banquet and carouse and swill
> Amongst the students.
> (xviii.1–2, 5–7)

Faustus knew from the outset what he would eventually incur. He willingly 'surrenders up ... his soul' for twenty-four years of 'voluptuousness' in the knowledge that 'eternal death' will be the result (iii.90–4). At the end of the first scene he exits declaring 'This night I'll conjure though I die therefor'. Later he reflects: 'long ere this I should have done the deed [i.e. suicide]/ Had not sweet pleasure conquer'd deep despair' (vi.24–5). This is a despairing hedonism rooted in the fatalism of his opening soliloquy: 'If we say that we have no sin, we deceive ourselves, and there's no truth in us. Why, then, belike we must sin, and so consequently die' (i.41–4). Half-serious, half-facetious, Faustus registers a sense of human-kind as miscreated.

Tamburlaine's will to power leads to liberation through transgression. Faustus' pact with the devil, because an act of transgression without hope of liberation, is at once rebellious, masochistic and despairing. The protestant God – 'an arbitrary and wilful, omnipotent and universal tyrant'[11] – demanded of each subject that s/he submit personally and without mediation. The modes of power formerly incorporated in mediating institutions and practices now devolve on Him and, to some extent and unintentionally, on His subject: abject before God, the subject takes on a new importance in virtue of just this direct relation.[12] Further, although God is remote and inscrutable he is also intimately conceived: 'The principal worship of God hath two parts. One is to yield subjection to him, the other to draw near to him and to cleave unto him'.[13] Such perhaps are the conditions for masochistic transgression: intimacy becomes the means of a defiance of power, the new found importance of the subject the impetus of that defiance, the abjectness of the subject its self-sacrificial nature. (We may even see here the origins of subcultural transgression: the identity conferred upon the deviant by the dominant culture enables resistance as well as oppression.)

Foucault has written: 'limit and transgression depend on each other for whatever density of being they possess: a limit could not exist if it were absolutely uncrossable and, reciprocally, transgression would be pointless if it merely crossed a limit composed of illusions and shadows.'[14] It is a phenomenon of which the anti-essentialist writers of the Renaissance were aware: 'Superiority and inferiority, maistry and subjection, are joyntly tied unto a naturall kinde of envy and contestation: they must perpetually enter-spoile one another'.[15]

In the morality plays sin tended to involve blindness to the rightness of God's law, while repentance and redemption involved a renewed apprehension of it. In *Dr Faustus* however sin is not the error of fallen judgement but a conscious and deliberate transgression of limit. It is a limit which, among other things, renders God remote and inscrutable yet subjects the individual to constant surveillance and correction, which holds the individual subject terrifyingly responsible for the fallen human condition while disallowing him or her any subjective power of redemption. Out of such conditions is born a mode of transgression identifiably protestant in origin: despairing yet defiant, masochistic yet wilful.

Faustus is abject yet his is an abjectness which is strangely inseparable from arrogance, which reproaches the authority which
demands it, which is not so much subdued as incited by that same
authority:

> **Faustus**   I gave ... my soul for my cunning.
> **All**   *God* forbid!
> **Faustus:**   God forbade it indeed; but Faustus hath done it.
>
> (xix. 61–4)

Mephostophilis well understands transgressive desire; it is why he
does not deceive Faustus about the reality of hell. It suggests too why
he conceives of hell in the way he does; although his sense of it as a
state of being and consciousness can be seen as a powerful recuperation of hell at a time when its material existence as a *place* of future
punishment was being questioned, it is also an arrogant appropriation
of hell, an incorporating of it into the consciousness of the subject.

A ritual pact advances a desire which cancels fear long enough to
pass the point of no return:

> Lo, Mephostophilis, for love of thee
> Faustus hath cut his arm, and with his proper blood
> Assures his soul to be great Lucifer's,
> Chief lord and regent of perpetual night.
> View here this blood that trickles from mine arm,
> And let it be propitious for my wish.
>
> (v.54–8)

But his blood congeals, preventing him from signing the pact.
Mephostophilis exits to fetch 'fire to dissolve it'. It is a simple yet
brilliant moment of dramatic suspense, one which invites us to
dwell on the full extent of the violation about to be enacted.
Faustus finally signs but only after the most daring blasphemy of
all: 'Now will I make an end immediately/ ... *Consummatum est*:
this bill is ended' (v.72–4). In transgressing utterly and desperately
God's law, he appropriates Christianity's supreme image of
masochistic sacrifice:[16] Christ dying on the cross – and his dying
words (cf. John xix. 30). Faustus is not liberating himself, he is
ending himself: 'it is finished'. Stephen Greenblatt is surely right to
find in Marlowe's work 'a subversive identification with the alien',
one which 'flaunts society's cherished orthodoxies, embraces what
the culture finds loathsome or frightening'.[17] But what is also worth
remarking about this particular moment is the way that a subver-

sive identification with the alien is achieved and heightened through travesty of one such cherished orthodoxy.

Power and the unitary soul

For Augustine the conflict which man experiences is not (as the Manichean heresy insisted) between two contrary souls or two contrary substances – rather, one soul fluctuates between contrary wills. On some occasions *Dr Faustus* clearly assumes the Augustinian conception of the soul; on others – those expressive of or consonant with the Manichean implications of universal conflict – it presents Faustus as divided and, indeed, constituted by that division. The distinction which Augustine makes between the will as opposed to the soul as the site of conflict and division may now seem to be semantic merely; in fact it was and remains of the utmost importance. For one thing, as *Dr Faustus* makes clear, the unitary soul – unitary in the sense of being essentially indivisible and eternal – is the absolute precondition for the exercise of divine power:

> O, no end is limited to damned souls.
> Why wert thou not a creature wanting soul?
> O, why is this immortal that thou hast?
> Ah, Pythagoras' *metempsychosis*, were that true,
> This soul should fly from me and I be chang'd
> Unto some brutish beast: all beasts are happy,
> For when they die
> Their souls are soon dissolv'd in elements;
> But mine must live still to be plagu'd in hell.
> (xix.171–9)

Further, the unitary soul – unitary now in the sense of being essentially incorruptible – figures even in those manifestations of Christianity which depict the human condition in the most pessimistic of terms and human freedom as thereby intensely problematic. In a passage quoted below, the English Calvinist William Perkins indicates why, even for a theology as severe as his, this had to be so: if sin were a corruption of man's 'substance' then not only could he not be immortal (and thereby subjected to the eternal torment which Faustus incurs), but Christ could not have taken on his nature.[18]

Once sin or evil is allowed to penetrate to the core of God's subject (as opposed to being, say, an inextricable part of that subject's fallen *condition*) the most fundamental contradiction in Christian theology is reactivated: evil is of the essence of God's creation. This is of course only a more extreme instance of another familiar problem: how is evil possible in a world created by an omnipotent God? To put the blame on Adam only begs the further question: Why did God make Adam potentially evil? (Compare Nashe's impudent gloss: 'Adam never fell till God made fools'.[19])

Calvin, however, comes close to allowing what Perkins and Augustine felt it necessary to deny: evil and conflict do penetrate to the core of God's subject. For Calvin the soul is an essence, immortal and created by God. But to suggest that it partakes of *God's* essence is a 'monstrous' blasphemy: 'if the soul of man is a portion transmitted from the essence of God, the divine nature must not only be liable to passion and change, but also to ignorance, evil desires, infirmity, and all kinds of Vice'.[20] Given the implication that these imperfections actually constitute the soul, it is not surprising that 'everyone feels that the soul itself is a receptacle for all kinds of pollution'. Elsewhere we are told that the soul, 'teeming with ... seeds of vice ... is altogether devoid of good'.[21] Here is yet another stress point in protestantism and one which plays like *Dr Faustus* (and *Mustapha*) exploit: if human beings perpetuate disorder it is because they have been created disordered.

The final chorus of the play tells us that Dr Faustus involved himself with 'unlawful things' and thereby practised 'more than heavenly power permits' (II.6,8). It is a transgression which has revealed the limiting structure of Faustus' universe for what it is, namely, 'heavenly *power*'. Faustus has to be destroyed since in a very real sense the credibility of that heavenly power depends upon it. And yet the punitive intervention which validates divine power also compromises it: far from justice, law and authority being what legitimates power, it appears, by the end of the play, to be the other way around: power establishes the limits of all those things.

It might be objected that the distinction between justice and power is a modern one and, in Elizabethan England, even if entertained, would be easily absorbed in one or another of the paradoxes which constituted the Christian faith. And yet: if there is one thing that can be said with certainty about this period it is that God in the form of 'mere arbitrary will omnipotent' could not 'keep men in awe'. We can infer as much from many texts, one of which was

Lawne's *Abridgement* of Calvin's *Institutes*, translated in 1587 –
around the time of the writing of *Dr Faustus*. The book presents
and tries to answer in dialogue form, objections to Calvin's theology. On the question of predestination the Objector contends that
'to adjudge to destruction whom he will, is more agreeable to the
lust of a tyrant, than to the lawful sentence of a judge'. The 'Reply'
to this is as arbitrary and tyrannical as the God which the Objector
envisages as unsatisfactory: 'it is a point of bold wickedness even so
much as to inquire the causes of God's will'.[22] It is an exchange
which addresses directly the question of whether a tyrannical God
is or is not grounds for discontent. Even more important perhaps is
its unintentional foregrounding of the fact that, as embodiment of
naked power alone, God could so easily be collapsed into those
tyrants who, we are repeatedly told by writers in this period, exploited Him as ideological mystification of their own power. Not
surprisingly, the concept of 'heavenly power' interrogated in *Dr
Faustus* was soon to lose credibility, and it did so in part precisely
because of such interrogation.

Dr Faustus is important for subsequent tragedy for these reasons
and at least one other: in transgressing and demystifying the limiting
structure of his world without there ever existing the possibility of his
escaping it, Faustus can be seen as an important precursor of the mal-
contented protagonist of Jacobean tragedy. Only for the latter, the
limiting structure comes to be primarily a socio-political one.

Lastly, if it is correct that censorship resulted in *Dr Faustus* being
one of the last plays of its kind – it being forbidden thereafter to in-
terrogate religious issues so directly – we might expect the transgressive impulse in the later plays to take on different forms. This is
in fact exactly what we do find; and one such form involves a strategy already referred to – the inscribing of a subversive discourse
within an orthodox one, a vindication of the letter of an orthodoxy
while subverting its spirit.

From Jonathan Dollimore, *Radical Tragedy: Religion, Ideology and
Power in the Drama of Shakespeare and his Contemporaries* (New
York and London, 1989), pp. 109–19.

Notes

[Jonathan Dollimore's project in his influential *Radical Tragedy* (1984) is
to challenge essentialist humanism and demonstrate how early modern

English tragedy marks a process of subversion and transgression, whereby man is decentred from the place he occupied in the view of Christian orthodoxy. Some of the Elizabethan and Jacobean playwrights, Dollimore argues, consciously decentred both religion and humankind in order to stress the role of culture, and especially politics. Influenced by positions taken by writers such as Foucault, Brecht and Raymond Williams, his approach is informed by what has been termed as Cultural Materialism. Ed.]

1. Christopher Marlowe, *Dr Faustus*, ed. Roma Gill (London, 1965), p. xix [All quotations are from *Dr Faustus*, ed. John Jump (London, 1962). Ed.]

2. This concept, originating in a classification of Benveniste's, is developed by Catherine Belsey in *Critical Practice* (London, 1980), ch. 4.

3. Max Bluestone, '*Libido Speculandi*: Doctrine and Dramaturgy in Contemporary Interpretations of Marlowe's *Dr Faustus*', in N. Rabkin (ed.), *Reinterpretations of Elizabethan Drama* (New York, 1969), p. 55.

4. Raymond Williams, 'Forms of English Fiction in 1848', in *1848: The Sociology of Literature*, ed. F. Barker (Colchester, 1977), p. 287.

5. Still important for this perspective is Nicholas Brooke's 1952 article, 'The Moral Tragedy of Doctor Faustus', *Cambridge Journal*, 5 (1952), 662–87.

6. Stevie Davies (ed.), *Renaissance Views of Man* (Manchester, 1978), p. 92.

7. Christopher Marlowe, *Dr. Faustus 1604–16, Parallel Texts*, ed. W. W. Greg (Oxford, 1950), p. 330.

8. The Manichean implications of protestantism are apparent from this assertion of Luther's: 'Christians know there are two kingdoms in the world, which are bitterly opposed to each other. 'In one of them Satan reigns ... He holds captive to his will all who are not snatched away from him by the Spirit of Christ ... In the other Kingdom, Christ reigns, and his kingdom ceaselessly resists and makes war on the kingdom of Satan' (E. Gordon Rupp (ed.), *Luther and Erasmus: Free Will and Salvation* [London, 1969], pp. 327–8; see also Peter Lake, *Moderate Puritans and the Elizabethan Church* [Cambridge, 1982], pp. 144–5). J. P. Brockbank, in a discussion of the Manichean background of *Dr Faustus*, notes similarities between Faustus and the Manichean Bishop of the same name mentioned by Augustine in the *Confessions* – himself an ardent of the Manichean faith for nine years; on Manicheanism generally, see also John Hick, *Evil and the God of Love* (Glasgow, 1968), ch. 3.

9. Cf. Michael Walzer: 'The imagery of warfare was constant in Calvin's writing'; specifically of course, warfare between God and Satan (*The*

Revolution of the Saints: A Study in the Origins of Radical Politics [London, 1966], p. 65).

10. Pico della Mirandola, *Oration On the Dignity of Man*, in Stevie Davies (ed.), *Renaissance Views of Man*, pp. 69–70.

11. Walzer, *Revolution of the Saints*, p. 151.

12. Cf. C. Burges, *The First Sermon* (1641): 'A man once married to the Lord by covenant may without arrogancy say: this righteousness is my righteousness … this loving kindness, these mercies, this faithfulness, which I see in thee … is mine, for my comfort … direction, salvation, and what not' (quoted from Conrad Russell, *Crisis of Parliaments* [London, 1971], p. 204).

13. William Perkins, *An* Instruction *Touching Religion; or Divine Worship*, in *Works*, ed. I. Breward (Abingdon, 1970), p. 313.

14. Michel Foucault, *Language, Counter-Memory, Practice* (Ithaca and London, 1977), p. 34.

15. Michel de Montaigne, *Essays*, trans. John Florio, 3 vols (London, 1965), III. 153.

16. Margaret Walters reminds us how Christian iconography came to glorify masochism, especially in its treatment of crucifixion. Adoration is transferred from aggressor to victim, the latter suffering in order to propitiate a vengeful, patriarchal God (*The Nude Male: A New Perspective* [New York and London, 1978], p. 10; see also pp. 72–5). Faustus' transgression becomes subversive in being submissive yet the reverse of propitiatory.

17. Stephen Greenblatt, *Renaissance Self-Fashioning* (Chicago, 1980), pp. 203, 220.

18. [The passage referred to is from Perkins' *A Golden Chain*: 'Sin is not a corruption of man's substance, but only of faculties. Otherwise neither could men's souls be immortal, nor Christ take upon him man's nature (*Works*, p. 192). Ed.]

19. Thomas Nashe, *The Unfortunate Traveller and Other Works*, ed. J. B. Steane (Harmondsworth, 1972), p. 269.

20. John Calvin, *Institutes*, trans. Henry Beveridge, 2 vols (London, 1949), I. xv. 5.

21. Ibid., I. xv; ii, iii.

22. William Lawne, *An Abridgement of the Institution of Christian Religion*, trans. Christopher Fetherstone (Edinburgh, 1587), p. 222; quoted in Alan Sinfield, *Literature in Protestant England 1560–1660* (London, 1982), p. 171.

8

Doctor Faustus and Knowledge in Conflict

CATHERINE BELSEY

Discursive knowledge

The subject of liberal humanism is required to know. Its knowledge is won, possessed, an entitlement, a definition. Knowledge is the ground of the democratic right of electoral choice, and its analogue in the marketplace, consumer choice. It is not innate, but is planted in the subject by 'experience' as well as by education, the press, advertising and all the other sources of information indispensable to the free west. But the growth of knowledge in the individual depends on the condition of the subject itself – its sanity and maturity (lunatics and children are not entitled to vote), and its intelligence (there is no point in educating a person beyond his or her capacity). Some subjects are thus more knowing than others and this entitles them to audibility, authority and a relatively high price for their labour-power. Knowledge is knowledge of things and people – science, technology, psychology, worldly wisdom. It thus differentiates the subject from the objects of its knowledge, defines the subject as that which knows in contradistinction to that which is known. But knowledge is also the abstraction and introjection of the essence of the object. The subject thus contains the world it knows, the world of its knowledge. When it achieves self-knowledge, knowledge in its highest form, the subject becomes its own object and thus expands to touch the horizon of its understanding.

And then, still climbing after knowledge infinite, it pushes back that horizon too, exceeding all known limits. The subject of liberal humanism literally knows no bounds.

It was not always so. In the Middle Ages knowledge was ultimately knowledge not of the world and the self but of God, by means of theology, the queen of the sciences, culminating discipline of the trivium and the quadrivium. To know God was not to master an object of knowledge, but to apprehend a meaning which was also truth. God, the *Logos*, at once divinity, concept and word, was pure meaning and pure being, the transcendental signified and referent, and fully to know God was not to differentiate oneself from the objects of knowledge but, on the contrary, to become absorbed in total presence, to be transformed and ultimately dissolved. Knowledge was also practice, uniting meaning and being in submission to the discourse and the discipline of salvation. It was thus absorption into the institution of the church and the body of the faithful. Knowledge was release into dispossession.

Absolute presence, eliminating difference, is precisely the dissolution of the subject. The nearest approach to such a condition in this life is in the cloud of unknowing, where the soul moves beyond preliminary earthly understanding, beyond the instruction of the church, and in knowing only that it knows nothing, knows all that can be known of God.[1]

The cloud of unknowing is a special prerogative, a way of perfection, of ecstasy which is neither available nor necessary outside the life of contemplation. But the knowledge which is a necessary prelude to unknowing is a condition of salvation. This knowledge is inscribed in a discourse which does not pretend to transparency since it is itself the location of truth. The effectivity of the (Latin) liturgy lies not beyond it in a process which it *expresses*, but in the participation of the faithful in its performance, in the process which it enacts and re-enacts. When in *Mankind* Mercy invites the audience to live in accordance with the implications of the Atonement, he does so in an aureate manner which invests his words with weight and authority. Clarity, more or less synonymous with transparency, is highly prized only later, when language becomes a *medium* through which, as through glass, thought is made visible.

If virtue foregrounds the signifying process in this way, it is also at the level of signification that the Vices work to efface the knowledge which leads to salvation. The characteristic eloquence of vice in the morality plays is a strongly accentual, incantatory nonsense, which celebrates the process of enunciation Itself. This engaging nonsense which scrambles the discourse of salvation reverberates through the moralities. The effect of the Reformation was to trans-   ⊄ form the discourse of redemption from a liturgical to a scriptural one, but not immediately to challenge the notion of knowledge as inscription. The guarantee of virtue was the Word of God. Correspondingly, the Vices continue the practice of obscuring the signified. Nearly a hundred years after *Mankind* when Haphazard, the Vice of *Apius and Virginia*, has driven Conscience out of Judge Apius, he confirms his victory by dissipating in nonsense the meaning of the event:

> For Conscience was carelesse, and sayling by seas
> Was drowned in a basket and had a disease.
> Sore mooved for pitye when he would graunt none
> For beyng hard harted was turned to a stone.
> And sayling by Sandwitche he sunke for his sin.
> Then care not for Conscience the worth of a pin.
>
> (ll. 438–43)

As Robert Weimann points out, Vice-nonsense sometimes indicates an alternative set of meanings, points to another knowledge which is in conflict with Christian teaching. In this sense it is not only impertinent, subverting the authority of virtue, and not merely impertinent in its irrelevance, but a grotesque inversion of the otherworldly knowledge which leads to salvation. Thus in *Mankind* Mercy concludes his address to the audience with an invocation of John the Baptist's prophecy that the corn will be saved but the chaff will be burnt (Matt. 3:12; Luke 3:17). Mischief counters this by announcing that he has been taken on as a cornthresher and invoking an alternative authority who reveals that 'Corn servit bredibus, chaffe horsibus, straw fyrybusque'. Which is to say, he explains, that corn is used to make bread, chaff to feed horses, and straw to provide fire in winter (ll. 54–9) – Mischief here not only celebrates the play of signification but in doing so confronts the symbolism of Christian knowledge with the literal, secular, physical knowledge which has to do with survival in an agricultural community.[2] Vice in this instance is not simply nonsense, though it is that: it is also a parody of sense which offers at the same time a competing and contradictory sense.

The project of the Vices from the beginning is to replace the discourse of salvation with the wisdom of this world which is foolishness with God (I Cor. 3:19). In *The Castle of Perseverance* Covetousness wins Mankind not in the outright battle against the virtues but by persuading him that in his old age he will need the comforts money can bring. In *Wisdom* Lucifer works by appropriating patristic discussions of scripture. The adoption of pseudonyms, an almost invariable practice of the Vices in the sixteenth-century moralities, is an elaboration of this identification of the process of temptation as the construction of a rival discourse which legitimates sin and leads to hell. The contest between these rival discourses is nowhere more evident than in the parapraxes which are a recurrent feature of Vice-comedy. The Vice proffers his victim a glimpse of what is at stake, then hastily withdraws it, insisting that he really said something quite different. Two antithetical knowledges are set side by side before the audience, with the effect of drawing attention to the implications of the opposition between divine and worldly wisdom.

The play of meaning in the world after Babel permits evil to challenge the knowledge which is guaranteed by God and ensures salvation. The gap opened by the Fall, the space between signifier and signified, signifier and referent, the place of difference, is also the place of death. Emptied of God, the discourses of evil circulate endlessly about an eternal absence. The wisdom of this world, *self-*centred, is finally centred on an eternal absence, the dissipation of the self imaged in the torments of hell. The knowledge of salvation, centred on God, implies the ultimate dissolution of the self in undifferentiated presence. Discursive knowledge does not recognise the knowing subject of liberal humanism, differentiated from the objects of its knowledge, the unified self which is the origin and proprietor of what it knows.

Empirical knowledge

But there was meanwhile an alternative tradition which can be traced back to Plato by way of St Paul. The creator, author of the book of nature, is intelligible in and through his creation. The natural world is thus a signifying system offering access to the transcendental signified, the divine authorial intention. In this form the tradition of empirical knowledge is not in conflict with discursive knowledge since in each case the project is the same: to read God in his inscriptions, the world or the church. In the Middle Ages empirical knowledge was subordinate to discursive knowledge and was constantly policed by the church wherever it threatened to lay claim to an alternative institution or institutional powers. But the ideological and institutional uncertainties which immediately followed the breakdown of control by the Catholic church offered a space in which empirical knowledge, not apparently in conflict with either Catholic or Protestant orthodoxy, was developed and modified to the point where experience was finally to supplant discourse as the source of truth.

In the course of this development and modification certain areas of conflict with the earlier orthodoxy gradually emerged and proved to be decisive for the history of the subject. First, the book of nature requires a reader as well as a writer. Empirical knowledge thus inaugurates a difference between the knowing subject and the objects of its knowledge, and this difference becomes definitive for the subject. The subject is now defined as that which knows, in contradistinction to that which is known. Secondly, language ceases to be the location of knowledge and becomes its instrument. Discourse is thus no longer constitutive but expressive. It is experience, lodged in the subject itself, which is now the source of knowledge and thus constitutive of being. The subject consequently takes the place of God and becomes the author and guarantee of its own (subjective) truth. And thirdly, the question, 'what can it *do?*', always implicitly addressed to discursive knowledge and confidently answered by the promise of salvation, is also addressed to empirical knowledge, but, then and now, more evasively met. The resolution in the late seventeenth century of these three areas of conflict was the triumph of liberal humanism – and the subsequent interrogation of the resolution then adopted has consistently been identified as a threat to its hegemony.

In response to the implicit question, 'what can it do?', a humanist text naturally claims that there is a connection between knowledge and virtue. But the nature of the connection is slightly elusive. A similar uncertainty about whether the value of knowledge is primarily moral or material can be traced through a group of allegorical plays which seem to have been designed for school performance at intervals during nearly fifty years of the sixteenth century. In *The Marriage Between Wit and Wisdom* (1579) a substantial part of the action concerns the comic activities of Idleness, who picks Wit's pocket, steals a porridge pot, appears disguised as a quack doctor, a ratcatcher and then a priest, is outwitted by Snatch and Catch who are clever criminals, and is finally repudiated when Wit marries

Wisdom. These exploits display the shifts that must be made in order to survive without education. Like *Nice Wanton* (c. 1550), *The Disobedient Child* (1560s) and Gascoigne's *The Glass of Government* (1575), the text sets out to demonstrate that idleness in youth leads to enforced idleness and so to crime in adult life. Conversely, the market value of knowledge guarantees those who possess it a good, steady job.

Knowledges in conflict

The education Idleness neglects remains primarily discursive. Latin grammar, rhetoric and logic constituted the school curriculum, and in the universities divinity retained its pre-eminence as the culminating discipline of the quadrivium. Knowledge is thus the place in this period of a major contest for meaning. Either empirical or discursive, dissolving the self on the one hand or installing the subject on the other, its motivation may be eschatological, moral or material. These meanings converge and conflict in a number of plays of the period in specific but distinct ways, with implications in each case for the identity of the subject.

Knowledges in conflict produce the tragedy of Doctor Faustus who, from inside the framework of a predominantly discursive knowledge, repudiates its promise of salvation and seeks the worldly fruits of empirical knowledge. Within a framework which allots sovereignty to heaven or hell, Faustus, in quest of wealth and dominion, sets out to become more than man – and ends longing to be less.

The implied question which runs through Faustus's opening soliloquy is, 'what can knowledge do?' One by one he rejects the traditional disciplines on the grounds that the power inscribed in them is not absolute, not transcendental:

> Is to dispute well logickes chiefest end?
> Affoords this art no greater miracle?
> Then read no more ...
> Couldst thou make men to live eternally,
> Or being dead, raise them to life againe,
> Then this profession were to be esteem'd.
> 　　*(Doctor Faustus*, ll. 36–8, 52–4)[3]

Only God can legitimately transcend nature, and the miracle promised by the discourse of salvation is precisely eternal life. But when Faustus finally reaches divinity, he dismisses it in a false syllogism which rejects exactly that promise:

> The reward of sin is death ...
> If we say that we have no sinne we deceive our selves, and
> there is no truth in us. Why then belike
> We must sinne, and so consequently die.
> I, we must die an everlasting death.
> What doctrine call you this?
>
> (ll. 67–74)

In invoking each of these premises, Faustus omits the second half of the quotation, which in each case tempers the divine justice with Christian mercy and promises redemption (Rom. 6:23: I John I:8–9). He concludes that orthodox knowledges can do nothing worth doing, and turns to magic as a source of riches and power:

> Oh, what a world of profite and delight,
> Of power, of honour, and omnipotence,
> Is promised to the studious artizan?
> All things that move betweene the quiet poles
> Shall be at my command: emperors and kings
> Are but obey'd in their severall provinces:
> Nor can they raise the winde, or rend the cloudes:
> But his dominion that exceeds in this,
> Stretcheth as farre as doth the mind of man.
>
> (ll. 80–8)

The syllogism, which for Faustus is decisive, is the primary instrument of deduction in scholastic logic, and within the framework of discursive knowledge logic itself is an authoritative source of truth. Both Bacon and Locke would later resist the attribution of such importance to the syllogism, on the grounds that it demonstrates no truth which is not already implied in the premises. The empiricist separation of meaning from truth renders the syllogism merely instrumental. While modern logic is seen as a formal system for testing the validity of an argument on the basis of the relations between the propositions, where the criteria for judging the truth of the propositions lie outside the sphere of logic itself, scholastic logic holds dialectics to be a ground of knowledge. In a problematic which defines language as opaque and identifies (true) meaning with truth, the syllogism is not transparent but is the location of truth. Where God is the transcendental meaning-as-truth, falsehood is synonymous with evil, and consequently finds its signified, which is also its referent, in hell.

Faustus rejects the discourse of salvation anchored in heaven and replaces it with the hellish signifying nonsense of magic:

> These metaphisicks of magitians,
> And negromantick bookes are heavenly.
> Lines, circles, signes, letters, and characters,
> These are those that Faustus most desires.
> (*Doctor Faustus*, ll. 76–9)

Later we see him performing the ceremonies and Latin invocations which constitute a travesty of the signifying practices of Christian knowledge. But the discourse of salvation constantly returns to haunt him, not only in the words of the Good Angel and the Old Man, but in the very moment when, in a parody of the Atonement, Faustus seals his difference from God in writing and in blood. His blood congeals and the words 'Homo fuge' are momentarily inscribed on his body. The devils distract him with 'crownes and rich apparell', the emblems of wealth and power (l. 471 SD).

In the problematic of discursive knowledge understanding is a preparation for the dissolution of the self. It is empirical knowledge which promises dominion. In empiricism as Locke would define it a century later, the subject of humanism takes, in effect, the place of God. Faustus seeks to be a knowing subject. He has mastered the objects of knowledge to a certain point, yet he is still 'but Faustus, and a man' (l. 51). His project is a greater one: 'Here tire my braines to get a deity' (l. 90). When he seeks empirical knowledge, however, Faustus is rapidly brought up against its limits. The discourse of evil cannot tell him anything he does not already know: 'These slender questions Wagner can decide: / Hath Mephostophilis no greater skill?' (ll. 600–1). The signifying practices of hell forbid him to know who made the world (ll. 618–23). In the sphere of satanic knowledge the book of nature does not point to eternal power and Godhead. And human dominion is in practice no more than a series of conjuring tricks.

The anguish Faustus constantly rehearses, and dissipates in vain delights, is a recognition of the limits which confine the subject who usurps the place of God. The play is poised between two problematics, a discursive knowledge which does not lead to power, and an empirical knowledge which is not yet certain of its own project or its authority. Faustus, aspiring to more than discursive knowledge permits, cannot become an autonomous knowing subject, because as yet the only fully articulated, coherent alternative to Christian knowledge is the discourse of hell which is service to Lucifer. At the critical moment when his blood congeals it is this autonomy that is in question:

> What might the staying of my bloud portend?
> Is it unwilling I should write this byll?
> Why streames it not, that I may write afresh?
> Faustus gives to thee his soule: ah there it staid.
> Why shouldst thou not? is not thy soule thine owne?
>
> (ll. 453–7)

From the moment of his signature, as the rest of the play makes clear, his soul, previously heaven's, belongs to hell. Lucifer is now his sovereign lord, and though a return to the service of God remains a perpetual possibility until the point of death, there is as yet no place of full ownership, no place of true and legitimate dominion for the knowing subject. At last, in terror, Faustus, who sought a deity, longs to be a beast without a soul (l. 1964), or to be dissolved, though not with Christ (ll. 1970, 1977–8). He is finally torn to pieces by the devils, dispersed in hell.

From Catherine Belsey, *The Subject of Tragedy: Identity and Difference in Renaissance Drama* (London and New York, 1985), pp. 55–75.

Notes

[Catherine Belsey's seminal work, *The Subject of Tragedy* (1985) explores the development of subjectivity in early modern drama. Her argument, informed by concepts of subject and knowledge such as Foucault's and other poststructural thinkers, powerfully suggests the distinction between the unified 'I' cherished by traditional, liberal-humanist criticism – namely, autonomous and self-determining – and the more complex subjectivity betrayed by early modern authors through the perspectives of poststructuralist scrutiny, capable of discerning in the given texts a radically different sense of identity. Ed.]

1. Phyllis Hodgson (ed.), *The Cloud of Unknowing and Related Treatises* (Salzburg, 1982), p. 70.

2. Robert Weimann, *Shakespeare and the Popular Tradition in the Theater* (Baltimore, 1978), pp. 119–20.

3. [All quotations from Christopher Marlowe, *The Complete Works*, ed. Fredson Bowers (Cambridge, 1973), vol. 2. Ed.]

9

Reading Faustus's God

ALAN SINFIELD

The Tragical History of Doctor Faustus has afforded a marvellous interpretive challenge to Christian humanists who feel they should discover Marlowe to be endorsing a nice, decent kind of god.[1] However, my argument should suggest another plausible Christian reading. Elizabethan orthodoxy would make Faustus's damnation more challenging than most modern readers might expect, by denying that Faustus had a choice anyway: it would regard Faustus, not as damned because he makes a pact with the devil, but as making a pact with the devil because he is already damned. 'Before the foundations of the world were laid', it says in the seventeenth of the Thirty-nine Articles, 'he hath constantly decreed by his counsel secret to us, to deliver from curse and damnation those whom he hath chosen.' And Faustus, an Elizabethan might infer from his blasphemous, dissolute, and finally desperate behaviour, exemplifies the fate of the reprobate. The article continues: 'So, for curious and carnal persons, lacking the Spirit of Christ, to have continually before their eyes the sentence of God's predestination is a most dangerous downfall, whereby the devil doth thrust them either into desperation, or into wretchlessness of most unclean living, no less perilous than desperation.' In Kyd's *The First Part of Hieronimo* (c. 1585), the villainous Lazarotto declares himself just such a person:

> Dare I? Ha! ha!
> I have no hope of everlasting height;
> My soul's a Moor, you know, salvation's white.
> What dare I not enact, then? Tush, he dies.[2]

172

That Faustus might be in such a condition is supported by Mephostophilis's claim:

> 'Twas I that, when thou were't i' the way to heaven,
> Damm'd up thy passage; when thou took'st the book
> To view the scriptures, then I turn'd the leaves
> And led thine eye.
>
> (V.ii.86–9)

If Faustus was guided by Mephostophilis, the decision was God's. For protestant thought could not tolerate devils wandering round the world at whim: God does not just allow their activities, he contracts out tasks to them. They are 'God's hang-men', King James wrote, 'to execute such turns as he employs them in'.[3] However, Calvin says, it is only the reprobate who are ultimately subject to them – God 'does not allow Satan to have dominion over the souls of believers, but only gives over to his sway the impious and unbelieving, whom he deigns not to number among his flock'.[4] So Mephostophilis's intervention would be part of Faustus's punishment within the divine predetermination.

The issue is focused in Faustus's first speech when he juxtaposes two texts: 'The reward of sin is death', and 'If we say that we have no sin we deceive ourselves, and there is no truth in us'. It appears that it has been arranged who shall sin and die; Faustus concludes:

> Why then, belike we must sin, and so consequently die.
> Ay, we must die an everlasting death.
> What doctrine call you this? *Che sera, sera.*
> What will be, shall be.
>
> (I.i.40–6)

Christians who wish usually manage to evade this discouraging thought. Douglas Cole says Faustus's texts are 'glaring half-truths, for each of the propositions he cites from the Bible is drawn from contexts and passages which unite the helplessness of the sinner with the redeeming grace of God'; Cole's implication is that Faustus is so eager to damn himself that he disregards God's generous offers.[5] To be sure, 'the wages of sin is death' continues: 'but the gift of God is eternal life'; and the second quotation, about everyone sinning and dying, continues: 'If we confess our sins, he is faithful and just to forgive us our sins, and to cleanse us from all unrighteousness.' But Calvin uses the first text – all of it – to emphasise that salvation is entirely God's decision: the desert of all is death but some receive eternal life through 'the gift of God' *(Institutes* 3.14.21). And Tyndale in his *Exposition of the First Epistle of St John* (1531) uses the second text to demonstrate that we have no say in the success of our confession: 'our nature cannot but sin, if occasions be given, except that God of his especial grace keep us back: which pronity to sin is damnable sin in the law of God.'[6] So God may indeed forgive us our sins if we repent, but some at least will be damned for sins to which they have, in their nature, a 'pronity'. Faustus's summary, 'What will be, shall be', may be irreverent, but it is in the mainstream of Reformation thought. If he draws not comfort but blasphemy from his reading, that will perhaps be for the reason given by Tyndale in a rubric in the Prologue to the first edition of his *Exposition of ... John:* 'If God lighten not our hearts, we read the scripture in vain.'[7]

If Faustus is damned from before the start (to pursue the hypothesis), what then of his efforts to repent? For modern readers and audiences who do not already know the story, there is a question: will he change or not? For Elizabethan orthodoxy the answer was the same again: repentance is not something for the individual to achieve, but a divine gift. 'It is not in our powers to repent when we will. It is the Lord that giveth the gift, when, where, and to whom it pleaseth him', Phillip Stubbes declares.[8] So if Faustus does not have it, there is nothing he can do. Yet there are the injunctions of the Good Angel, which appear to represent, like the personifications in a morality play, a choice open to Faustus:

> **Good Angel**   Faustus, repent; yet God will pity thee.
> **Bad Angel**   Thou art a spirit [sc. devil]; God cannot pity thee.
> **Faustus**   Who buzzeth in mine ears I am a spirit?
>   Be I a devil, yet God may pity me;
>   Yea, God will pity me if I repent.
> **Bad Angel**   Ay, but Faustus never shall repent.
>   *Exeunt Angels.*
> **Faustus**   My heart's so harden'd I cannot repent.
>   (II.ii.12–18)

If Faustus's heart is hardened and he cannot repent, who has hardened it? This was a key question in the theology of election and reprobation. In Exodus (chapters 7–14) it is stated repeatedly that God hardens Pharoah's heart against the Israelites, so that he refuses to let them go despite divine smiting of the Egyptians with diverse plagues. This was taken as a paradigm of the way God treats the reprobate. Paul alludes to it when he confronts the question in the Epistle to the Romans: 'Therefore hath he mercy on whom he will have mercy, and whom he will he hardeneth' (Rom. 9:18). Luther stressed this text, and Erasmus was obliged to admit that it appears to leave nothing to human choice.[9] For Calvin it was plain: 'When God is said to visit in mercy or harden whom he will, men are reminded that they are not to seek for any cause beyond his will' *(Institutes* 3.22.11). Hence Donne's lines: 'grace, if thou repent, thou canst not lack; / But who shall give thee that grace to begin?' (Holy Sonnet 4). And that is why Faustus can speak repentant words and it makes no difference. He actually calls upon Jesus: 'Ah, Christ my saviour, my saviour, / Help to save distressed Faustus' soul.' But the response is the entrance of Lucifer, Belzebub, and Mephostophilis: 'Christ cannot save thy soul, for he is just', says Lucifer (II.ii.83–5). Is this a devilish manipulation or a theological commonplace? It may be both – as Banquo says, instruments of darkness may tell us truths; it is the argument offered by Lawne's apologist for the *institutes*.

Why then the appeals of the Good Angel? 'What purpose, then, is served by exhortations?' Calvin asks himself. It is this: 'As the wicked, with obstinate heart, despise them, they will be a testimony against them when they stand at the judgment-seat of God; nay, they even now strike and lash their consciences' *(Institutes* 2.5.5). On this argument, the role of the Good Angel is to tell Faustus what he ought to do but cannot, so that he will be unable to claim ignorance when God taxes him with his wickedness. This may well seem perverse to the modern reader, but is quite characteristic of the strategies by which the orthodox deity was said to manoeuvre himself into the right and humankind into the wrong. Perkins declares:

> Now the commandment of believing and applying the Gospel, is by God given to all within the Church; but not in the same manner to all. It is given to the Elect, that by believing they might indeed be saved; God enabling them to do that which he commands. To the rest, whom God in justice will refuse, the same commandment is given not for the same cause, but to another end, that they might see how they could not believe, and by this means be bereft of all excuse in the day of judgment.[10]

Such doctrine was preached from almost every pulpit.

Faustus is amenable at every point, I think, to a determined orthodox reading. Yet the play might do more to promote anxiety about such doctrine than to reinforce it. For although I have felt it necessary to argue for the Reformation reading, *Faustus* is in my view *entirely ambiguous* – altogether open to the more usual, modern, free-will reading. The theological implications of *Faustus* are radically and provocatively indeterminate.

A good deal might depend on which version is being used, for many of the exchanges added in the B text seem to sharpen the theological polarity. They include the lines where Lucifer, Belzebub, and Mephostophilis gloat over Faustus (V.ii.1–19), and the speeches where Mephostophilis says he led Faustus's eye when he read the Bible and where the Good and Bad Angels vaunt over Faustus (V.ii.80–125). These additions enhance the impression that the Reformation god is at work; William Empson argues that they were demanded by the censor, who wanted it clear that Faustus must suffer and be damned for his conjuring. Empson calls them 'the sadistic additions', finding their 'petty, spiteful, cosy and intensely self-righteous hatred' untypical of Marlowe.[11] Given the intermittent nature of the evidence, Empson's theory must be regarded as a stimulating indication of the awkward status of orthodoxy in the play, rather than as right or wrong. In any event, what Empson does not quite take on board is that the B text adds also two major passages that are *more* sympathetic to Faustus: the kind and gentle exhortation of the Old Man (V.i.36–52), and the scene after Faustus's removal to hell in which the Scholars resolve to mourn and give him due burial (V.iii). These passages plant in the play a moral perspective alternative to God's. The Old Man and the Scholars pray for Faustus right up to the end, though theologians like Tyndale say we should not pray for apostates – except for their destruction, 'as Paul prayed for Alexander the coppersmith (the ii Timothy, the last), "that God would reward him according to his works" '.[12] The Old Man speaks

> not in wrath,
> Or envy of thee, but in tender love,
> And pity of thy future misery.
>   (V.i.48–50)

Unlike in the A text at this point, the Old Man is far gentler than the Good Angel, who anyway has not visited Faustus for nine hundred lines and has only reproaches left to contribute (V.ii.92–108; B text only). The Scholars, in the face of the horrific evidence of Faustus's destruction ('See, here are Faustus' limbs, / All torn asunder by the hand of death' [V.iii.6–7]), agree to hold a noble funeral. It is rather like the endings of Euripides' *Hippolytus* and *Bacchae*, where the gods stand aside after their disastrous intrusions upon human affairs and the people draw together in sorrow and compassion.

This is why I say the B text sharpens the theological polarity, whereas Empson says it is only more sadistic: both the Reformation god and a more genial alternative are presented more vividly. This produces the possibility, which would also fit the sense most readers have of Marlowe as an author, that at some stage at least the play was written to embarrass protestant doctrine. Richard Baines alleged that in order to persuade men to atheism, Marlowe 'quoted a number of contrarieties out of the scripture',[13] and the strenuous efforts of Christian humanist critics to tame the play to their kind of order suffice to make it worth considering whether *Faustus* dwells provocatively upon such contrarieties. However, there need not have been a precise intention in either direction, and no version of the play may represent, or ever have represented, a single coherent point of view. Substantial texts are in principle likely to be written across ideological faultlines because that is the most interesting kind of writing; they may well not be susceptible to any decisive reading. Their cultural power was partly in their indeterminacy – they spoke to and facilitated debate. But whoever rewrote parts of *Faustus*, and from whatever motive, the revisions indicate an unease with Reformation theology and help to make plain the extent to which any extended treatment cannot but allow contradictions to be heard – by those situated to hear them.

A similar confusion appears in the text of Nathaniel Woodes's *The Conflict of Conscience* (1581), a play usually adduced to set off Marlowe's superior verse and humanity. It is based on the story of one Francesco Spiera, which was translated in 1550 and reissued in 1569–70 with a preface by Calvin. In Woodes's play, Philologus, despite good protestant beginnings, is tempted and indulges in worldly delights, and concludes that he is 'reprobate' and cannot be saved: 'I am secluded clean from grace, my heart is hardened quite.'[14] But the play appeared in print in 1581 in two issues of the same quarto edition, and with two contrasting endings. In the first Philologus kills himself and is indeed damned; in the second, a joyful messenger reports that he renounced his blasphemies at the last moment. (Both versions are headed on the title page 'An excellent new Commedie'.) Evidently someone involved in the publication was worried. The two endings of *The Conflict of Conscience* correspond to the main alternatives in the Christian dilemma: either God must know who is to be damned and therefore, since he created everyone, must be responsible for people going to hell; or God has set the world going but has left it to myriad individual people to decide how it will all turn out. In the former version it is hard to discern his goodness; in the latter, he may be good but is disconcertingly impotent (perhaps rather than paring his fingernails, as James Joyce has it, he is gnawing them in suspense). Historically, each of these two theologies has fed on the inadequacy of the other. And so with the predestinarian and free-will readings of *Faustus*. In Marlowe's play they are, in effect, simultaneously present, but they cannot be read simultaneously; instead they obstruct, entangle, and choke each other. In performance, one or the other may be closed down, but the texts as we have them offer to nudge audiences first this way then that, not allowing interpretation to settle. *Faustus* exacerbates contrarieties in the protestant god so that divine purposes appear not just mysterious but incoherent.

Even critics who believe Faustus is able to choose freely do not thereby prevent the play from provoking embarrassment about God. They cannot settle the point at which Faustus is irrevocably committed, and this is related to God's goodness – the later the decision, the more chance Faustus seems to have. Many theologians have held apostasy to be irrevocable – the 'sin against the Holy Ghost', the one that cannot be forgiven. The homily 'Of Repentance' declares, 'they that do utterly forsake the known truth do hate Christ and his word, they do crucify and mock him (but to their utter destruction), and therefore fall into desperation, and cannot repent'. Richard Hooker said the same.[15] If this is so, Faustus's fate is settled very early, and most of the play shows God denying him further chance to repent; the effect is quite close to a predestinarian reading. No doubt this is why others have maintained that Faustus's situation becomes irretrievable when he conjures; or when he signs; or when he rejects the Good Angel; or when he visits hell; or when he despairs; or when he consorts with Helen; or not until the last hour. Such interpretive scope hardly makes for a persuasive theology. It may lead to the thought that there is no coherent or consistent answer because we are on an ideological faultline where the churches have had to struggle to render their notions adequate. It may suggest not only that Faustus is caught in a cat-and-mouse game played by God at the expense of people, but also that God makes up the rules as he goes along.

Finally, *Faustus* disrupts any complacent view of orthodox theology through its very nature as a dramatic performance. Even for an audience that finds Faustus's blasphemy horrifying, an actor might very well establish a sufficient empathic human presence to make eternal damnation seem unfair. Faustus himself manifests at one point a morality provocatively superior to God's. Anticipating the terror of his last hour, he refuses the support of the Scholars: 'Gentlemen, away, lest you perish with me' (there is no knowing what God might do) – 'Talk not of me, but save yourselves and depart' (V.ii.67–70). At this moment, when human companionship might be most desired, Faustus puts first his friends' safety. As with the Old Man and the Scholars, a generous concern for others is shown persisting in people beyond the point (whenever that is) where the Reformation god has decided that eternal punishment is the only proper outcome. It is one thing to argue in principle that the reprobate are destined for everlasting torment, but when Faustus is shown wriggling on the pin and panic-stricken in his last hour, members of an audience may think again. If this is what happened, for some at least, then there are two traps in the play. One is set by God for Dr Faustus; the other is set by Marlowe, for *God*.

From Alan Sinfield, *Faultlines: Cultural Materialism and the Politics of Dissident Reading* (Oxford, 1992), pp. 230–7.

Notes

[Alan Sinfield's critical writing is yet another sample of Cultural Materialism in our collection. Sinfield reads early modern drama in the light of the ideologies of its time. Here he delineates in particular the ambivalence inherent in *Doctor Faustus'* complex attitudes toward Calvinism, in terms of the controversy between predestination and free will. Ed.]

1. For a good selection, including James Smith, W. W. Greg, J. C. Maxwell, Helen Gardner, Cleanth Brooks, J. B. Steane, and L. C. Knights, see John Jump (ed.), *Marlowe: 'Dr Faustus': A Casebook* (London, 1969). However, Una Ellis Fermor found the God of *Faustus* to be 'sadistic' and revolt against him only proper (Jump, p. 43). For more recent attitudes, see Stephen Greenblatt, *Renaissance Self-*

Fashioning (Chicago, 1980), ch. 5; Jonathan Dollimore, *Radical Tragedy*, 2nd edn (Hemel Hempstead, 1989), ch. 6; Simon Shepherd, *Marlowe and the Politics of Elizabethan Theatre* (New York, 1986), pp. 100–8, 136–41. I come shortly to Empson.

2. Thomas Kyd, *The First Part of Hieronimo and The Spanish Tragedy*, ed. Andrew S. Cairncross (London, 1967), *First Part of Hieronimo*, 3.59–62.

3. King James I, *Daemonologie* (1597), *Newes from Scotland* (1591) (London, 1924), p. 20.

4. John Calvin, *Calvin's Institutes*, trans. Henry Beveridge (Florida, n.d.), 1.14.18; cited hereafter in the text as *Institutes*.

5. Douglas Cole, *Suffering and Evil in the Plays of Christopher Marlowe* (Princeton, NJ, 1962), p. 198. Cole recognises that Faustus's behaviour is typical of the reprobate, but still believes he makes 'his original choice by himself' (pp. 199–201). See also Helen Gardner and J. B. Steane, in Jump (ed.), *Marlowe*, pp. 95, 181–2. Malcolm Kelsall says Faustus's tone and failure to complete his quotations show a superficial attitude and 'would be picked on by any school child' (*Christopher Marlowe* [Leiden, 1981], p. 163). The texts are I John 1:8–9 and Rom. 6:23.

6. T. H. L. Parker, *English Reformers* (London, 1966), p. 111.

7. G. E. Duffield (ed.), *The Work of William Tyndale* (Appleford, Berks, 1964), p. 175.

8. Philip Stubbes, *The Anatomie of Abuses*, ed. Frederick J. Furnivall (London, 1877–79), 1:190. However, Calvin seems uneasy at *Institutes* 3.3.24.

9. E. Gordon Rupp and Philip S. Watson (eds), *Luther and Erasmus* (London, 1969), pp. 230–1, 64. Sidney's theory of poetry centres upon the claim that people are moved by it, but he accepts nevertheless that in Alexander Pheraeus, it 'wrought no further good in him' beyond that he 'withdrew himself from hearkening to that which might mollify his hardened heart' (*The Miscellaneous Prose of Sir Philip Sidney*, ed. Katherine Duncan-Jones and Jan van Dorsten (Oxford, 1973), pp. 96–7.

10. William Perkins, 'A Discourse of Conscience', in Thomas F. Merrill (ed.), *William Perkins* (Nieuwkoop, 1966), pp. 20–1; see William Lawne, *An Abridgement of the Institution of Christian Religion written by John Calvin*, trans. Christopher Fetherstone (Edinburgh, 1587), pp. 53, 72–3, 221. Apropos of the second commandment, where God promises to visit 'the iniquity of the fathers upon the children unto the third and fourth generation' (Deut. 5:9), Lawne's objector is told that children are justly punished for the iniquity they

themselves commit 'when God taketh away grace and other helps of salvation from a family' (Lawne, *Abridgement*, pp. 86–87).

11. William Empson, *Faustus and the Censor* (Oxford, 1987), p. 168 and ch.6. Empson dismisses as insignificant Faustus's uncompleted biblical quotations (discussed above), on the ground that 'to accept the promises of God requires a miracle' anyway, 'and it had been vouchsafed to Luther but not to Faust' (p. 169).

12. In T. H. L. Parker (ed.), *English Reformers* (London, 1966), p. 142.

13. Richard Baines's allegation, quoted from Paul Kocher, *Christopher Marlowe* (New York, 1962), p. 36.

14. Nathaniel Woodes, *The Conflict of Conscience* (Oxford, 1952), 11. 2116, 2151. See Celesta Wine, 'Nathaniel Wood's *Conflict of Conscience*', *PMLA*, 67 (1952), 219–39.

15. *Certain Sermons or Homilies of Ecclesiastical Polity*, intro. C. Morris (London, 1969), I:295. See also Calvin, *Institutes* 3.3.22; Ian Breward (ed.), *The Work of William Perkins* (Abingdon, 1970), p. 254. And see *Plays of Christopher Marlowe*, ed. Roma Gill (Oxford, 1971), p. xxii.

10

The Terms of Gender: 'Gay' and 'Feminist' Edward II

DYMPNA CALLAGHAN

I wish to address the terms of gender in relation to two early modern treatments of the history of Edward II. With the release of Derek Jarman's film (1991), Christopher Marlowe's play, *Edward II* (c. 1592),[1] has achieved an almost iconic status in gay criticism, its author identified as proto-Queer, while the 'proto-feminist' history *The Raign and Death of Edward II* (written 1626), has provoked an intense debate about whether Elizabeth Cary, Countess of Falkland, was in fact its author. My own position does not depend on Cary's authorship (though for convenience's sake I will refer to the text as 'Cary's' throughout): it depends on the feminist interest and investment in Cary having written it.[2] Marlowe and Cary can, of course, only anachronistically be described as 'gay' and 'feminist', and feminist and queer cultural representations and identities do not have early modern 'equivalents'.[3] However, one can lay claim to these terms in order to ascertain those continuities that do exist within the sexualised terms of gender. Marlowe was a spy, brawler, notorious atheist, and sodomite, while Cary inhabited that emergent and transgressive identity of woman writer and had the temerity to convert to Catholicism while her subsequently estranged husband was Lord Deputy of Ireland, an act for which he reduced her to such penury that the Privy Council was obliged to intervene on her behalf.

That both authors wrote about Edward II, however, is not in itself remarkable. Edward's reign (1307–27) appears to have been one of perennial fascination. That a condensed octavo version of Cary's *Raign and Death*, entitled *The History of the Life Reign and Death of Edward II*, was published in the same year that the full-length one saw print (1680) indicates that it was as relevant a political lesson for the late seventeenth century as it had been for the Elizabethan and Jacobean era. Indeed, Marlowe's play, though written during the reign of Elizabeth, has been taken as a commentary on James' problems with his favourites in Scotland. Similarly, Cary, writing in 1626, is thought to be disapprovingly pointing toward James' relation to his favourites in England.[4] Much of the interest in Edward's downfall from Holinshed's *Chronicles* through the late seventeenth century, then, was in its extensible capacity for political allegory. However, the allegorical dimension of Marlowe and Cary's reworking of the past as an intervention in the politics of the present does not take the conventional form of allegorical didacticism directed at an erring ruler. In Marlowe's play, what is at stake is how to demystify Elizabethan erotic politics by making the sovereign a man whose most significant erotic alliances are with male favourites. And what is at issue in Cary's text, which patently disapproves of Edward's misgovernance as Marlowe's does not, is how a wife may legitimately usurp the personal and political sovereignty of her husband. Thus, what distinguishes Cary and Marlowe from other early modern treatments of the story of Edward II as a crisis of sovereignty is that, for them, this crisis hinges on a juxtaposition between representations of femininity and homoerotic masculinity.

Current interest in Marlowe clearly rests on the fact that sexual practices which have been consistently persecuted, suppressed and marginalised since the eighteenth century (and intermittently prior to it) take centre stage in *Edward II*, and it may seem perverse to argue that the drama is more about patriarchy than it is about sexuality. But in the play, sexuality is always overtly bound up with dominant institutions and practices of power. Indeed, only the modern ideology of sexuality allows it to be perceived as such – as sexuality, rather than say, patronage – at all. As John Michael Archer argues, Edward's power is a commentary on – though not an allegory of – Elizabeth's court, because the connection is insisted on in Gaveston's remark that London after exile, 'Is as Elysium to a new come soule':

> *Edward II* both underwrites the political erotics of Elizabeth's court ... and criticises its compulsory heterosociality by imagining a male

monarch, courted by male suitors, and threatened by over-mighty male subjects. In doing so, it once again both conceals and reveals the paradoxical link between patronage and homoeroticism as subversive practice and social bond.[5]

While Edward II is not merely a cipher for Elizabeth, there is an undeniable resemblance between Edward and Elizabeth's sovereignty. Marlowe shows that patriarchal sovereignty is never, in practice, a clear and prescriptive relation of domination and subordination (though the ideal articulation of sovereignty nonetheless accompanies the practice).[6] Thus, even the radical ambiguation of sexual dominance or binary differences entailed in the rule of a female or sodomitical monarch indicates the adaptability of patriarchal sovereignty rather than its absolute subversion.

Throughout, the play's ideological project is determined by the juxtaposition of femininity and male homoeroticism, and not merely by the sodomitical exclusion of the feminine, rendering the position of women in this structure a fascinating one. When Edward brands Isabella with adultery, what is at stake is less a matter of personal betrayal than alternative allegiance:

> **Queen Isabella** Thus do you still suspect me without cause?
> **Niece** Sweet uncle, speak more kindly to the queen.
> (II.ii.227–8)

That another woman – the only other woman in the play apart from that backdrop of patriarchal history, the silent ladies in attendance – comes to Isabella's defence is significant. It is she, Edward's niece, the Duke of Gloucester's daughter, who is in a position structurally parallel to that of the Queen. She is introduced in Act II, in a scene framed by Baldock and Spenser's talk of the latter's homoerotic attachments to Gaveston. From the perspective of conventional sexual relations, we have here a young woman sadly unaware of court politics who expresses genuine longing to marry her duplicitous beloved: 'since he was exil'd, / She neither walks abroad nor comes in sight' (II.i.23–4). She then enters rejoicing at the return of her beloved and reading passages from his amorous missives which, in contrast to the lines from Edward's letter which open the play ('*My father is deceas'd. Come, Gaveston, / And share the kingdom with thy dearest friend*'), are replete with all the tired and overblown rhetoric

characteristic of that genre: 'When I forsake thee, death seize on
my heart!' (II.i.63). It is when she has been married to Gaveston,
given as a gift by Edward, that she speaks her one-line defence of
Isabella. However, Edward's niece is not just a gullible young
woman to whom sodomy is unintelligible, but someone who in
the next scene actively participates in the alliances it generates,
belying any suspicion that her union with Gaveston is anything
other than felicitous. Her agency and investment in sodomitical
power relations which constitute the status quo become apparent
when she begs patronage for Spenser and Baldock from the king:
'Two of my father's servants whilst he liv'd: / May't please your
grace to entertain them now' (II.ii.240–1). In this episode,
Gaveston and his bride work together, he seconding her request
on behalf of Spenser, with whom we know him to have had a
significant personal connection from the opening of Act II: 'For
my sake let him wait upon your grace' (II.ii.251). Homoerotic attachment and the apparatus of heterosexual alliance both enforce
patriarchy in attempts to buttress their own positions.[7]

Male homoerotic bonds are represented in Marlowe's play as
within rather than outside patriarchy, and making them is acknowl-
edged to be one of its most pervasive practices. When the Elder
Mortimer famously advises his discontented and Machiavellian
nephew:

> seeing his mind so dotes on Gaveston,
> Let him without controlment have his will.
> The mightiest kings have had their minions
> (I.iv.391–3)

he shows homoeroticism and power to be perfectly compatible:
famous men from Achilles to Socrates have had male lovers.
Crucially, for Mortimer these same sex attachments are not
sodomitical, as such. For sodomy, as Jonathan Goldberg's
Sodometries has so valuably demonstrated, consists of male–male
sexual love plus disorder. Archer observes that Mortimer's speech
indicates 'an earlier and alien realm of sexual possibility remote
from present realities'.[8] In fact, the list of famous lovers of their
own sex suggests what is almost unthinkable at a moment of
intense homophobia such as our own, namely, that overt male
sexual alliances with other men once buttressed power far more
than they contested it. Younger Mortimer's response affirms that

same-sex relations do not inherently pose a threat to the social order:

> Uncle, his wanton humour grieves not me;
> But this I scorn, that one so basely born
> Should by his sovereign's favour grow so pert.
>
> (I.iv.404–6)

It is the combination of homoeroticism and class transgression that makes *sodomy* both visible and transgressive here.[9] Mortimer's riposte is to argue that Gaveston is not a 'minion'. No servile dependent he; there is nothing diminutive about his social carriage. Yet as he expands upon what he finds so troubling, it is neither sodomy nor class status that bother Mortimer, but Gaveston's mastery of the techniques of self-display that ordinarily constitute authority. In the wrong hands these become foppery:

> While soldiers mutiny for want of pay,
> He wears a lord's revenue on his back,
> And, Midas-like, he jets it in the court,
> With base outlandish cullions at his heels,
> Whose proud fantastic liveries make such show
> As if that Proteus, god of shapes, appear'd.
>
> (I.iv.408–13)

In violation of sumptuary proprietary and law, Gaveston, as Emily Bartels has observed, stages a spectacle of power.[10] It is a capacity for transformation that Gaveston has signalled at the opening of the play with the expressed purpose of manipulating the King, 'And drawing the pliant king which way I please' (I.i.53). This is not the studied indeterminacy of postmodern theories about the performance of identity, but an appropriation of one of the most powerful apparatuses of power, that of spectacle, in order to effect a transformation of class status. This manipulation is quite outside Mortimer's repertoire of Machiavellian strategy, and one for which he will profess not outright envy, but only moral disdain.

It is the malleability of Gaveston's self-representation that makes him so desirable and so beloved of Edward. The political end of this spectacle, according to his own motivation, however, is not consolidation of an already established sovereign power – though this is of course its ultimate effect – but the display of the illicit power of a social climber. Isabella, in contrast, while not desiring control over the forces of cultural and social representation, remains trapped in a residual paradigm of the ritual display of court culture:

> O miserable and distressed Queen!
> Would, when I left sweet France, and was embarked,
> That charming Circe, walking on the waves,
> Had chang'd my shape! or at the marriage-day
> The cup of Hymen had been full of poison!
> Or with those arms, that twin'd about my neck,
> I had been stifled, and not liv'd to see
> The king my lord thus abandon me!
> Like frantic Juno will I fill the earth
> With ghastly murmur of my sighs and cries;
> For never doted Jove on Ganymede
> So much as he on cursed Gaveston.
> But that will more exasperate his wrath.
>
> (I.iv.171–84)

Isabella claims that the self-destructive histrionics of Juno are the sole theatricals to which she has recourse. Gaveston's power lies in his access to representational mechanisms in the play, while Isabella's power appears to take cover behind the stereotypical constructions of the victimised woman and the abandoned wife. And while these histrionics may have no influence on the king, they certainly have the desired effect on the barons with whom she subsequently develops an enormously powerful alliance: 'Look, where the sister of the king of France / Sits wringing of her hands and beats her breast!' (I.iv. 188–89); 'Hard is the heart that injures such a saint' (I.iv.191). At this juncture, Isabella may become an ambivalent figure for the audience – a hapless victim or a strategic manipulator – depending on how far her performance corresponds with these conventional descriptions. Isabella bases her bid for power on an older mode of feudal alliance and its attendant ritualised self-representation, whereas Gaveston relies on making a spectacle of his sexual access to the king.

Gaveston endeavours to control how Isabella is represented. He trumps up the charge that she has committed adultery with Mortimer. In a virulently misogynist episode, the King and Gaveston mercilessly bait Isabella:

> **King Edward** Fawn not on me, French strumpet; get thee gone!
> **Isabella** On whom but on my husband should I fawn?
> **Gaveston** On Mortimer; with whom, ungentle queen, – I
> say no more – judge you the rest, my lord.

> **Isabella** In saying this, thou wrong'st me, Gaveston.
>
> (I.iv.146–50)

Edward clearly holds Isabella responsible for the demand for
Gaveston's exile, and argues, very plausibly, that she has the
power to revoke it. Isabella's power lies in her alliance with the
barons:

> **King Edward**   by thy means is Gaveston exil'd
>   But I would wish thee reconcile the lords,
>   Or thou shall ne'er be reconcil'd to me.
> **Queen Isabella** Your highness knows, it lies not in my power.
> **King Edward** Away, then! Touch me not. – Come, Gaveston.
> **Queen Isabella** Villain, 'tis thou that robb'st me of my lord.
> **Gaveston** Madam, 'tis you that rob me of my lord.
> **Queen Isabella** Wherein, my lord, have I deserv'd these words?
>   Witness the tears that Isabella sheds,
>   Witness the heart that sighing for thee, breaks,
>   How dear my lord is to poor Isabel!
> **King Edward** And witness heaven how dear thou art of me.
>   There weep; for till my Gaveston be repeal'd
>   Assure thyself thou com'st not in my sight.
>
> (I.iv.156–70)

Gaveston's attempts at presenting to Edward a sexually repellent
Isabella are enormously successful. Throughout the play, we get a
sense of Edward's physical revulsion for Isabella as opposed to his
physical intimacy with Gaveston: 'Touch me not', 'Com'st not in
my sight.' 'My lord' clearly belongs to 'my Gaveston': 'He claps his
cheeks, and hangs about his neck, / Smiles in his face, and whispers
in his ears' (I.ii.51–2). Sexuality is not the issue here, so much as
access to the king's body, and in early modern England these could
take the form of any number of lowly or exalted relations of
service, none of which were necessarily or inherently eroticised.
Isabella's power lies, then, in a genuinely powerful alliance with
Edward's political opponents.

Isabella trades her covert alliance with the barons for the less
politically potent influence to be had from sexual access to a man,
Young Mortimer: 'The Prince I rule, the queen do I command'
(V.iv.46).[11] When Isabella returns to England, she briefly rallies
before the assembled multitude at Harwich, trying unsuccessfully
and belatedly to retain her grasp on power, this time through public
address. While her previous speeches have been private and often

soliloquised lamentations on her loss of Edward's love, she begins this speech, all too soon interrupted by Mortimer, in the manner of Elizabeth I's address to the troops at Tilbury:

> Now, lords, our loving friends and countrymen,
> Welcome to England all, with prosperous winds!
>   ... a heavy case
> When force to force is knit, and sword and glaive
> In civil broils make kin and countrymen
> Slaughter themselves in others, and their sides
> With their own weapons gor'd! But what's the help?
> Misgovern'd kings are the cause of all this wrack;
>   (IV.iv.1–9)

The speech is a vivid description of civil war as self-mutilation, and it prophetically invokes the *contrapasso* of Edward's own final disfigurement, 'With their own weapons gor'd!' Despite the fact that this is the most stringent and comprehensive critique of Edward's reign in the play, it is also the moment when the queen loses her power to Mortimer. Once Isabella enters the domestic sphere as Mortimer's surrogate wife, all her power over the instruments of representation is lost. After Harwich, all Isabella's performances are strictly controlled by her lover: 'Finely dissembled! Do so still, sweet queen' (V.ii.76). The fifteen minutes of fame atop Fortune's wheel are allotted to Mortimer, not Isabella. He justifies his *coup*, not as Isabella has done as a matter of dire exigency, but as an act of belligerent indignation against sodomitical sycophants who 'havok England's wealth and treasure'. Silence is enforced upon Isabella, and the sense that it may be coercively enforced is indicated when she tells her son, 'I dare not speak a word' (V.iv.96).

Edward's misogyny, of course, is superficially premised on the notion that Isabella has cuckolded him with Mortimer. For everyone but Edward, the real issue is that a male consort has power, which Isabella by virtue of her gender alone cannot have in a culture that defines femininity and power as mutually exclusive, antithetical entities, brought together only in enormous contradiction and with a vast national apparatus of mythology-as-ideology in the figure of the Virgin Queen. 'Mortimer / And Isabel do kiss while they conspire. / And yet she bears a face of love, forsooth' (IV.v.21–3).

The conclusion of Marlowe's play shows the restoration of patriarchal order with the final emphasis on dynastic continuity: 'Ah, nothing grieves me, but my little boy / Is thus misled to countenance their ills!' (IV.iii.51–2). This 'little boy' has an unnerving awareness of posterity:

> The king of England, nor the court of France,
> Shall have me from my gracious mother's side,
> Till I be strong enough to break a staff,
>   (IV.ii.24–6)

When young Edward comes to power, the juxtaposition of femininity and masculine homoeroticism gives way to a familial and dynastic configuration, that is, to the renegotiated and reinforced terms of gender, but only at the price of the chilling spectacle of Edward III's allegiance to his father before the gory head of the decapitated Mortimer, and the rebuke and imprisonment of his mother: 'Sweet father, here unto thy murder'd ghost / I offer up this wicked traitor's head' (V.vi.99–100). Edward thus renounces his mother and pleads allegiance to his dead father before the image of what is, in Freudian terms, his own displaced castration, the severed head. Dynasty reasserts itself through gender's disciplinary mechanisms:

>   Accursed head,
> Could I have rul'd thee then, as I do now,
> Thou hadst not hatch'd this monstrous treachery!
>   (V.vi.95–7)

Sexual and dynastic control are consolidated here by addressing Mortimer as the formerly unruly member of the body politic. Mortimer is feminised, first in the sense of being symbolically castrated, and secondly, in being capable of gestation and generation. Curiously, Mortimer, the closest approximation we have in the play to the idea of dominant masculinity, becomes a figure who has been unnaturally impregnated by treachery. Symbolically, then, Edward III is asserting his own desire to subjugate, 'Could I have rul'd thee then'. Gregory Bredbeck has brilliantly argued that 'Sodomy does not create disorder; rather disorder demands sodomy'.[12] In this sense, castration, the inaugural and ultimate discipline of gender, articulates itself simultaneously with the homoerotic practice of government: men on top – of a hierarchy of other men. Thus, sodomy converts its disorderliness into a dominant practice rather than a subversive identity, and as Archer points out, 'finally it is regicide and not sodomy that is fully recognised and punished'.[13] So, having banished his mother and promised her execution, Edward directly addresses two symbolic absences – the

dead head and his dead father.[14] The last word of the play is 'innocency', the new king's exculpation from the sins of his predecessor:
'I offer up this wicked traitor's head; / And let these tears, distilling
from mine eyes, / Be witness of my grief and innocency'
(V.vi.100–3). Edward's testament constitutes both the punishment
and repression of sodomy, the figure of regicide, because Mortimer,
in having Edward impaled by Lightbourne, becomes figuratively the
instrument of sodomy, that unnatural instrument now cut off and
bleeding before the new king. As Judith Haber has powerfully
argued, Marlowe's play is about the submission to history defined
as the dominant ideology. Her paradigmatic example of this is the
manner of Edward II's murder: '[N]ot only is the manner of
Edward's murder literally true but, in its logical "punishment-
fitting-the-crime" aspect, it is a figure *for* the literal truth, the intelligible, the determinate, the (patri)lineal, the causal – the historical.'[15]

In contrast to Marlowe's play, in which Isabella is hastily
dispatched to the tower to leave the scene free for the continuation of
Edward III's kingship, Cary places central importance on Isabel and
on her reactions to the execution. Phyllis Rackin argues that most
Renaissance history 'was not simply written without women; it was
also written against them'.[16] Cary's text is exceptional in offering as
it does a female perspective on turbulent historical events. In part, her
narrative form, rather than Marlowe's dramatic one, allows Cary full
access to Isabel's subjectivity. Certainly, Cary's turgid history is en-
livened by Isabel's appearance. From this point on, Edward ceases to
be the text's protagonist, and instead, Isabel's response to events is
vividly imagined and recorded. Cary becomes Isabel's advocate and
records the history from her point of view. The notorious 'invisibility'
of the manner of Edward's death, which Cary dwells on with sala-
cious relish, replaces the conventional invisibility and erasure of the
feminine typical of male-authored texts. In a sense, Cary uses sodomy
to make femininity visible.

What is significant in Cary's account is that a king who has insistently somaticised sovereignty, is disciplined by a practice which at
once reproduces his crime *and* erases it. The somatisation of sovereignty thus vies with the mythic notion of divine right, which
continues irrespective of the mortal body of any individual king.
The invisibility of the manner of death parallels Isabel's status as a
marginal inscription on both the crime and its history. Further, its
marginal, erasable status parallels the status of the feminine where
female subjects, no matter how saturated by their gender, nonetheless, leave no impression on the patriarchal record. In accordance

with the Foucaultian paradigm of discourse repression and production, the murderous act itself must not be spoken of, but is endlessly talked about as that about which one must be silent. For an act without apparent trace (historically and perhaps corporeally), it has left an indelible mark. As Cary rightly points out, poisoning would have been the discreet way to kill the king, so clearly the main goal was not discretion. The phrasing of the passage is such that Mortimer sounds unschooled in some *sexual* 'Italian trick' of Spencer's.

Cary's text has a moral project – the outright condemnation of Edward and justification of his wife's treason – as Marlowe's does not. Regicide is evil, but Cary leaves us in no doubt that in this instance it was fully justified. Cary's *Raign and Death* makes clear from the outset that Edward is degenerate and that women are not morally culpable in his downfall; and in so doing, she enfranchises the domestic sphere.

The source of Edward's perversion is 'Gaveston his Ganymede, a man as base in birth as in condition' (p. 4), 'his left-handed Servant' (p. 24). Cary clearly disparages Gaveston because she regards sodomy as an inherently degenerate practice, and, in the rhetoric with which she rationalises this position, sodomy is posited not as a personal idiosyncrasy of Edward (or, as in Marlowe's Old Mortimer's speech, of monarchs in general), but as a structural weakness in the system of absolute monarchy: '[It] is the general Disease of Greatness, and a kinde of Royal Fever, when they fall upon an indulgent Dotage, to patronize and advance the corrupt ends of their Minions, though the whole Society of State and Body of the Kingdom run in a direct opposition' (p. 16). Edward fails to display his proper sovereignty to his people: '[T]he King appear'd so little himself, that the Subjects thought him a Royal Shadow without a Real Substance' (p. 20) and publicly 'he slubbers o'er his private Passion' (p. 23). That is, though Cary's formal charge against Edward is that he has confused private desire with public government – 'his private Appetite should subscribe to publick necessity' (p. 9) – there is an implicit suggestion that with sodomy it could not be otherwise. Such a suggestion leads Cary to posit in somewhat contradictory fashion a norm of male sexual behaviour that is not absolutely 'heterosexual'. Excessive love, rather than specifically homosexual desire, becomes the object of her critique: 'Such a masculine Affection and rapture was in those times without president, where Love went in the natural strain, fully as firm, yet far less violent' (p. 28). This excessive love constitutes effeminacy, and as Alan Sinfield reminds us, effeminacy, though it rarely correlates with same-sex passion in the Renaissance to the degree that it does in accounts of Gaveston, is founded in misogyny: 'the root idea is of a male falling away from the purposeful reasonableness that is supposed to constitute manliness, into the laxity and weakness conventionally attributed to women.'[17] Cary overturns this convention and makes Isabel the corrective to effeminate sovereignty.

When Isabel escapes the snares of Spencer to France with Mortimer, we are told 'his Craft and Care, that taught him all those lessons of Cunning Greatness, here fell apparent short of all Discretion, to be thus overreached by one weak Woman' (p. 92). Baldock too falls prey to the error of underestimating her: '*Alas, what can the Queen a wandering Woman compas, that hath nor Arms, nor means, nor Men, nor Money?*' (p. 93). Even though Cary has made clear earlier that the queen indeed 'had cast a wandering eye upon the gallant *Mortimer*' (p. 89), once his wife has flown, Edward's public taints upon her reputation are ridiculed by Cary:

> [A] Declaration is sent out to all the Kingdom, that taints the Honour of the Queen, but more his Judgement. The ports are all stopt up, that none should follow: a Medicine much too late; a help improper, to shut the Stable-door, the Steed being stol'n: but 'tis the nature of a bought Experience, to come a day too late, the market ended.
>
> (p. 94)

Spencer's conflict with Isabel is described in terms of a contest of wits between Eve and the serpent: '*Spencer*, that was as cunning as a Serpent, findes here a female Wit that went beyond him, one that with his own Weapons wounds his Wisdome' (p. 91). Spencer has, however, wit enough to fear Isabel: 'He knew her to be a Woman of a strong Brain, and a stout Stomack, apt on all occasions to trip up his heels, if once she found him reeling' (pp. 86–7). Cary intervenes here to rewrite history and place the queen's power over Spencer in the most positive possible light – not as devious manipulation but as political ingenuity.

Cary's Isabel is a warrior queen who frequently outwits the men around her, and whose paramour is barely mentioned. Indeed, Mortimer is little more than an accessory to Edward's downfall. Isabel presents the major *political* challenge to Edward's reign; her sexual liaison with Mortimer is of remarkably little significance. She is the self-composed diplomat, who overcomes her passion for revenge and assuages Mortimer, restraining him from rash action, as she strategises their return to England (p. 104). Far less the spurned wife than the rebellious queen, 'Her Army still grows greater, like a beginning Cloud that doth fore-run a Shower' (p. 123), Isabel gains a specifically military victory, 'the Queen having thus attained to the full of her desire, resolves to use it to the best advantage' (p. 127). It is Isabel, and not Mortimer, who defeats Edward, who can only hope in vain for mercy at her hands (p. 125). She heads for London in a victorious parade whereupon 'A world of people do strain their wider throats to bid her welcome' (p. 128). Cary argues for women's statecraft and intellectual capacities, 'Thus Womens Wit sometimes can cozen Statesmen' (p. 109), instead of offering a defensive apologia for traditional female virtues.

There can be no question that the female-authored Isabel is the plucky victor whereas Marlowe's Isabella functions as the rather stereotypically forlorn queen who cannot survive without male support. Rejected by Edward and then her brother, Valois, Marlowe's Isabella finally turns to Mortimer. While this does not, of course, mean that positive images of women necessarily make for more radical or even better texts, it does show how history is read differently by an author who foregrounds female political agency. For all that, Cary's championing of Isabel is an argument for a strong, ideal patriarchy. Had Edward exercised proper manly power, there would have been a perfect balance between the reciprocal duties of sovereign and subjects. But Edward, as well as being the possessor of 'many *puny* vices', is also a 'cruel Tyrant' (p. 74) in the 'bloody Hurly-burlies' (p. 76) of the realm.

Contrary to the claims of feminist critical appraisals of the text, it is not an heroic nature that allows Isabel to resist tyranny. Rather, her resistance – aligned with that of Edward's subjects – comes about as a natural effect of the King's weakness. In sharp contrast to the bowmen and pikes who take up Edward's cause in Marlowe, Cary leaves Edward without even the semblance of military support. Again, private vanities as such are not the issue but, rather that 'all things at home, under his Government, were out of rule and order; and nothing successful that he undertook by forraign Employment' (p. 39). Edward has virtually ceded all power to Gaveston, 'He thus assuming the administration of Royal affairs, his Master giving way to all his actions' (p. 53). Cary states that it was 'not altogether improbable' that this was the result of witch-craft, 'for never was Servant more insolently fortunate, nor Master unreasonably indulgent' (p. 49). It is the kingdom which must pay for Edward's excesses, 'making the Subject groan under the unjust Tyranny of an insolent oppression' (p. 40).

But the pseudo-sexual instrument of this disorder is not the phallus, the patriarchal organ of government, so to speak, but the tongue, by which Edward is sexually manipulated first by Gaveston, and then by Spencer. A loyal subject declares: '*I am no tongue man*' (p. 55) while the evil of the realm is seen to emanate from the tongue: 'Admission of the Royal ear to *one Tongue* only, ties all the rest' (p. 62).[18] Spencer, like his predecessor, 'made his tongue a guide to lead his actions' (p. 86). Even though Edward is the 'feminine' recipient of the tongue, the Machiavellianism of those who manipulate with it is almost feminine power gone public – that is, the influence of the '*Harpy* with his *Lycean* eyes' (p. 54), which in the properly ordered state is normally kept within the confines of the private realm.

When the queen manufactures a spectacle of her power, Cary voices her one criticism of Isabel, which is that she leads Spencer in triumph. This is an astonishing moment in the narrative: not only is Isabel's honour totally divorced from the question of chastity, but also the death sentence she has meted out to Spencer is corroborated. The style of Isabel's justice, however, is severely criticised – specifically, the way she grasps the reins of representation. Spencer deserves death, but one more fitting his class position, 'Though not by Birth, yet by Creation he was a Peer of the Kingdom' (p. 129). Cary continues, 'it was at best too great and deep a blemish to suit a Queen, a Woman, and a Victor' (p. 129), but then, as she adds in a passage about Isabel's execution of Arundel on the following page, 'we may not properly expect Reason in Womens actions' (p.130). In Cary's narrative, the queen and Mortimer reign on unpunished. In this sense, Isabel's victory is the antithesis of conventional patriarchal history where 'Depicted as blank pages awaiting the inscription of patriarchal texts, silenced by the discourse of patriarchal authority, the women could never tell their own stories',[19] and yet her role is to consolidate the powers she ostensibly challenges.[20] Cary presents Isabel as a figure of legitimate resistance to cruelty and wantonness, whose only real sin is not adultery but her display of Spencer and her own power after she defeats him. Women too, it seems, can be the instruments of strong patriarchy, and the unpunished victory is a fantasy of how they can be absorbed within it.

I have been pursuing the juxtaposition of male homoeroticism and femininity in order to determine where such a configuration places women. Jonathan Goldberg valuably endeavours to disclose the limits of feminist discussions which treat 'gender as if the only forms of power involved were those that determine the inequality between the sexes (arguments ... which collapse questions of sexuality in to questions of gender)'.[21] Goldberg's valid and significant objective here is to make homoeroticism visible in the Renaissance, a visibility contingent upon the degree to which it can be made distinct from gender. Yet, Goldberg claims that attention to women's subordination is *in itself* tantamount to homophobia. A focus on the restrictions of gender, which constrain women more than men, is seen itself to perpetuate those restrictions. Thus, in criticising the way feminist critics subsume sexuality under the category of gender, Goldberg reverses the manoeuvre and collapses gender into sexuality. Crucially, that sexuality is ungendered. The result is a postmodern rendition of the allegedly gender-neutral, universal subject – man; nothing less than a covert return to masculinity.[22] Heterosexuality, defined as 'the relations between men and women',[23] flattens out, so that the specificity of feminine sexuality, whether heterosexual or homoerotic, gets lumped in with masculine heterosexuality. The trajectory of his argument leads Goldberg in his analysis of Marlowe's *Edward II* to make the astonishing claim that Isabella is a sodomite.

Phyllis Rackin has argued in her analysis of Shakespeare's history plays that 'In the central scene of historical representation, women have no place'.[24] Marginal as the roles of wife, mother, and England's queen may be, even these dynastic roles are unavailable to Marlowe's Isabella – Kent even wins her son from her in Act V. Marlowe's queen is caught in the interstices of male power, never really able to wield it on her own behalf. Isabella's adultery, far from being an act of *resistance to* the constraints of marriage, is rather a last ditch resistance against her *exclusion from* conjugality. The price of Jonathan Goldberg's insistence on sexuality as distinct from gender is the erasure of the discipline of gender *and* the possibility of a specifically female resistance.[25] In Goldberg's reading of the relation between the feminine and the male homoerotic, women disappear. In Marlowe and Cary's texts, in contrast, both male homoeroticism and gender hierarchy become hyper-visible in the exacerbated conditions of Edward's reign.

Of particular concern to my argument is the way femininity and homoerotic masculinity are set against one another. This manifests itself as an unsettling alignment between feminism and homophobia, homoeroticism and misogyny, and does so in spite of the shared political agenda of much feminist and queer theory. Such an opposition constricts interventions and isolates their effects so that work against either sexism or homophobia produces interventions that may challenge certain practices within patriarchy, but not the structure itself, and only serves, however unwittingly, inadvertently, or reluctantly, to reproduce the patriarchal order.

The configuration of sexuality and gender, male homoeroticism and feminity, as juxtapositions rather than antagonistic antitheses suggests a contiguity which recognises that 'divide and conquer' is one of patriarchy's most enduring strategies. I hope also to register that there is a powerful patriarchal projection which saddles woman with both the mark of gender and blame for its discipline; by extension, feminism is seen as having a unique investment in enforcing gender's terms. As psychoanalytic theory has demonstrated, it is femininity that threatens to disrupt gender, while the Law of the Father sets the terms.

From *Feminist Readings of Early Modern Culture*, ed. Valerie Traub, M. Lindsay Kaplan and Dympna Callaghan (Cambridge, 1996), pp. 281–97.

Notes

[Dympna Callaghan's essay best represents in our collection the feminist approach to early modern drama. When reading Marlowe or, for that matter, Elizabeth Cary's work in terms of gender politics, be it queer theory or feminism, one does not necessarily suggest the original texts consciously, or even unconsciously, pertained to such discourse. However, employing such notions does enlighten us as readers of the early modern texts, since they attest, as Callaghan puts it, to 'those continuities that do exist within the sexualised terms of gender'. Ed.]

1. Christopher Marlowe, *The Complete Plays*, ed. J. B. Steane (1969; rpt. Harmondsworth 1986).

2. Elizabeth Cary, *The Raign and Death of Edward II* (London, 1680); STC. 313, and *The History of the Most Unfortunate Prince King Edward II* (London, 1680), STC 314.

3. For the debate on historicising the category of homosexuality since Foucault's claim that it emerged only in the nineteenth century, see:

Terry Castle, *The Apparitional Lesbian: Female Homosexuality and Modern Culture* (New York, 1993), ch. I; and Claude Summers' introduction to *Homosexuality in Renaissance and Enlightenment England: Literary Representations in Historical Context, Journal of Homosexuality*, 23, I/2, 1992 (New York). See also in that volume, Joseph Cady, ' "Masculine Love", Renaissance Writing, and the "New Invention" of Homosexuality', pp. 9–40. I would argue that in some sense the debate is based on the erroneous assumption that Foucault is speaking only of homosexuality. Since homosexuality is what defines and produces the discrete category of heterosexuality, it is more accurate to say sexuality itself can be dated as a recent event.

4. See Tina Krontiris, *Oppositional Voices* (New York, 1992), p. 91. One of James' Scottish cousins, Esmé Stuart, was, like Gaveston, actually banished from the realm. See Jonathan Goldberg, *Sodometries: Renaissance Texts, Modern Sexualities* (Stanford, CA, 1993), p. 271.

5. John Archer, *Sovereignty and Intelligence: Spying and Court Culture in the English Renaissance* (Stanford, CA, 1993), p. 77.

6. For Jonathan Dollimore, who uses both lesbian and gay texts to extrapolate his thesis, the epistemological and political rupturing wrought by a repeated unsettling of the opposition between dominant and subordinate 'operating in terms of gender' is what constitutes sexual dissidence (*Sexual Dissidence* [Oxford, 1991], p. 21).

7. Goldberg notes the play allows for 'ways of conceiving sexual relations and gender construction that cannot be reduced to the normative structure of male/female relations under the modern regimes of heterosexuality' (*Sodometries*, p. 129).

8. Archer, *Sovereignty and Intelligence*, p. 81.

9. Sharon Tyler notes that Marlowe emphasises that Gaveston is low-born even though his sources do not, 'Bedfellows Make Strange Politics: Christopher Marlowe's *Edward II*', in *Drama, Sex and Politics*, James Redmond (ed.), *Themes in Drama* 7 (Cambridge, 1985), p. 57.

10. Emily Bartels, *Spectacles of Strangeness: Imperialism, Alienation, and Marlowe* (Philadelphia, 1994) pp. 143–72.

11. Of course even as an adulteress, the queen remains dangerous. Phyllis Rackin has argued that women in patriarchal historiography represent a physicality that men can neither capture nor control, and that the adulterous woman in particular threatens to disrupt and destroy the dynastic scheme and 'at any point could make a mockery of the whole story of patriarchal succession'. *Stages of History: Shakespeare's English Chronicles* (Ithaca, NY, 1990), p. 160.

12. Gregory Bredbeck, *Sodomy and Interpretation* (Ithaca, NY, 1991), p. 77.

13. Archer, *Sovereignty and Intelligence*, p. 86.

14. Judith Haber remarks about Edward III's threatening his mother with execution: 'His painfully firm resolution is particularly striking in a play in which almost everyone has been presented as "slack" or "drooping",' 'Submitting to History: Marlowe's *Edward II*', in *Enclosure Acts: Sexuality, Property, and Culture in Early Modern England*, Richard Burt and John Michael Archer (eds) (Ithaca, NY, 1994), p. 179.

15. Ibid., p. 180.

16. Rackin, *Stages of History* p. 160.

17. Alan Sinfield, *Cultural Politics* (Philadelphia, 1994), p. 15. For an analysis of motifs of clothing and the body in relation to effeminacy, see Gregory Woods, 'The Body, Costume, and Desire in Christopher Marlowe', in *Homosexuality in Renaissance and Enlightenment England*, Summers (ed.), pp. 24–5.

18. Edward, however, actively employs, as well as being passively manipulated by, the politics of the tongue: 'Thus *Kings* can play their parts, and hide their Secrets, making the Tongue the instrument of sweetness, when that the Heart is full of bitter Gall and Wormwood' (p. 64).

19. Rackin, *Stages of History*, p. 147.

20. Dollimore points out: 'dissidence may not only be repressed by the dominant (coercively and ideologically), but in a sense actually produced by it, hence consolidating the powers which it ostensibly challenges' (*Sexual Dissidence*, p. 27).

21. Goldberg, *Sodometries*, p. 21.

22. Ibid., p. 106.

23. Ibid., p. 107.

24. Rackin, *Stages of History*, p. 147

25. Challenging new historicist notions of containment, Barbara Lewalski argues that Cary's history, like the writings of Jacobean women in general, is inherently a text of resistance: Although these writers were subsequently ignored or suppressed, I take it that their literary gestures of resistance matter. Attention to these women writers will also help us recognise that authorship may be the process as well as the product of asserting subjectivity and agency. (*Writing Women in Jacobean England*, p. 11).

11

Queer Edward II: Postmodern Sexualities and the Early Modern Subject

THOMAS CARTELLI

Queer Edward II is the title of the book that Derek Jarman published as a companion piece to his recent film, *Edward II* (1991), in order to itemise and emphasise points that he wanted to make in excess of those he felt able to make in the film.[1] I have put the book's title to work in the heading of this essay because it highlights, in a direct and aggressive manner, the film's affinities with contemporary queer theory which it is at least part of my purpose to examine here. According to Michael Warner, the 'preference for "queer" ' in contemporary gay discourse 'represents, among other things, an aggressive impulse of generalisation; it rejects a minoritising logic of toleration or simple political interest-representation in favour of a more thorough resistance to regimes of the normal'.[2] Jarman's affiliation with queer theory is evinced less by his film's predictably sympathetic representation of the relationship of Edward and Gaveston than by his vigorous integration into the film of militant gay liberation positions, including actions of resistance undertaken in their behalf by actual members of OutRage, described as '*the* Gay Activist Group' in the book's introductory matter. The *book's* debt to positions associated with the contemporary queer movement is even more pronounced, and is paraded in the aggressive slogans that frame Jarman's generally more anecdotal commentary on the successive sequences of the film, the film's development, and his own, now concluded, struggle with AIDS.

These slogans operate in a wry but conscientiously polarising manner, and aim to privilege both homosexual and homosexist positions at the expense of the insistently demystified protocols of heterosexuality. Most of the slogans – YOUR CLOSET *IS* YOUR COFFIN';[3] 'gender is apartheid' (p. 36); 'DEVIATE or *die*' (p. 88); 'LAWS MAKE NATURE' (p. 150); 'HETEROPHOBIA *liberates*, HOMOSEXISM *empowers*' (p. 168) – plainly reject accommodation to the residual biases of the resisting heterosexual reader. In their insistence on a thoroughgoing transformation of the 'regimes of the normal', the slogans also underwrite the similarly unaccommodating construction of the heteronormative in Jarman's film.

But what, Jarman provokes one to ask, does all this have to do with Marlowe's *Edward II*, the presumptive occasion around which both book and film are assembled? In *Queer Edward II* Jarman offers competing answers to the same question. On his dedication page, Jarman rather archly writes: 'How to make a film of a gay love affair and get it commissioned. Find a dusty old play and violate it.' Marlowe's play becomes, in this formulation, merely an enabling medium or ruse that affords Jarman the means/financial backing to stage something else entirely, 'a film of a gay love affair'. A few lines down, however, Jarman adds, 'Marlowe outs the past – why don't we out the present?', thereby appearing to enlist Marlowe as a kindred spirit or collaborator who has done for the past what Jarman hopes to do for the present. Throughout both book and film, Jarman maintains this same casual ambivalence about his actual debt to Marlowe. One gets the sense that should Jarman attribute too much to Marlowe as a violator of his age's presumed heterosexual consensus, Jarman will have less to claim for his own violations or interventions. There is, on this account, quite a bit of strategic self-congratulation on Jarman's part, premised on a recognisably postmodern embarrassment at having to deal at all with 'a dusty old play' that may have helped get his film funded but lacks the panache of the 'pop songs' which, as he says elsewhere, only 'the best lines in Marlowe sound like'.

Although Jarman would undoubtedly prefer to sustain both the mystery and erotic charge carried by the word *violation*, he provides a more accurate – and modest – explanation of his aims in the running-head printed across each of the facing pages of *Queer Edward II*, which reads 'EDWARD II *improved by* DEREK

JARMAN'. In the sections of *Queer Edward II* that refer directly to Marlowe's play, Jarman promotes his film as an improvement of *Edward II* in two primary respects: (1) It unqualifiedly displays and celebrates, in the best postmodern manner, homoerotic behaviours that Marlowe allegedly presents in a more qualified, constrained way; (2) It replaces Marlowe's allegedly neutral perspective on the play's 'action' with a militantly partisan point of view that champions homosexuality and demonises heterosexism, if not heterosexuality itself. Having measured Jarman's claims against my own understanding of Marlowe's play, I would suggest that by selectively foregrounding issues that the play's critics – as opposed to Marlowe himself – have chosen either to marginalise or to treat from a moralised perspective, Jarman has done more to hasten the demise of an already unravelling critical consensus on *Edward II* than he has to improve a play that, in many respects, invites the treatment Jarman has given it.[4]

This is not to suggest that Jarman brings nothing new to *Edward II's* realisation. Jarman makes a series of political interventions that do, indeed, 'improve' on Marlowe by substituting a clearly positioned emphasis on gay victimisation and empowerment in place of Marlowe's generally unpositioned fascination with power and the powerful. Although Marlowe initially situates his audience in sympathetic relation to Edward and Gaveston's carnivalesque reign of misrule, playgoers are ultimately directed to accommodate themselves to the drama's often shifting fields of force and the dramatic agents who command them. As I have argued elsewhere, gravitation to power, not to sexual orientation, is the play's prevailing medium of receptive engagement.[5] Jarman, however, appears to assume that the homosexual subject – even in the guise of a king – is always the victimised object of an established heterosexist power structure. He consequently positions the filmgoer in sympathetic relation to whatever forces of resistance he can enlist to recuperate the play's potential to promote the cause of dissident sexualities. Superimposing a militantly homoerotic point of view on the play's reconstruction, Jarman energises its dramatically foreclosed capacity to stage resistance to heterosexist aggression.

That Marlowe's play succumbs to an identification with power is at least in part owing to the historical untenability of exactly the kind of oppositional sexual politics Jarman's film provides.[6] By the same token, Marlowe's capacity to generate, most notably through his characterisation of Gaveston, a staging-ground for the operation

and development of homosexual agency provides Jarman with a
fertile site on which to structure his improvements.[7] While scholars
like Alan Bray consider it 'anachronistic and ruinously misleading'
to identify 'an individual in [the early modern] period as being or
not being "a homosexual"' (pp. 16–17), and while neither Edward
nor Gaveston confine themselves to same-sex encounters, it
nonetheless seems clear, as Bruce Smith has argued, that in his
constructions of both characters, 'Marlowe introduces us to the
possibility of a homosexual subjectivity' (p. 223).[8] Moreover, he
does so in a manner that stands in much the same relation to other
early modern constructions of Edward and Gaveston as Jarman
stands in relationship to Marlowe.

As in other histories of Edward's reign, Marlowe casts Gaveston
as the more profoundly sexualised figure, unmoored from the
normative attachments of family, social, and political obligation.[9]
Unlike them, he does not seek to explain, clarify, or judge
Gaveston's sexual or social exceptionalism. It is, on this account
and others, worth comparing Marlowe's conception with Michael
Drayton's construction of Gaveston in a poem datable to 1593–94
whose dedication suggestively states that Gaveston's name 'hath
been obscured so many yeeres, and over-past by the Tragedians of
these latter times'.[10] Gaveston notably speaks in his own voice
throughout this sustained dramatic monologue, and is given a
good deal of sympathetic access to his readers in shaping his
versions of events. Implicitly countering the conventional charge
of unnaturalness levelled against his relationship with Edward,
Gaveston speaks of a 'naturall attracting *Sympathie*' (p. 164),
adding

> O depth of nature, who can looke into thee?
> O who is he that hath thy doome controuled?
> Or hath the key of reason to undoe thee:
> Thy workes divine which powers alone doe knowe,
> Our shallow wittes too short for things belowe.
>
> (p. 164)

The naturalness of Edward and Gaveston's love appears to extend
to its physical realisation as Gaveston states, 'And like two Lambes
we sport in every place, / Where neither joy nor love could well be
hid / That might be seal'd with any sweet embrace' (p. 182). But
Drayton's Gaveston is elsewhere made to proclaim 'What act so
vile, that we attempted not?' (p. 167) and to moralise regretfully on

sexual practices that are now graphically presented as unnatural acts:

> My soule now in the heavens eternall glory,
> Beholds the scarrs and botches of her sin,
> How filthy, uglie, and deformed shee was,
> The lothsome dunghill that shee wallowed in.
>
> (p. 202)

A similar ambivalence attends the representation of Gaveston and his relationship to Edward in the history of Edward II authored by one E. F. in 1627, but now generally attributed to Elizabeth Cary. Cary mines what we will recognise as a stereotypical vein of homosexual inscription in stating of Gaveston that 'the most curious eye could not discover any manifest errour, unles it were in his Sex alone since he had too much for a man, and Perfection enough to haue equal'd the fairest Female splendour that breath'd within the confines of this Kingdom'.[11] But Cary puts this overendowed sexuality into play in relation to Edward in a manner that romantically idealises their attachment: 'A short passage of time had so cemented their hearts, that they seem'd to beat with one and the self-same motion; so that the one seem'd without the other, like a Body without a Soul, or a Shadow without a Substance' (pp. 4–5). She later adds that 'their Affections, nay their very *Intentions* seem'd to go hand in hand' (p. 20), thereby appearing to naturalise what she had initially presented as a kind of excess of, or deformity in, nature itself. Cary's initial difficulty in accepting as natural these indisputable signs of reciprocal attachment is, however, recuperated in a still later formulation where she writes that 'Such a masculine Affection and rapture was in those times without precedent, where Love went in the natural strain, fully as firm, yet far less violent' (p. 28). *Excess* seems, finally, the distinguishing marker employed by Cary to designate where the natural ends and the unnatural begins. As such, it serves to map that space of difference a later age will come to identify – in other words, through other signs – as homosexuality.

Excess and the unnatural operate as the privileged spaces of homosexual activity in Francis Hubert's unqualifiedly negative appraisal of Gaveston in his 1629 *History of Edward II*, which, like Drayton's *Peirs Gaveston*, is also structured as a verse monologue but this time spoken by Edward himself. In Hubert we discover the

fully demonised face of the professed sodomite, appraised by
Edward as the 'This highest Scholler in the School of Sinne, / This
Centaure, halfe a man, and halfe a Beast', who 'acted all' as
'*Plantaganet* was turn'd to *Gaveston*'.[12] Seductive as the serpent in
the garden, Hubert's Gaveston pleads the case of pleasure as allur-
ing bait 'to tye [Edward]still in streighter bands' (p. 13), reducing
civil laws to 'servile observations / Of this, or that, what pleas'd the
Makers mind' (p. 14) and making 'the golden law of Nature, /
Sweet Nature, (sweetest Mother of us all)' (p. 15) the sole arbiter of
approved behaviour.

These competing representations of Gaveston and 'masculine'
love demonstrate how simultaneously settled and unsettled the categories for representing homosexuality were in the early modern
period. For his part, Marlowe, in *Edward II*, effectively obviates
the dispute regarding the natural and unnatural by representing
homosexual behaviour as one among many material practices that
are motivated by irregular blends of affection, compulsion, and
opportunism and that operate beyond the reach of moral or idealist
categories. Where Drayton and Cary inscribe Edward and Gaveston
as both sexually other and romantically the same, as at once
perfectly and imperfectly natural, Marlowe approaches difference
itself from the point of view of indifference, thereby implicitly
normalising the avowedly exceptional acts of the homosexual
subject. And it is, I would submit, precisely in this refusal to impose
normative binaries on homosexual practices that Marlowe's violation of his age's heterosexual bias becomes most apparent.[13]

The materialist basis of Marlowe's position may, in fact, be said
to constitute another salient early modern marker of homosexual
agency, as Hubert's conflation of Gaveston's Machiavellian discourse and sodomitical behaviour indicates. The argument Hubert
delegates to Gaveston regarding the social construction of laws –
which he terms 'scar Crowes [invented] to keepe [men] in some
awe' (p.14) – falls squarely in the range of damnable opinions that
were characteristically delegated to atheists and sodomites alike
in the period, and that were specifically attributed to Marlowe in
the wake of his violent death.[14] Indeed, the argument is remarkably consistent with statements regarding the social construction
of religion attributed to Marlowe in the Baines deposition ('That
the first beginning of religion was only to keep men in awe')
which appear alongside even more provocative celebrations of homosexual practices. The Baines deposition itself may either be

construed as a particularly rich repository of early modern queer theory – if we accept Marlowe's authorship of its notorious opinions – or of early modern theory about queers – if we assume, instead, that it was deliberately constructed to implicate Marlowe. I assume that it is both and that its travesties of normative beliefs and behaviours in claims like 'St John the Evangelist was bedfellow to Christ and leaned alwaies in his bosom, [and] used him as the sinners of Sodoma' need not have been exactly rendered by Marlowe to be considered Marlovian.[15] Should we, nonetheless, choose to accept Marlowe's authority for such pronouncements, we will have established an early modern precedent for Jarman's postmodern sloganeering, one that makes Marlowe a more outspoken advocate of transgressive knowledge and practices than Jarman would appear to allow.

The role played by travesty in marking the space of transgression is, of course, equally prominent in Marlowe's *Edward II* where it is less their lovemaking than the practice of Edward and Gaveston to 'flout our train, and jest at our attire'[16] that Mortimer finds objectionable. Compelled by the peers to stand outside the socially constituted realm of the natural, Edward and Gaveston play at, and against, orders of behaviour that are established and dictated by the heteronormative consensus. Sexual difference thus becomes the enabling site for the production of both emulative and alternative discourses and behaviours. This is made even more abundantly clear in Jarman's film in scenes which feature Edward and Gaveston's exuberantly abandoned dancing to the music of a string quartet, their respective entertainment of a sensuous snake-charmer and a poet's suggestive re-signifying of Dante's 'I came to myself in a dark wood where the straight way was lost', and in their wholesale reconfiguration of court life as a privileged preserve of play and fantasy. In such scenes, the 'straight way' is travestied in the very act of being superseded by a 'crookedness' that has developed aesthetic and moral parameters of its own.

It is particularly through his elaboration of alternative subject positions for Edward and Gaveston to inhabit that Jarman is able to extend and move beyond the circuit of Marlowe's comparatively more emulative travesties of the heterosexual consensus. Whereas Marlowe's Gaveston is, for the most part, a reactive character, miming and mocking the sober behaviours of the peers, Jarman's Gaveston is a decidedly more unpredictable figure, who draws on passions and resources that are conspicuously different from those of Mortimer and his supporters. As played by Andrew Tiernan, Jarman's Gaveston operates both within and against contemporary stereotypes of homosexual behaviours. In the first place he betrays a good deal more passion and commitment for Edward than Gaveston does even in Marlowe's play, transforming the early modern space of sexual excess and Machiavellian opportunism into a site of erotic preference and romantic solidarity. In keeping with Jarman's desire to insist on differences to which Marlowe was indifferent, Tiernan's Gaveston generally keeps the space of lovemaking free of the impulse to travesty that characterises his other appearances. For example, in the farewell scene that features Annie Lennox singing a Cole Porter lovesong and that would consequently appear ripe for parody, Tiernan chooses to play Gaveston romantically 'straight', unsettling even further the stereotypes within which he would otherwise be confined.

In other appearances, Tiernan variously plays Gaveston as loutish, vicious, and demonic. For example, in taunting Mortimer by performing naked acrobatics on Edward's throne (sequence 15), Tiernan, as Jarman writes, 'pulled out all the stops, turning himself into a frightful clucking demon' (p. 30). In another sequence (#22) in which he thuggishly supervises the merciless beating of the archbishop, Tiernan 'looked as if he'd stepped from "The Krays" ' (p. 44), a recent film that conflates homosexual practices and homicidal pathologies. Tiernan is so adept at sexually arousing, and subsequently taunting, Isabella in the next sequence that he provokes Jarman to remark, rather defensively, that 'Not all gay men are attractive. I am not going to make this an easy ride. Marlowe didn't' (p. 46).

In refusing to ennoble Gaveston, Jarman reminds us that homosexual subjectivity does not consist of one or more enduring attributes, but issues from the conditioned force of homosexual agency which has historically been compelled to operate in – and as – resistance to enforced constraints.[17] Jarman does not allow these constraints to rationalise Gaveston's behaviour. But in exaggerating their strength in scenes like the one in which an exiled Gaveston is first made to pass through a gauntlet of cursing and spitting priests, Jarman makes palpable the fierce repressiveness that church, state, and 'civil' society can muster in the face of resistance and also indicates why resistance may come to resemble what it opposes. As the closing sections of his film make plain, Gaveston's enjoyment of the licence to brutalise is, in any event, summarily revoked when this heterosexist consensus re-establishes its control over king and court. Aware of the raised stakes of this moment, Jarman chooses to transpose several of these scenes to the present, and to stage Edward's final contention with Mortimer in the form of militant gay resistance to police repression. His decision to delegate Edward's actual execution to the province of nightmare is, however, altogether more problematic.

While consistent with his transformation of Edward's long-lost struggle against members of his own ruling class into a more hopeful contemporary battle between opposed sexualities, Jarman's ending magically elides the very relation between past and present oppressions that he otherwise seeks to document. (History, in this respect, becomes a nightmare from which we all too easily awaken.) Jarman seems specifically unwilling to allow a too powerful imaging of the material oppression of homosexuals to carry over into the present without simultaneously providing a way out. His decision to have Lightborne cast his hot-poker away, and to embrace Edward as a lover, has the added effect of making fantasy seem the preferred medium of resistance in the battle for homosexual rights. This particular 'improvement' of *Edward II* arguably constitutes the most indisputable violation of Marlowe's play in Jarman's film.[18]

It is, moreover, decidedly less effective than Jarman's inspired imaging of the future in the cross-sexed person of Edward III who, at the end of Jarman's film, orchestrates the demise of the caged Mortimer and Isabella to the tune of 'The Sugar Plum Fairy'. Although just as fantastical as the elision of Edward's murder, this is a victory that the film may claim to have earned. I say this in light of Jarman's similarly inspired treatment of the young Edward throughout the film, whose questions, perceptions, and experiments in gender displacement speak eloquently on behalf of subjects and sexualities still in the process of formation.

Jarman's construction of Isabella is, however, considerably more problematic and symptomatic of his indifference to contemporary efforts to reconcile queer and feminist political agendas. Jonathan Goldberg, for example, argues that in embracing adultery, Marlowe's Isabella 'refuses the boundaries of the licit' and operates in much the same transgressive space as Edward. According to Goldberg, 'what Marlowe intimates, insofar as it is possible to think of Isabella as a sodomite, is that the possibility for 'strong' female behaviour lies outside of marriage and its regularisation of gender' (p. 123). He pointedly concludes that 'her "strength" *as a woman* lies in refusing the limits of marriage' (p. 126).

Although Jarman brings similar conceptions of Isabella to bear in the course of his film, in the end he resists Goldberg's reconciliation of feminist and queer agendas by transforming the Queen into a bloodsucking vampire in evening dress, bent on exacting the cruellest revenge on Edward and his supporters. Moreover, he does so while extending, in a predictably extreme manner, the conventional appraisal of the love-sick queen into the representation of a scorned woman who, however illicit her adulterous arrangements, remains firmly committed to the established regimes of the normative, if not the normal.[19] Dressed to kill any suggestion of normality, Jarman's Isabella is nonetheless presented as well-practised in the protocols of self-regarding mastery and royal control, and repeatedly placed in the company of the most banal representatives of social conformity. Heterosexual adultery in no way qualifies the Queen to operate in the space of sodomy Goldberg explores which, as far as Jarman is concerned, has 'men only' inscribed on the door, as the slogan that closes the book on *Queer Edward II* indicates. While the slogan – HETEROPHOBIA *liberates*, HOMOSEXISM *empowers* – is no doubt meant to function in the same wryly overstated manner as are the others scattered through the book, it also suggests that as far as women are concerned, it is every man for himself.

From *Marlowe, History, and Sexuality*, ed. Paul Whitfield White (New York, 1998), pp. 213–21.

Notes

[In studying the aftermath of Marlowe's text, and the ways in which it is transformed into later modes of artistic production – in this case its conversion into film – Thomas Cartelli marks the possibilities of enriching the original text by further layers of theoretical and critical reading. Derek Jarman's treatment of *Edward II* serves as an instance to demonstrate how modern queer theory can be used to reread early modern texts. Ed.]

1. In his repeated attacks on the vicissitudes of dissident film-making in Britain, Jarman indicates that he was unable to be as forthright in making his positions clear in *Edward II* as he was in *Queer Edward II*. Indeed, although the film starts with two of the play's 'poor men' making unabashed love as Gaveston reads Edward's letter, the film is

generally a good deal more inhibited in its representation of homo-sexual practices than Jarman indicates in his book.

2. Michael Warner, 'Fear of a Queer Planet', *Social Text*, 29 (1991), 3–17 (16).

3. Derek Jarman, *Queer Edward II* (London, 1991), p. 8. All subsequent references to Jarman's text will be to this edition and placed in parentheses.

4. The already unravelling critical consensus on *Edward II* was consider-ably intensified by three books published by avowedly gay literary scholars in the same period (1991–92) in which Jarman's book and film were distributed. See the sections devoted to the play in Gregory Bredbeck, *Sodomy and Interpretation: Marlowe to Milton* (Ithaca, NY, 1991; Jonathan Goldberg, *Sodometries: Renaissance Texts, Modern Sexualities* (Stanford, CA, 1992); and Bruce Smith, *Homosexual Desire in Shakespeare's England* (Chicago, 1991).

5. See the chapter devoted to *Edward II* in Thomas Cartelli, *Marlowe, Shakespeare, and the Economy of Theatrical Experience* (Philadelphia, 1991).

6. According to Alan Bray, 'What determined the skewed and recurring features of homosexual relationships [in the early modern period] was the prevailing distribution of power, economic power and social power, not the fact of homosexuality itself'. See Alan Bray, *Homosexuality in Renaissance England* (London, 1982), p. 56.

7. As Jonathan Goldberg, *Sodometries*, observes, 'it is possible, impera-tive, to recognise in Marlowe a site of political resistance' (p. 141).

8. Bruce Smith, *Homosexual Desire*, p. 223. It is, according to Smith, worthy of note that 'In Edward and Gaveston we have, not a man and a boy, but two men' (pp. 213–14).

9. Bredbeck notes that 'a number of anecdotal summaries of the king's life, all written between 1590 and 1650, were widely reprinted', and offers illuminating accounts of several of them in *Sodomy and Interpretation* (pp. 48–50; 53–6).

10. Michael Drayton, 'Peirs Gaveston' (orig. 1593–94). In *The Works of Michael Drayton*, 5 vols, ed. J. William Hebel (Oxford, 1931), 1:158.

11. Elizabeth Cary, *The History of the Life, Reign and Death of Edward II, King of England, and Lord of Ireland. With the Rise & Fall of his great favourites, Gaveston & the Spencers. Written by E. F. in the year 1627. And Printed verbatim from the Original* (London, 1680), p. 4. All subsequent references are to this edition.

12. Francis Hubert, *The History of Edward II* (London, 1629), p. 13. All subsequent references are to this edition.

13. Cf. Goldberg, *Sodometries*: 'On the basis of the illicit, a defoundational site that cannot be read through or merely as a reflection of the licit, Marlowe's play negotiates difference – in gender and in sexuality – differently. Modern heterosexist presumptions are not in place' (p. 125).

14. The full text of Gaveston's argument reads as follows:

> For what are Lawes, but servile observations
> Of this, or that, what pleas'd the Makers mind?
> The selfe-conceited sowers Imaginations
> Of working braines, which did in freedom find
> Our humaine state, wch they forsooth would bind
> To what they lik't, what lik't not, was forbidden
> So Horse and Mule, with bitt are ridden.
>
> (p. 14)

15. Cf. Bray, *Homosexuality*: 'Baines's depositions should ... be taken as documents which have been carefully constructed but which are none the less based on Marlowe's actual opinions' (p. 63).

16. Christopher Marlowe, *Edward II*. Ed. Irving Ribner (New York, 1970), I.iv.417.

17. I am attempting to work here with Paul Smith's distinction between the human agent, on the one hand, and the human *subject*, on the other. According to Smith, the *agent* may be seen as 'the place from which resistance to the ideological is produced or played out, and thus as *not* equivalent to either the "subject" or the "individual" ' See Paul Smith, *Discerning the Subject* (Minneapolis, 1988), p. xxxv. The *subject* may be understood 'to describe what is actually the series or the conglomeration of *positions*, subject-positions, provisional and not necessarily indefeasible, into which a person is called momentarily by the discourses and the world that he/she inhabits' (p. xxxv).

18. As Goldberg, *Sodometries*, writes, 'Marlowe affirms *as proper* what his society sees as warranting death; his unflinching representation of the death of Edward is one sign of this, a making manifest of sodomy as the ungrounded truth of the play' (p. 129).

19. Kathleen Anderson has recently made a strong case for abandoning the commonplace appraisal of Marlowe's Isabella as 'an inconsistent, lovesick' character, 'motivated mainly by her need to have a man love her' (p. 31) in favour of a more expressly Marlovian conception of 'a powerful political figure who uses her sexuality, her son, her position, and all of the gender stereotypes available to her to get and hold on to power' (p. 39). See Kathleen Anderson, ' "Stab as Occasion Serves": The Real Isabella in Marlowe's *Edward II*'; *Renaissance Papers* (1992), 29–39.

Further Reading

Editions

Marlowe, Christopher, *Collected Works*, ed. David Fuller and Edward J. Esche (Oxford: Clarendon Press, 1998).

Marlowe, Christopher, *Complete Plays and Poems*, ed. E. D. Pendry; textual adviser J. C. Maxwell. Everyman Edition (London: Dent, 1976).

Marlowe, Christopher, *The Complete Plays*, ed. Mark Thornton. Everyman Edition (London: Dent, 1999).

Marlowe, Christopher, *Tamburlaine the Great*, ed. J. S. Cunningham. The Revels Plays (Manchester and New York: Manchester University Press, 1981).

Marlowe, Christopher, *The Jew of Malta*, ed. James R. Siemon. New Mermaids (London: A & C Black, 1994).

Marlowe, Christopher, *Edward the Second*, ed. Charles R. Forker. The Revels Plays (Manchester and New York: Manchester University Press, 1995).

Sources

Thomas, Vivien and William Tydeman (eds) *Christopher Marlowe: The Plays and Their Sources* (London and New York: Routledge, 1994). An invaluable reference volume for the sources of Marlowe's plays.

Concordances

Crawford, Charles, *The Marlowe Concordance* (Louvain: A. Vystpruyst, 1911–32). Fehrenbach, Robert et al., *A Concordance to the Plays, Poems, and Translations of Christopher Marlowe* (Ithaca, NY: Cornell University Press, 1982).

Ule, Louis, *A Concordance to the Works of Christopher Marlowe* (Hildesheim, New York: Olms, 1979).

Biographies

Bakeless, John, *Christopher Marlowe* (London: Jonathan Cape, 1938).

Boas, Frederick, *Christopher Marlowe: A Biographical and Critical Study* (Oxford: Clarendon Press, 1940).

Brooke, C. F. Tucker, *The Life of Marlowe and the 'Tragedy of Dido, Queen of Carthage'* (New York: Gordion Press, 1930).

Eccles, Mark, *Christopher Marlowe in London* (Cambridge, MA: Harvard University Press, 1934).

Henderson, Philip, *Christopher Marlowe*. 2nd edn (Brighton: Harvester Press, 1974). A passionate biography of Marlowe.

Hopkins, Lisa, *Christopher Marlowe* (Basingstoke and New York: Palgrave – now Palgrave Macmillan, 2000). An up-to-date, lucid review of Marlowe's biography, which situates the individual works of Marlowe within the context of his overall literary career.

Kuriyama, Constance Brown, *Christopher Marlowe: A Renaissance Life* (Ithaca, NY: Cornell University Press, 2002). The author attempts to speculatively reconstruct Marlowe's personality (in a similar way to that used in her criticism of his work – see below), while arguing against points raised in former biographies.

Nicholl, Charles, *The Reckoning: The Murder of Christopher Marlowe* (London: Jonathan Cape, 1992). The most comprehensive investigation to date into the circumstances of Marlowe's death. Reads like a thriller, but gets speculative at times.

Norman, Charles, *The Muses' Darling: The Life of Christopher Marlowe* (London: Falcon Press, 1947).

Riggs, David, 'The Killing of Christopher Marlowe.' *Stanford Humanities Review*, 8.1 (2000), 239–51. Part of Riggs' forthcoming volume *Nasty, Brutish and Brilliant: Life of Christopher Marlowe*.

Urry, William, *Christopher Marlowe and Canterbury*, ed. Andrew Butcher (London and Boston: Faber & Faber, 1988). Urry has collected a lot of new biographical material, especially concerning Marlowe's connections to his town of birth, and his family and people he must have come across.

Wraight, A. D., *In Search of Christopher Marlowe: A Pictorial Biography* (1965; Chichester, UK: Adam Hart, 1993).

Works of Fiction Inspired by Marlowe's Biography

Burgess, Anthony, *A Dead Man in Deptford* (London: Vintage, 1994). A novel by the celebrated author of *Clockwork Orange*, placing Marlowe and the events leading to his murder in a rich depiction of Elizabethan London.

Cook, Judith, *The Slicing Edge of Death* (London: Simon & Schuster, 1993). A novel mixing fact and fiction, offering a solution to the mystery of Marlowe's death.

Demaria, Robert, *To Be a King* (1999). A novel about Christopher Marlowe.

Garrett, George, *Entered from the Sun: The Murder of Marlowe* (San Diego, New York, London: Harvest/HBJ Books, 1990). A book of historical fiction, set in 1597 London, where Hunnyman, an actor, and Barfoot, a soldier/spy set out to unravel the mystery of Marlowe's death.

Norman, Marc and Tom Stoppard, *Shakespeare in Love* (London: Faber & Faber, 1999). The Oscar-winning film, wittily forwarding a theory as if Marlowe's murder was caused by Shakespeare's attempt to save his own life, threatened by a jealous husband.

Wichelns, Lee, *The Shadow of the Earth* (Elysian Press, 1988). An historical novel based on the life of Christopher Marlowe.

Bibliographies

Chan, Lois Mai, with the assistance of Sarah A. Pedersen, *Marlowe
Criticism: A Bibliography* (Boston: G. K. Hall, 1978).
Friedenreich, Kenneth, *Christopher Marlowe: An Annotated Bibliography
of Criticism Since 1950* (Metuchen, NJ & London: Scarecrow Press,
1979).
Welsh, Robert Ford, *The Printing of the Early Editions of Marlowe's Plays*
(Ann Arbor, MI: University microfilms, 1966).

Marlowe, General Criticism

Altman, Joel B., *The Tudor Play of Mind: Rhetorical Inquiry and the
Development of Elizabethan Drama* (Berkeley, CA: University of
California Press, 1978). Habits of mind engendered by training in formal
rhetoric, especially arguing for both sides, shape the dramatist's practice.
The last chapter is devoted to Marlowe, showing his passage from hope
for discoveries to a sceptical view about such a project.
Andrews, Michael Cameron, *This Action of Our Death: The Performance
of Death in English Renaissance Drama* (Newark, DE: University of
Delaware Press, 1989). Focuses on death speeches in several Renaissance
playwrights. Marlowe is 'the first Renaissance playwright to capitalise on
the dramatic potential of death'.
Archer, John Michael, *Sovereignty and Intelligence: Spying and Court
Culture in the English Renaissance* (Stanford, CA: Stanford University
Press, 1993). Contains a chapter on 'Marlowe and the Observation of
Men'.
Asibong, Emmanuel B., *Comic Sensibility in the Plays of Christopher
Marlowe* (Ilfracombe, UK: Stockwell, 1979). Finds in Marlowe's drama
various patterns of the comic; comedy of cruelty, comedy of passion, and
comedy of inversion.
Bartels, Emily C., *Spectacles of Strangeness: Imperialism, Alienation, and
Marlowe* (Philadelphia: University of Pennsylvania Press, 1993). Discusses
the view of otherness and alienation in Marlowe's dramatic work.
Bosonnet, Felix, *The Function of Stage Properties in Christopher
Marlowe's Plays* (Bern: Francke, 1978). Marks the significance of notable
stage props in Marlowe's plays, such as crowns in Tamburlaine, daggers
and books in *Dr Faustus*, Letters in *The Jew of Malta*, swords in *Edward
II*, etc.
Breight, Curtis C., *Surveillance, Militarism and Drama in the Elizabethan
Era* (Basingstoke, and London: Macmillan – now Palgrave Macmillan,
1996).
Brown, John Russell, 'Marlowe and the Actors', *Tulane Drama Review*, 8
(1964), 155–73.
—— (ed.), *Marlowe: Tamburlaine the Great, Edward the Second and The
Jew of Malta: A Casebook* (London: Macmillan – now Palgrave

Macmillan, 1982). A rich and varied collection of essays on those three plays of which the present one serves as a sequel.

Cartelli, Thomas, *Marlowe, Shakespeare, and the Economy of Theatrical Experience* (Philadelphia: University of Pennsylvania Press, 1991).

Cheney, Patrick, *Marlowe's Counterfeit Profession: Ovid, Spenser, Counter-Nationhood* (Toronto, Buffalo and London: University of Toronto Press, 1997). Traces in Marlowe's writing three interlocking themes: the idea of a literary career; the practice of professional rivalry; and the writing of nationhood (and counter-nationhood).

Cole, Douglas, *Suffering and Evil in the Plays of Christopher Marlowe* (Princeton, NJ: Princeton University Press, 1962).

——, *Christopher Marlowe and the Renaissance of Tragedy* (Westport, CT and London: Praeger, 1995).

Cutts, John P., *The Left Hand of God: A Critical Interpretation of the Plays of Christopher Marlowe* (Haddonfield, NJ: Haddonfield House, 1973). Attempts to delineate the double image-figures on which the plays of Marlowe focus, whose deeply rooted inner frustrations may be traced beyond their overt glamour and bravado.

Dabbs, Thomas, *Reforming Marlowe: The Nineteenth-Century Canonization of a Renaissance Dramatist* (Lewisburg: Bucknell University Press, 1991). Explores Marlowe's rediscovery and canonisation in the nineteenth century.

Deats, Sara Munson, *Sex, Gender, and Desire in the Plays of Christopher Marlowe* (Newark, DE: University of Delaware Press, 1997).

—— and Robert A. Logan (eds), *Marlowe's Empery: Expanding his Critical Contexts* (Newark, DE: University of Delaware Press, 2002). A collection of critical essays on Marlowe.

Downie, James Alan and J. T. Parnell (eds), *Constructing Christopher Marlowe* (Cambridge: Cambridge University Press, 2000). An up-to-date collection of essays on Marlowe, ranging from recovering facts about his own career to later interpretation and reworking of his work in criticism and in film.

Ellis-Fermor, Una, *Christopher Marlowe* (London: Methuen, 1927).

Fanta, Christopher G., *Marlowe's 'Agonists': An Approach to Ambiguity of his Plays* (Cambridge, MA: Harvard University Press, 1970). Stresses the ambiguity resulting from Marlowe's own ambivalence toward his characters and themes.

Friedenreich, Kenneth, Constance Kuriyama and Roma Gill (eds), *'A Poet and a Filthy Play-Maker': New Essays on Christopher Marlowe* (New York: AMS Press, 1988). A collection of essays on Marlowe.

Garber, Marjorie, 'Infinite Riches in a Little Room: Closure and Enclosure in Marlowe' in Kernan 1977 (see below).

Godshalk, William Leigh, *The Marlovian World Picture* (The Hague: Mouton, 1974). Suggests a rearrangement of the canon's received order according to the author's idea that the thrust of Marlowe's plays is toward the dominance of the stage by a single, powerful character. Thus he places *Edward II* as an early play, whereas *Tamburlaine* is a later link towards the two most powerful and isolated characters in the Marlovian world: Faustus and Barabas, situated within a world of evil dissected by Marlowe, who is perceived as a savage moralist in the vein of Swift.

Goldberg, Jonathan, 'Sodomy and Society: The Case of Christopher Marlowe', *Southwest Review*, 69 (1984), 371–8.

Grantley, Darryll and Peter Roberts (eds), *Christopher Marlowe and English Renaissance Culture* (Aldershot, UK, and Brookfield, VT: Scolar Press, 1996). A good collection of modern essays on Marlowe's work.

Greenblatt, Stephen, *Renaissance Self-Fashioning: From More to Shakespeare* (Chicago: University of Chicago Press, 1980).

Healy, Thomas, *Christopher Marlowe* (Plymouth: Northcote House, 1994).

Kelsall, Malcolm, *Christopher Marlowe* (Leiden: Brill, 1981). Kelsall doubts whether, in the light of our scant knowledge of Marlowe's life or the order of his work, we can come to any general conclusions regarding his thought or character. He stresses the theatrical complexity of the plays.

Kernan, Alvin (ed.), *Two Renaissance Mythmakers:Christopher Marlowe and Ben Jonson* (Baltimore and London: Johns Hopkins University Press, 1977).

Kocher, Paul, *Christopher Marlowe: A Study of his Thought, Learning, and Character* (Chapel Hill, NC: University of North Carolina Press, 1946). A thorough study of the plays, interpreting Marlowe's religion and secular thought, his politics, ethics and views on other related issues, on the basis of the plays themselves and the author's reading of biographical evidence.

Kuriyama, Constance Brown, *Hammer or Anvil: Psychological Patterns in Christopher Marlowe's Plays* (New Brunswick, NJ: Rutgers University Press, 1980). Attempts to trace in Marlowe's plays dominant psychological themes, or indeed, psychoanalytical traits underlying the text.

Leech, Clifford, *Christopher Marlowe: Poet for the Stage*, ed. Ann Lancashire (New York: AMS Press, 1986).

Levin, Harry, *Christopher Marlowe: The Overreacher* (London: Faber and Faber, 1961).

Lunney, Ruth, *Marlowe and the Popular Tradition: Innovation in the English Drama Before 1595* (Manchester and New York: Manchester University Press, 2002). The author explores Marlowe's engagement with the popular traditions of the stage in the late 1580s and early 1590s, and offers a reading of his major plays in terms of staging and audience response.

Maclure, Millar (ed.), *Marlowe: The Critical Heritage 1588–1896* (London, Boston and Henley: Routledge and Kegan Paul, 1979). A rich selection of Marlowe criticism and references, from Robert Greene's complaints during Marlowe's lifetime to George Bernard Shaw over three hundred years later.

Masinton, Charles, *Christopher Marlowe's Tragic Vision: A Study in Damnation* (Athens, OH: Ohio University Press, 1972). Focuses on the theme of damnation, which he regards of a central importance to the tragic vision in Marlowe's five major plays.

Meehan, Virginia Mary, *Christopher Marlowe, Poet and Playwright: Studies in Poetical Method* (The Hague and Paris: Mouton, 1974). Approaching Marlowe's work through his poetic technique, style, imagery and rhetoric, to reach its poetic meaning.

Prosser, Matthew, *The Gift of Fire; Aggression and the Plays of Christopher Marlowe* (New York: Peter Lang, 1995). The author concentrates on Marlowe's alleged aggressiveness, supported by bigraphical evidence, as a disruptive force in his creative process, and marks its thematic implication in his work, as well as the strategies adopted by the playwright to contain and control its effects.

Ritchie, Brian B., *The Plays of Christopher Marlowe and George Peele: Rhetoric and Renaissance Sensibility* (Dissertation.com, 1999). In this published dissertation, the author compares the verbal rhetoric of the two Elizabethan playwrights, linking their rhetorical devices to the visual aspects of their plays.

Sales, Roger, *Christopher Marlowe* (Basingstoke: Macmillan – now Palgrave Macmillan, 1991).

Sanders, Wilbur, *The Dramatist and the Received Idea: Studies in the Plays of Marlowe and Shakespeare* (London: Cambridge University Press, 1968).

Shapiro, James, *Rival Playwrights: Marlowe, Jonson, Shakespeare* (New York: Columbia University Press, 1991).

Shepard, Alan, *Marlowe's Soldiers: Rhetorics of Masculinity in the Age of the Armada* (Aldershot: Ashgate, 2002).

Shepherd, Simon, *Marlowe and the Politics of Elizabethan Theatre* (Brighton: Harvester Press, 1986).

Simkin, Stevie, *Marlowe: The Plays* (Basingstoke: Palgrave – now Palgrave Macmillan, 2001).

Steane, J. B., *Marlowe: A Critical Study* (London: Cambridge University Press, 1978).

Summers, Claude J., *Christopher Marlowe and the Politics of Power* (Salzburg: Institut für Englische Sprache und Literatur, 1974).

Tromly, Fred B., *Playing with Desire: Christopher Marlowe and the Art of Tantalization* (Toronto, Buffalo and London: University of Toronto Press, 1998). Tromly discusses Marlowe's preoccupation with games of tantalisation in which enticing objects and ideas are offered, teasing the imagination, and then withdrawn before they can be grasped.

Weil, Judith, *Christopher Marlowe: Merlin's Prophet* (Cambridge: Cambridge University Press, 1977). A study of what the author defines as Marlowe's prophetic style, whereby the catastrophes anticipated and fulfilled serve to adjust plot to character, and trap the protagonists within a rigorously moral form.

White, Paul Whitfield (ed.), *Marlowe, History, and Sexuality: New Critical Essays on Christopher Marlowe* (New York: AMS Press, 1998).

Wilson, Richard (ed.), *Christopher Marlowe* (London: Longman, 1999). An up-to-date collection of essays on Marlowe's work.

Zucker, David Hard, *Stage and Image in the Plays of Christopher Marlowe* (Salzburg: Salzburg Studies in English Literature, 1972).

Zunder, William, *Elizabethan Marlowe: Writing and Culture in the English Renaissance* (Hull: Unity Press, 1994). A short introduction to Marlowe's work, situating the major works in their historical and discursive context.

Individual Plays

Tamburlaine the Great

Armstrong, William A., *Tamburlaine: The Image and the Stage* (Hull: Hull University Press, 1966). A short inaugural lecture which focuses on the theatrical aspects of Marlowe's plays.

Barber, C. L., 'Theatrical Magic in *Tamburlaine*', in C. L. Barber, *Creating Elizabethan Tragedy: The Theater of Marlowe and Kyd*, ed. Richard P. Wheeler (Chicago and London: University of Chicago Press, 1988).

Battenhouse, Roy W., *Marlowe's Tamburlaine: A Study in Renaissance Moral Philosophy* (Nashville, TN: Vanderbilt University Press, 1941). A Christian approach to the play, that became very influential in its time.

Burton, Jonathan, 'Anglo-Ottoman Relations and the Image of the Turk in *Tamburlaine*', *Journal of Medieval and Early Modern Studies*, 30 (2000), 125–56.

Geckle, George L., *Tamburlaine and Edward II*: Text and Performance (Basingstoke and London: Macmillan – now Palgrave Macmillan, 1988). Outlines the potential in the text of dramatic performance, and then discusses a select number of productions of the play.

Howe, James Robinson, *Marlowe, Tamburlaine, and Magic* (Columbus, OH: Ohio University Press, 1976). Studies the play from the narrow strand of the Hermetic philosophy, that of magic. Marlowe was exploring the nature and limits of the Renaissance ideal man in relation to magic.

Stark, Lisa S., ' "Won with thy words and conquered with thy looks": Sadism, Masochism, and the Masochistic Gaze in *1 Tamburlaine*', White (ed.), 1998 (see above), pp. 179–93.

Wilson, Mary Floyd, '*Tamburlaine* and the Staging of White Barbarity', in her *English Ethnicity in Early Modern Drama* (Cambridge: Cambridge University Press, 2003). Mary Floyd Wilson's concern with Marlowe is primarily cultural: she explores in her essay how notions of race and ethnicity affect collective self-conciousness. Central to her argument is the charged concept of barbarism, not necessarily directed at exotic Eastern figures, but also close to home, at European and British ethnicities.

Wilson, Richard, 'Visible Bullets: Tamburlaine the Great and Ivan the Terrible', in Grantley and Roberts (eds), 1996 (see above), pp. 51–69. A remarkable piece of critical insight and contextualising the work.

The Jew of Malta

Babb, Howard B., '"Policy" in Marlowe's *The Jew of Malta*', *English Literary History*, 24 (1957), 85–94.

Jones, Robert C., *Engagement with Knavery* (Durham, NC: Duke University Press, 1986). In a chapter devoted to 'Barabas: Stagecraft vs. Statecraft', discusses the dramatic implications and the 'longer reach' of a

play in which the knavish hero directly engages the audience and affects
its point of view.

Rothstein, Eric, 'Structure as Meaning in *The Jew of Malta*', *Journal of
English and Germanic Philology*, 65 (1966), 260–73. Rothstein discusses
the structure of the play and its implications on reading it as a tragedy.

Segal, Erich, *Veins of Humor* (Cambridge, MA: Harvard University Press,
1972). Regards Barabas as a comic hero.

Doctor Faustus

Alexander, Nigel, 'The Performance of Christopher Marlowe's *Dr Faustus*',
Chatterton Lecture given at the British Academy (London: Oxford
University Press, 1971). Focuses on the theatrical values of the play, and
Marlowe's art of building audiences' suspense.

Barber, C. L., 'The forme of Faustus fortunes good or bad', in C. L. Barber,
Creating Elizabethan Tragedy: The Theater of Marlowe and Kyd, ed.
Richard P. Wheeler (Chicago and London: University of Chicago Press,
1988).

Campbell, Lily B., '*Dr Faustus*: A Case of Conscience', *PMLA*, 67 (1952),
219–39.

Empson, William, *Faustus and the Censor: The English Faust-Book and
Marlowe's 'Doctor Faustus'*, ed. John Henry Jones (Oxford: Blackwell,
1987).

Farnham, Willard (ed.), *Twentieth Century Interpretations of 'Doctor
Faustus'* (Englewood Cliffs, NJ: Prentice-Hall, 1969).

Heller, Otto, *Faust and Faustus: A Study of Goethe's Relation to Marlowe*
(St. Louis, MO: Washington University Press, 1931). A study of Goethe's
use of Marlowe's play as a source to his opus.

Jump, John (ed.), *Marlowe: 'Doctor Faustus'* (London: Macmillan, 1969).
A casebook of criticism on the play.

Kirscbaum, Leo, 'Marlowe's *Faustus*: A Reconsideration', *Review of
English Studies*, 19 (1943), 225–41. Contrary to former interpretations,
insists on the consistent hedonism of the character of Faustus to the very
end of the play, ending his passionate article by exclaiming: 'Wanton
Faustus!'

Mebane, John S., *Renaissance Magic and the Return of the Golden Age:
The Occult Tradition and Marlowe, Jonson, and Shakespeare* (Lincoln &
London: University of Nebraska Press, 1989). In a chapter about vision
and illusion in *Dr Faustus*, relates the play to the tradition of occultism in
the Renaissance, defines magic as a unifying symbol of Marlowe's chief
interests, but stresses the equivocal response Marlowe provides to this
question in the play.

Nuttall, A. D., 'Raising the Devil: Marlowe's *Dr Faustus*', in his *The
Alternative Trinity: Gnostic Heresy in Marlowe, Milton and Blake*
(Oxford: Oxford University Press, 1998), pp. 23–70. A. D. Nuttall's
criticism has always inclined to read the literary and the dramatic in
the light of abstract ideas drawn from philosophy or theology. In his
The Alternative Trinity he explores the subversive theology presenting
God as evil and Christ as antagonist back from the Gnostics of the

second century to its presence in the works of Marlowe, Milton and Blake.

Spivack, Charlotte (ed.), *Merlin Versus Faust: Contending Archetypes in Western Culture* (Lewiston / Queenstown / Lampeter: Edwin Mellen Press, 1992).

Streete, Adrian, '"Consummatum Est": Calvinist Exegesis, Mimesis and *Doctor Faustus*', *Literature and Theology*, 15 (2001), 140–58.

Tydeman, William, *Doctor Faustus: Text and Performance* (Basingstoke: Macmillan, 1984).

Weil, Judith, '"Full Possession": Service and Slavery in *Doctor Faustus*', in White (ed.), 1998 (see above), pp. 143–54.

Wilson, Luke, *Theaters of Intention: Drama and the Law in Early Modern England* (Stanford, CA : Stanford University Press, 2000).

Edward II

DiGangi, Mario, 'Marlowe, Queer Studies, and Renaissance Homoeroticism', in White (ed.) 1998 (see above), pp. 195–212.

Geckle, George L., *Tamburlaine and Edward II*: Text and Performance (Basingstoke and London: Macmillan – now Palgrave Macmillan, 1988). Outlines the potential in the text of dramatic performance, and then discusses a select number of productions of the play.

Parks, Joan, 'History, Tragedy, and Truth in Christopher Marlowe's *Edward II*', *Studies in English Literature*, 39 (1999), 275–90.

Smith, Bruce R., *Homosexual Desire in Shakespeare's England: A Cultural Poetics* (Chicago: University of Chicago Press, 1991).

A Marlowe Chronology

1564   6(?) February: Christopher Marlowe born at Canterbury, second child and elder son to John Marlowe, a cobbler, a member of the shoemakers and tanners of the city, and Katherine née Arthur.

26 February: Christopher Marlowe christened at the church of St George the Martyr, the same church where his parents were married.

April: John Marlowe becomes a freeman of the city of Canterbury.

23 April: William Shakespeare is born at Stratford-upon-Avon.

1572   23–24 August: the Massacre of St Bartholomew's Day in Paris.

1579   14 January: Christopher obtains a scholarship to enter King's School, Canterbury. He may have been a paying commoner at the school beforehand.

1579–80   Scholar at King's School, Canterbury.

1580   December: Arrives in Cambridge, holding a nomination to a scholarship in Corpus Christi College, given by Archbishop Matthew Parker, Archbishop of Canterbury between 1558 and 1585, intended for boys likely to become clergymen.

1580–7   Attends Corpus Christi College, Cambridge. Among other young scholars attending Cambridge at that time were poets and playwrights Thomas Nashe and Robert Greene, future politician Robert Cecil (son of Lord Burghley, the Lord Treasurer of England and Chancellor of the university), and rhetorician Gabriel Harvey was a fellow of Pembroke Hall. All of them will tie up with Marlowe's name when he moves to London.

1581   17 March: Matriculates.

24 March: Listed as a college commoner at Corpus Christi.

7–11 May: Officially awarded the Parker scholarship, intended to sustain him during his Cambridge years.

1584   Receives his BA degree.

1587   A controversy in Cambridge over Marlowe's frequent and lengthy absences from the university brings the decision to withhold his MA degree. Marlowe finally receives his degree, following a Privy Council certificate assuring the university that Marlowe's long absences from Cambridge were made in the service of Her Majesty. In November Dr Norgate, Master of Corpus Christi, probably the chief person behind the authorities' decision to withhold Marlowe's MA, dies, to be replaced by Dr Copcott, vice-chancellor of the University and an appointee of Lord Burghley (and thus a supporter of Marlowe).

May: 'The Children of Her Majesty's Chappel' perform at Norwich and Ipswich, both close enough to Cambridge for Marlowe to attend and possibly present them with a manuscript of his *Dido*, which they later performed, as the title page of the play states. *Tamburlaine the Great*, Parts One and Two, are performed by the Lord Admiral's Men.

1589   18 September: Marlowe is fighting on Hog Lane, in a suburb of London, with William Bradley, an innkeeper's son. Marlowe's friend Thomas Watson appears and intervenes in the brawl, which ends in his killing Bradley. Both Watson and Marlowe are arrested and committed to Newgate prison on suspicion of murder.

1 October: Marlowe is bailed for £40 until his case comes up in the next sessions. Watson remains in jail.

3 December: Watson and Marlowe's case heard. Marlowe is discharged. Watson will gain the Queen's pardon only two months later.

1590   *Tamburlaine the Great* published.

1591   Shares a chamber with playwright Thomas Kyd, both writing for the same company of actors, Lord Strange's Men.

1593	11 May: Thomas Kyd is arrested by the Privy Council on suspicion of heresy. He affirms that he had a short theological manuscript, allegedly 'denying the deity of Jesus Christ our saviour', seized among his papers, from Christopher Marlowe, with whom he shared a chamber in 1591.

18 May: A warrant issued by the Privy Council to Henry Maunder, one of the messengers of Her Majesty's Chamber, to repair to the house of Mr Thomas Walshingham in Kent, or to any other place where he shall understand Christopher Marlowe to be remaining, and by virtue thereof to apprehend and bring him to the court, on the suspicion of heresy.

20 May: Marlowe appears before the Council.

30 May: Marlowe spends the day at widow Eleanor Bull's eating-house in Deptford, with Ingram Frizer, Nicholas Skeres, and Robert Poley. Towards the evening an affray breaks out between Marlowe and Frizer. Frizer stabs Marlowe's left eye, and Marlowe dies on the spot. Frizer later claims self-defence. His claim is accepted, and he is pardoned by 28 June.

27 May, or 2 June: Richard Baines hands in his report, entitled 'A note containing the opinion of one Christopher Marly, concerning his damnable judgment of religion and scorn of God's word'.

1 June: Marlowe is buried at St Nicholas Church, Deptford, at the expense of the State.

1594   *Edward II* printed for William Jones.
Dido Queen of Carthage, written by Christopher Marlowe and Thomas Nashe [there is no convincing evidence, though, for Nashe's collaboration; he may have prepared the text for production by the Children of Her Majesty's Chapel, and probably for publication] printed by the Widdow Orwin for Thomas Woodcoke.

1598   'Hero and Leander' printed by Adam Islip, for Edward Blunt. 'Hero and Leander', begun by Christopher Marlowe and finished by George Chapman ... printed by Felix Kingston, for Paule Linley.

1599   Marlowe's translations of Ovid's elegies are burned by the order of the Bishop of London and the Archbishop of Canterbury.

1602(?)   *The Massacre at Paris* printed by E. A. for Edward White. Philip Henslowe pays the sum of £4 to William Birde and Samuel Rowley for additions to *Doctor Faustus*.

1604   A-text of *Doctor Faustus* printed by V. S. for Thomas Bushell.

1616   B-text of *Doctor Faustus* printed by John Wright.

1633   *The Jew of Malta* performed at the Cockpit and the Court; printed by I. B. for Nicholas Vavasour.

Notes on Contributors

Emily C. Bartels is Associate Professor of English at Rutgers University. She is the author of many articles on early modern drama, as well as *Spectacles of Strangeness: Imperialism, Alienation, and Marlowe* (1993) and the editor of *Critical Essays on Christopher Marlowe* (1977).

Catherine Belsey is Professor of English at Cardiff University, where she chairs the Centre for Critical and Cultural Theory. Her publications include *Critical Practice* (1980; rev. 2002), *The Subject of Tragedy: Identity and Difference in Renaissance Drama* (1985), *John Milton: Language, Gender, Power* (1998), *Desire: Love Stories in Western Culture* (1994), *Shakespeare and the Loss of Eden* (1999), and *Poststructuralism: A Very Short Introduction* (2002).

Dympna Callaghan is William Pearson Tolley Professor in the Humanities at Syracuse University. She is the author of *Woman and Gender in Renaissance Tragedy* (1989), *The Weyward Sisters: Shakespeare and the Feminist Politics* (co-author, 1994), *Shakespeare Without Women* (2000), co-editor of *Feminist Readings in Early Modern Drama* (1996) and editor of *The Feminist Companion to Shakespeare* (2001).

Thomas Cartelli is Professor of English and Chair of the Department of English and Humanities at Muhlenberg College. He is the author of *Marlowe, Shakespeare and the Economy of Theatrical Experience* (1991), *Repositioning Shakespeare: National Formations, Postcolonial Appropriations* (1999), as well as a number of articles on English Renaissance drama and postcolonial appropriations of Shakespeare.

Sara Munson Deats is Distinguished Professor of English and Director of the Center of Applied Humanities at the University of South Florida, a former President of the Marlowe Society of America and recipient of the Roma Gill Award for Outstanding Scholarship on Marlowe. She is the author of *Sex, Gender, and Desire in the Plays of Christopher Marlowe* (1997); over two dozen essays on Marlowe and Shakespeare; and the editor of several anthologies on feminist pedagogy, politics and literature. She is currently editing an anthology on *Antony and Cleopatra*.

Jonathan Dollimore is Professor of English and Related Literature at the University of York. Prior to going to York he was a professor in the Humanities Research Centre at the University of Sussex. He is the author of *Radical Tragedy: Religion, Ideology and Power in the Drama of Shakespeare and his Contemporaries* (Brighton, 1984, 2nd edn 1989); *Sexual Dissidence: Augustine to Wilde, Freud to Foucault* (London, 1991); *Death, Desire and Loss in Western Culture* (London, 1998); *and Sex, Literature and Censorship (2000)*. He is co-editor, with Alan Sinfield, of *Political Shakespeare: New Essays in Cultural Materialism* (1985).

Stephen Greenblatt is Professor of English at Harvard University, General Editor of the Norton Shakespeare, and President of the Modern Language Association of America. Formerly Class of 1932 Professor of English at the University of California, Berkeley, he is the author of numerous books, including: *Renaissance Self-Fashioning: From More to Shakespeare* (1980), *Power of Forms in the English Renaissance* (1982), *Shakespearean Negotiations: the Circulation of Social Energy in Renaissance England* (1988); *Learning to Curse: Essays in Early Modern Culture* (1990); *Marvelous Possessions: The Wonder of the New World* (1991), *Hamlet in Purgatory* (2000) and the forthcoming *Will in the World* (2002 – a tentative title while these lines are going to press). He is the editor of *Representing the English Renaissance* (1978), *Allegory and Representation* (1986), and *New World Encounters* (1993).

Michael Hattaway is Professor of English Literature at the University of Sheffield. He has taught at the Universities of Kent, British Columbia, and Massachusetts. He is the author of *Elizabethan Popular Theatre* (1982), *Hamlet (The Critics Debate)* (1987), co-editor of *The Cambridge Companion to English Renaissance Drama* (1990) and *Shakespeare in the New Europe* (1994); and is the editor of Shakespeare's *As You Like It*, and *1–3 Henry VI* for the New Cambridge Shakespeare, of plays by Jonson and Beaumont, of *A Companion to English Renaissance Literature and Culture* (2001), and of *Shakespeare's History Plays* (2002).

Avraham Oz is Professor of Drama at the University of Haifa, artistic director of Haifa University Theatre, and former head of the Departments of Theatre both at the University of Haifa and Tel Aviv University (where he teaches at the Department of Poetics and Comparative Literature). He has translated Shakespeare, Brecht and many other plays and operas into the Hebrew, and is the general editor of the Hebrew edition of Shakespeare, a founder of *Assaph: Studies in the Theatre*, and editor of *JTD: Journal of Theatre and Drama*. He is the author of *The Yoke of Love: Prophetic Riddles in 'The Merchant of Venice'* (1995), *The Political Theatre* (1999), and *Shakespeare and Nationhood* (forthcoming), and editor of *Strands Afar Remote: Israeli Perspectives on Shakespeare* (1998).

Alan Sinfield is Professor of English in the School of Cultural and Community Studies at the University of Sussex. He is the author of numerous books, including: *Literature in Protestant England, 1560–1660* (1983), *Literature, Politics, and Culture in Postwar Britain* (1989), *Alfred Tennyson* (1989), *Faultlines: Cultural Materialism and the Politics of Dissident Reading* (1992); *The Wilde Century: Effeminacy, Oscar Wilde and the Queer Moment* (1994); *Cultural Politics, Queer Readings* (1994), *Society and Literature, 1945–1970* (1994), *Gay and After* (1998), and *Out on Stage: Lesbian and Gay Theatre in the Twentieth Century* (1999). He is co-editor, with Jonathan Dollimore, of *Political Shakespeare: New Essays in Cultural Materialism* (1985), and with Alistair Davies, of *British Culture of the Postwar: An Introduction to Literature and Society, 1945–1999* (2001).

Lisa S. Starks is Assistant Professor of English at University of South Florida, St Petersburg. She has published on Marlowe, Shakespeare, film and psychoanalysis, in books and periodicals such as *Literature and Psychology, Early Modern Literary Studies, Shakespeare Quarterly* and *Post Script* (two special issues of which, on Shakespeare and Film, she edited), and co-edited, with Courtney Lehmann, two book collections: *Spectacular Shakespeare: Critical Theory and Popular Cinema* (2002) and *The Reel Shakespeare: Alternative Cinema and Theory* (2002).

David Thurn is Associate Professor of English at Princeton University where he teaches for the Humanities Council. He has published on Marlowe, Shakespeare, and Freud, and is currently working on a book about the treasures and imperial insignia of the Holy Roman Empire. David Thurn has written on Marlowe, Shakespeare, and Freud.

Index